JOHN DICKINSON

CONSERVATIVE

REVOLUTIONARY

John Dickinson

Conservative

Revolutionary

MILTON E. FLOWER

Milton E. Flower

Published for the Friends of
the John Dickinson Mansion by the
University Press of Virginia, Charlottesville

THE UNIVERSITY PRESS OF VIRGINIA
Copyright © 1983 by the Friends of John Dickinson Mansion, Inc.
First published 1983

Cover: John Dickinson, by Charles Willson Peale (1770).
The landscape background shows the Falls of the Schuylkill,
site of the Society of Fort St. David's tribute to Dickinson.
(Historical Society of Pennsylvania)

Library of Congress Cataloging in Publication Data

Flower, Milton Embick.
    John Dickinson, conservative revolutionary.

    Bibliography: p.
    Includes index.
    1. Dickinson, John, 1732-1808.   2. United States–History–
Revolution, 1775-1783–Causes.   3. United States–Politics
and government–Revolution, 1775-1783.   4. United States–
Constitutional history.   5. Statesmen–United States
–Biography.   I. Title
E302.6.D5F57   1982   973.3'092'4   [B]   82-11151
ISBN 0-8139-0966-X

Printed in the United States of America

Contents

Preface

In 1801 Vincent Bonsal and his partner, Hezekiah Niles, printers of Wilmington, Delaware, published two volumes entitled
The Political Writings of John Dickinson. The project had been
urged upon Dickinson by Dr. John Vaughan, an enthusiastic
young Wilmington physician, but the idea, both bold and imagi-
native, was that of the publishers. It was remarkable enough that
the young Republic should be able to publish a collection of
political writings, but all the more notable that they were from
the pen of one man. Collected works of any type were unusual at
that time. These essays, moreover, spanned the years from the
Stamp Act crisis through those of the Revolution to the establishment of the federal government and beyond. The publication underscored the extraordinary contributions Dickinson had made to
the growing country.

Volume 1, in addition to a preface, included the *Speech in the
House of Assembly*, 1764; *The Late Regulations respecting the
British Colonies on the Continent of America*, 1765; "The Rough
Draft of the Resolves of the First Congress," 1765; *An Address to
the Committee of Correspondence in Barbadoes*, 1766; and *The
Farmer's Letters*, 1767. Volume 2 republished the *Address of Con-
gress to the inhabitants of Quebec*, 1774; the *First* and *Second
Petitions to the King*, 1774 and 1775; *The Declaration by the Rep-
resentatives of the . . . Colonies . . . on the Causes and Necessity of*

Taking up Arms, 1775; the *Address of Congress . . . on the Present Situation of Affairs*, 1779; and the *Letters of Fabius*, first and second series, 1788 and 1797, the first of which were written in support of the new Constitution and the second concerning America's attitude toward France. The inclusions were a modest selection consisting of less than a third of the anonymous published letters, broadsides, official papers, and proclamations that Dickinson had written.

Dickinson has correctly been called the "Penman of the Revolution" by later historians. But his activities extended for two decades into the life of the new republic, years in which Dickinson's contributions were many. Dickinson's career began with his election to the Assembly in the Lower Counties (of Delaware) in 1759. Then, as a Pennsylvania legislator, he represented that colony at the Stamp Act Congress and later, until July 1776, in the Continental Congress. In 1767 as the "Farmer" he became America's first native political hero: the outstanding harbinger of American protest against arbitrary British measures and a true defender of liberty. Patience Wright modeled him in wax; Paul Revere engraved his likeness copied from an earlier Philadelphia print. Nor was Dickinson's reputation provincial. British leaders and those on the continent knew of him as well. His opposition to independence in July 1776 brought vilification by his political adversaries but did not keep Du Simitière in 1779 from drawing his profile as one of thirteen American celebrities of the Revolution—sketches later engraved in France and pirated in England.

Having left the Continental Congress for military service, Dickinson was not returned to that body by Pennsylvania. Instead Delaware elected him its congressional delegate, but he did not agree to serve until 1779. In 1781 he became president (governor) of Delaware, and the following year, having returned to political favor, he was chosen president of the Supreme Executive Council of Pennsylvania. At the conclusion of his term in Pennsylvania, he moved back to Delaware and took up residence at Wilmington.

Almost at once Delaware delegated him to attend the Annapolis Convention and shortly thereafter the Federal Convention. At the gathering in Philadelphia, Dickinson's voice was strong, setting forth a defense of small states, a position that led to the Great

Compromise in congressional representation. As a constitutional authority he had no equal and had been the author of the original Articles of Confederation, the country's first constitution. Dickinson's involvement in state and federal matters never slackened. He continued to act and to write, becoming chairman of Delaware's constitutional convention in 1791, writing under the pseudonym "Fabius" first in support of the Federal Constitution and then a decade later in espousing the French cause as opposed to England's. As an enthusiastic Democratic-Republican, he lent his support and advice to Jefferson.

Historians have labeled John Dickinson cautious and conservative. Cautious he was, in part too bound by his great dependence on lessons gained from both English and world history. To certain aspects of history he seemed blind, perhaps as a result of a temperamental revulsion to mass violence. His caution alone caused him to be called conservative. But his devotion to the rule of law and to the principles of liberty linked him to the radicals in the early days of the Revolution. Dickinson never changed his principles. A man of great moral courage, he refused to bow to popular clamor and support independence. A conservative stance which seeks to withstand the ongoing currents of a dynamic world cannot, inherently, be a popular one. It tends to obstruct and frustrate. Thus the defender earns calumny from the impatient. Such was the case with Dickinson in Pennsylvania at the time of independence, a fate reversed, however, once his moderation again proved desirable. His life thus is not that of the more familiar Founding Fathers, but of a man no less devoted to his country and important in its history.

A dozen years after John Dickinson's death in 1808, Deborah Norris Logan, his kinswoman and chronicler of her time, observed, "It has often been [a] matter of surprise to me that no biography of this eminent man has as yet been attempted." Not until 1891, when Charles J. Stillé at the request of the Historical Society of Pennsylvania wrote a life of John Dickinson, was a biography published. At that time less than a quarter of the vast collection of Dickinson papers were available. Subsequently both the Library Company of Philadelphia and the Historical Society of Pennsylvania greatly increased their holdings of Dickinson papers from the family's archives descending in the Logan-Loudoun families.

The late John H. Powell, beginning in 1934 when he was a graduate student at the University of Iowa, for thirty years was looked upon as the authority on John Dickinson. After writing his dissertation on this Philadelphia patriot, he was properly considered the future biographer of that notable. His articles and monographs on Dickinson were many, but unhappily he never completed a full biography.

In 1968 the current project was proposed to me by the late Theodore Marvin and Harriet Curtis Reese. Renewed interest in John Dickinson was first exhibited in the restoration of the Dickinson Mansion near Dover and subsequently in keeping Dickinson's memory and contributions alive through the Friends of the John Dickinson Mansion. Having suggested that I write a biography of John Dickinson, the Friends assisted me with a generous grant that enabled me to spend a sabbatical year in Philadelphia, where the great collections of Dickinson papers are now deposited. In addition, the Friends have provided other financial assistance and encouragement and have been unstinting in their support and kindness throughout this happy task. Without their aid this biography would remain unwritten.

The Faculty Research Fund of Dickinson College assisted me on several occasions with varying grants that enabled me to obtain photocopies of many letters and documents as well as visit other repositories, perhaps chief among them the Public Archives of the State of Delaware, for John Dickinson materials.

Such a task as this requires the cooperation of many people for their scholarly expertise and helpful suggestions, their sympathetic understanding, opinions, and even helpful concerns, some of which might seem only tangential to my project. The names of those to be thanked are beyond proper and complete listing. They include, however, most certainly the following:

Whitfield J. Bell, Jr., onetime colleague and now Director of the American Philosophical Society; the late Charles Coleman Sellers, friend and colleague, whose advice was ever valued; Leon de Valinger, the Director of the Public Archives of the State of Delaware, proved a fund of knowledge, particularly at the beginning of my research; Nicholas B. Wainwright, former Director of the Historical Society of Pennsylvania during my months of research there; and Edwin Wolf, 2nd, the able Librarian of the Library Company of Philadelphia, ever valuable in scholarly assistance.

Foremost among those assisting me in research were Tom Duncan and Conrad Wilson, then of the Historical Society of Pennsylvania, and Peter J. Parker, who succeeded Conrad Wilson as head of the Manuscript Division there; Mrs. Lillian Tonkin of the Library Company of Philadelphia; Murray Smith of the American Philosophical Society Library; Dorothy Bowers, Madelyn McDade Massey, and Yates Forbis of the Dickinson College Library; John A. Munroe of the University of Delaware; and William A. Hunter of the Pennsylvania State Archives. To this short list I should add the name of Kenneth Bowling, whose special interest, intelligence, and keen judgment have been helpfully supportive.

But there are more who must receive my thanks for reasons both academic or amicable, among them: Gladys Coghlan of the Delaware Historical Society, Charles Dorman, Mark Egnal, John R. Coleman, James D. Flower, Jr., Douglas Gatton, Warren Gates, Joseph L. Graham, K. Robert Nilsson, the M. P. Potamkins, the late Hannah L. Roach, Martha Slotten, Isabelle Hoover, Lida Strautnicks, Craig R. Thompson, Mrs. William A. Worth, and Henry J. Young, as well as certain former students, particularly Mary Grabill, Gary Greenblatt, and Joseph Lotwick. Three special technicians, Victoria Kuhn, Martha R. Wilson, and Barbara Miller, have transposed my handwritten pages and interpreted my interlinears with exactness. Finally, I cannot forbear noting that my late mother, Lenore Embick Flower, was ever helpful in her intelligent criticisms of the early chapters.

And in the end I once again return to the Friends of the John Dickinson Mansion my thanks for their generous and continued support in this project, the result and interpretation of which they quite properly have never questioned.

The preparation of this biography underscores certain important future considerations by scholars and writers. Selected letters of John Dickinson, perhaps those more especially written following his retirement from politics, must be published not only to broaden our understanding of the writer but to illuminate that period of our history. Essays, as well as certain letters and documents not yet attributed to Dickinson, deserve to be studied and then collected and published. Many yet remain unidentified.

The Dickinson Papers (in many collections) both in the Library Company of Philadelphia and in the Historical Society of Pennsylvania are a rich store for all students of the period this work covers. Dickinson did indeed "refine too much" as one colleague complained. The manuscripts often verge on illegibility due to interlinears. Moreover, capitalization and punctuation follow no present rule. Wherever quotations from such papers are included in the text, I have followed modern usage but carefully refrained from any addition or subtraction of words unless noted.

Portrait of John Dickinson, engraved by Benoit L. Prevost, Paris, 1781, after a drawing by Pierre Eugene Du Simitiere, Philadelphia, 1780. (Delaware Public Archives)

☆ 1 ☆

Building on
a Heritage

JOHN DICKINSON WAS A MAN of tradition who valued the rich treasures of the past. Conscious of his heritage, he never ceased to be interested in his family background. The 1658 Dickinson family Bible held the records of five generations, beginning with Samuel Dickinson's first notation: "Walter Dickinson, son of Charles Dickinson of London, baptized the 10th day of February 1621 in the Parish of St. Andrews, Holbourn."[1] Walter became the immigrant, arriving in America and settling first on the banks of the Rappahannock River of Virginia. There he "married a wife named Jane," who gave birth to a son, William, born in December 1658. This son became the father of Samuel. Thus John, Samuel's son, represented the fourth generation of the Dickinsons in America. Walter, the progenitor, early moved from Virginia to North Point in Maryland, where the Patapsco River flows into the Chesapeake, and thence to Talbot County on the Eastern Shore.

Walter Dickinson undoubtedly entered the Society of Friends and perhaps for that reason moved with his family across the bay. Following the birth of another son, Charles, who died in infancy, his wife Jane died. Soon afterwards he married again, this time to one Mary, who became the mother of a third son, named Walter.

The move to Talbot County in 1659 and the purchase of 400

[1] Family Bible, Logan Papers, Historical Society of Pennsylvania (hereafter cited as L/HSP).

[1]

acres on the Choptank River near Reed's Creek also meant putting down roots. The plantation was called Croisadore, a name often translated "cross of gold." A house was built not far from the riverbank; the opposite shore could be clearly seen, and before it the river traffic of sailing barges created an ever-changing landscape. The shores indented with coves and inlets, the deep and sparkling waters, and the many creeks and tributaries provided a special charm and culture. With good reason this has been called "Venetian Country." Transportation and communication were waterborne. Every plantation on the bay or its inlets had its own wharf where shallops and larger vessels docked. For Walter Dickinson the fertile shores yielded valuable harvests of tobacco, and his increase in wealth was in turn followed by extension of his property in Maryland and then into Delaware.

Encouraged by Lord Baltimore's subsidies, Walter Dickinson purchased 800 acres of land on the far side of the peninsula. The proprietor had urged all his settlers to establish holdings north into Pennsylvania and east toward the Delaware River and the Atlantic. His scheme was designed to narrow the claims of William Penn and thus increase his own. In consequence, the Whartons, the Chews, the Tilghmans, the Dickinsons, and many other families were to find their landholdings straddling two proprietary claims. In 1681 Walter died. The estates were divided, the elder son William receiving Croisadore and the younger Walter inheriting the lands on Jones Neck on the Delaware coast.

William flourished, married well, and laid the foundation of future Dickinson wealth. Elizabeth Powell Dickinson, his wife, was the daughter of Howell Powell, a Quaker leader in Talbot County, and the niece of onetime Governor Francis Lovelace of New York. The Dickinsons together became overseers of the Third Haven Quaker Meeting. William grew rich, happy in his marriage and the birth of children, Elizabeth, James, and Samuel. He increased his acreage sixfold, purchased slaves then being introduced into Maryland, developed varied farming and commercial interests, and became one of the great landholders of the Eastern Shore.[2]

[2] John H. Powell, *The House on Jones Neck* (Wilmington[?], 1954).

His son Samuel built upon his father's foundation. Sent to England for a year, he was guided there by the Hanburys and the Barclays, Quaker factors and merchants of London.[3] At the Quarterly Meeting at Third Haven, on November 4, 1710, the twenty-one-year-old Samuel was married to Judith Troth, the daughter of Andrew Troth of Troth's Folly in Talbot County, whose land was located on the North Choptank.

The marriage of these young neighbors was blessed with nine children. William, the eldest, was born in 1711, and the following year Walter arrived and was named for his paternal grandfather. Samuel was born in 1714; other children were Henry, born in 1718, and Elizabeth, who died in infancy. Four more daughters followed in succession, yet only Elizabeth (the second to be thus named), born in 1721, lived more than a few years.[4] The family prospered and grew in grace. Common interests in habitude and religion welded the Croisadore household. Along with two other Friends these earnest Quakers in 1718 were elected Society visitors, as William and Elizabeth had been, to oversee and superintend the Choptank Meeting of which they were members. The happy communion between Samuel and Judith Dickinson continued until her death in 1729. That year seemed enshrouded with gloom. First their six-year-old daughter Rebecca died, then on June 15 the mother, and in August three-year-old Rachel. Their sons had been sent to England to be educated. Walter died there shortly after arrival at the age of sixteen, and then came word of the death of Samuel, their third son.

Samuel Dickinson increased his Maryland acreage, and after the death of his Delaware cousin Walter, for whom he was administrator, he purchased land in Kent County. His activities as merchant and agent became more and more engrossing. Tobacco from the fields of Talbot County was forwarded to London on the sailing vessels that put into the deep waterways along the Chesapeake shores. Henry, aged thirteen in 1731, and ten-year-old Elizabeth

[3] Ibid. No primary evidence exists to indicate that Samuel Dickinson studied law in England or ever visited there.

[4] Genealogical Records, L/HSP.

were lively children at home. But a void remained. Children, slaves, indentured servants, and demanding business responsibilities failed to fill the gap left by the death of his wife.

Samuel Dickinson found a new companion in Mary Cadwalader of Philadelphia. Thirty-one, Mary Cadwalader was the daughter of John Cadwalader, who had migrated from Wales as a schoolmaster and had married Martha Jones, the daughter of Dr. Edward Jones.[5] In March 1731 Samuel was cleared by the Third Haven Meeting "in order to proceed in [the] Marriage," which took place in Philadelphia on November 4.[6] Mary, of an equally prominent family of Friends, also received the approval of the Society for her marriage.

The new mistress of Croisadore, a highly intelligent and mature young woman, at once set about forging a new life, one far different from that of Philadelphia. Soon news came from London of the death of her stepson William. Death in infancy was sorrowful yet common; but to lose three sons grown to adolescence and manhood so far from home was a bitter blow. This sad word was balanced somewhat by the joy of knowing that Mary expected a child in November. About three in the morning on the second day of that month a boy was born. Called John for his grandfather Cadwalader, he found devoted parents awaiting him. Two years later, another boy, Thomas, was born, but his life was cut off early.

Two matters were paramount in Samuel Dickinson's life, his family and its welfare. With renewed vigor following his second marriage Dickinson consolidated his Maryland holdings. To 4,000 acres gradually garnered in Talbot County he had added 2,000 more in Dorchester and Queen Anne counties. He also continued to purchase tracts on the Delaware side. Samuel's uncle, who had inherited the 800 acres of Delaware land from his father, had added another 400 after moving to that plantation. However, Samuel's cousin Walter, grandson of the first purchaser, found the acreage, much of which was uncleared marshland, a burden. He had become a carpenter. An exchange of property soon took place.

[5] *Pennsylvania Magazine of History and Biography* (hereafter cited as *PMHB*) 6 (1882):209, footnote re. Cadwalader genealogy.

[6] Copy of Third Haven Records, L/HSP.

In 1732 Samuel Dickinson sold Walter a small farm of 200 acres for £10 while buying Walter's inheritance of 1,000 acres for £50.[7] In the meantime, under Maryland patents Samuel came into possession of 1,368 more acres in Delaware, and in the decades that followed he spent many hours in quieting titles. Vincent Loockerman, "his trusty and well beloved friend," acting as his attorney, assisted in this process. The Delaware tracts included Burton's Delight, Poplar Ridge, Berry's Delight, and Brother's Portion, the last adjoining the town of Dover. By the end of the 1730s, Samuel Dickinson's plantation, made up of so many separate yet adjoining farms, had been consolidated into one stretching from Dover to the St. Jones River near its entrance into the bay. Although comprising only a third of the combined acreage of his Maryland estates, the plantation's six-square-mile area, made up of forest, stream, marsh, and fertile field, was of commanding size.

With the death of his three sons in England, Samuel Dickinson determined that another course must be followed in the education of his son Henry and, indeed, his daughter Betsy. In 1735 Henry was seventeen, Elizabeth fourteen, and John three. Mary Cadwalader Dickinson also knew the value of learning. For them both the question was important, and on a trip to Philadelphia the name of Francis Alison, a postulant for the Presbyterian ministry about to come to America, was suggested as a likely tutor. Thus, on his arrival in America, Francis Alison briefly came to live with the Dickinsons.[8] Alison later became founder of the distinguished New London Academy, vice-provost of the University of Pennsylvania, and a notable classical scholar. Many years later he noted that when he arrived not only were there no colleges or good grammar schools in the middle provinces, but those who "made any pretensions to learning were branded as letter-learned Pharisees."[9] Not so the Dickinson family.

[7] Powell, *The House on Jones Neck*, pp. 13–15; L/HSP, XXIV, 22.

[8] Burton Alva Konkle, *Benjamin Chew* (Philadelphia, 1932). This is the earliest source to suggest that Alison was a tutor in the Dickinson household. A few other secondary accounts also suggest that John studied at Alison's academy at New London.

[9] Francis Alison to Ezra Stiles, Dec. 12, 1767, Manuscript Collection, Yale University Library (hereafter cited as YU).

Elizabeth, called Betsy by the family, as their only living daughter was a jewel to her father's eye. Love, knowing no boundaries, placed her in the path of Charles Goldsborough, son of a prominent and prosperous planter as well as a near Talbot County neighbor. The match was perect save for one serious difficulty. The Goldsboroughs were Anglican and to that faith as devoted as the Dickinsons were to the Society of Friends. Although the Dickinsons failed to receive the sanction of the Third Haven Meeting, in 1739 the marriage was performed in the church of the bridegroom.

The close, indeed often tense, relationships of the Society of Friends made that community responsible for the discipline and conduct of its members. No matter how pious, devoted, or well connected the member, one was bound by the Society's judgment. There were no personal options, whether in disputes between members or in marriage decisions. It was not surprising, then, that the Third Haven Meeting seriously discussed the Dickinson-Goldsborough marriage. No approval had been given. The Quarterly Meeting considered it a "disorderly marriage," and worse was Samuel Dickinson's "concession thereto after the refusal by the Quarterly Meeting of their passing amongst Friends."[10] The matter was postponed for determination until the subsequent Quarterly Meeting. The Society's disapproval deeply wounded the ever faithful planter and merchant and his family. Nearly fifty years later his concerned son John inquired about the incident and learned his father at least had not been "disowned."

Henry, Samuel Dickinson's eldest living son, was twenty-one in 1739. Elizabeth now had left home, and John, serious, perhaps even precocious at seven, was a joy. Early in April a third son, Philemon, was born. Samuel Dickinson, merchant, owner of 9,000 acres lying along the Choptank River in Talbot County and rivers in Dorchester and Queen Anne counties, by 1739 was also lord of 3,000 acres in Delaware.[11] He made a momentous decision: he would move his family to Kent, leaving his son Henry in charge

[10] Samuel Troth, Clerk of Third Haven, to JD, Dec. 17, 1798, Family Papers, L/HSP.

[11] Powell, *The House on Jones Neck*, pp. 11–14.

of the Maryland estates. Henry and Betsy would inherit those lands. For Samuel himself it would, at age fifty-five, be a new life.

Life at Croisadore had been stable in its roots, watered by the orthodoxy of religion, and expansive in the rich yield of the tobacco fields and the shipments to England. The tenantry was basic to Samuel Dickinson's success as were the slaves who furnished the manpower. The major tasks were harvesting and collecting the tobacco, baling, and loading it. Vessels arriving from England brought goods that enriched the lives and homes of tenants and plantation owners. Associations with forwarding agents in London and elsewhere in England as well as in the West Indies were also significant. Samuel Dickinson had close contact and warm personal relationships with Quaker agents abroad and with Quaker merchants in Philadelphia. The interwoven fabric of economics and religion was a sturdy one.

The society of this Chesapeake region was solid and friendly, differing from that of the southern bay area in its lack of a center such as Williamsburg. It was equally isolated from the western shore and set apart by religious design.[12] The ebbing tide of prosperity which for so long had been based upon tobacco was not generally recognized. Samuel Dickinson's efforts to build a new domain in the 1730s were in part undoubtedly due to the increasing drop in tobacco prices, but he also thought in terms of two families and two estates. Mary Cadwalader Dickinson would be closer to Philadelphia, but the calm and isolation of Kent meant fewer neighboring friends. Nor would she see ships, shallops and barks, as silent as they were majestic, moving back and forth on the Choptank, an ever-changing panorama so close to the manor house. If ever Samuel Dickinson hesitated over his decision, the cool and critical voices of the Third Haven Meeting, particularly in regard to his daughter's marriage, were convincing.

Samuel Dickinson had been contemplating the move to Kent for some time. He had busily set to work going through endless litigation and recoveries to make sure that the land was his and the titles were clear. Now he was building a home. Set in the broad flat plain three hundred yards from the twisting St. Jones

---

[12] Carl Bridenbaugh, *Myths and Realities* (Baton Rouge, La., 1952), pp. 1–53.

River that snaked its way from the Delaware Bay to beyond Dover, the pedimented mansion faced due south. Built in Chesapeake style, it was perfectly proportioned, plain on the exterior, rising above the elevated cellar to a third floor and a triangulated roofline. The interior was more elaborate. The doorway entered into a spacious hallway with staircase. To the one side was a paneled parlor, while on the opposite side were two small rooms, each with fireplace. On the second story was the master's large bedroom, two small bedrooms, and over the hall and doorway a bright room for sewing and other necessary household chores. From here one could see the shallops as they moved up and down the river to the piers of the farms and plantations it served. A few years later a large dining room was built on the western end with an enclosed stairway to another room above it. The family named the mansion Poplar Hall.

Two years before his removal to Delaware in 1738 Samuel Dickinson had been appointed judge of the Court of Common Pleas for Kent County, and in 1744 he became a justice of the peace.[13] Formal training in the law was not necessary for appointment to either office; judicial temper, position, and prosperity were the considerations. Dickinson possessed all these attributes, and in addition he had learned much in the previous decade about land titles, suits, countersuits, and docking details. As judge he assumed a new role. The secular now supplanted the religious interest. Political justice replaced a morality established for a more personal community.

So it was that Samuel and Mary Cadwalader Dickinson and their two sons, John and Philemon, set out on a January day for their new home in Jones Neck. The journey, accompanied by their slaves and a wagon train carrying their goods, was deliberate. Leaving behind the waterways that flowed to the Chesapeake, they traveled toward the Lower Counties, the land now flat, the horizon marked only by edgings of the Delaware forests. Samuel Dickinson carefully recorded in the family Bible the act "that I and my wife and children came up to my plantation in Kent to live the 18th

---

[13] Powell, *The House on Jones Neck*, p. 22.

day of January 1740—old style which is the 29th day of January 1741 new style."

Continuing to profit by the tobacco market from his fields in Maryland and to some extent in Delaware, Samuel found the sandy soil of Kent more suitable to the raising of wheat and corn. New crops meant new business ties. From the pier on the St. Jones the shallops were filled with grain and dispatched northward to Christiana or Philadelphia, where it was ground into flour. Marshes and savannahs were many, and the tall reeds and rushes harbored birds, ducks, and other wildlife. There was a quiet beauty to this new, half-cultivated land, but in the summer the mosquitoes were unbearable, and the swamps both in the spring and autumn added a dampness that clung to man and beast. Nature was not kind, but the Dickinsons persisted.

Dickinson neighbors were now the Wilsons, the Rodneys, and the Whartons. The Loockermans and Ridgelys both in concern and taste were friends. There was a Quaker Meeting House, too, which Mary Dickinson attended, her letter of transfer having been properly sent. Samuel Dickinson did not request such a certificate.

Young John, slight in build and ever prey to the miasmatic air, was seven years older than his brother Philemon. In 1740 he was aged eight and his education already underway. One suspects that Mary Dickinson was the boys' earliest tutor, with Samuel teaching them at the dinner table and at the hearthside the lessons he himself was experiencing in business and in court. Several young men came and went as instructors. In the spring of 1745 James Orr, an Irishman, entered the Dickinson household "to teach school." For three years he was the dominant figure for John and young Philemon. During the first two years he also taught Sammy Chew, whose father, Samuel Chew, a Quaker physician, had been disowned by the Friends when as chief justice of New Castle he had charged the grand jury concerning the legality of resistance to an armed enemy.[14] After the death of Dr. Chew in 1744, Mary Chew, his widow, in 1745 paid for the young lad's "board and schooling" while he stayed with the Dickinsons, and the next year his brother Benja-

[14] *Appleton's Cyclopedia of American Biography* (New York, 1887), 1:601.

min, the future chief justice of Pennsylvania, assumed the responsibility.[15]

The Dickinson household also welcomed another young man, William Killen. He had known the Dickinson family since his arrival in America from Ireland nine years before. Now in 1746, aged twenty-four, he again entered the Dickinson home, studying informally with Orr, perhaps only mathematics, and learning to survey. In addition, he helped instruct young John in Latin. Intellectually alert and personally engaging, he was a happy companion for fourteen-year-old John. The friendship was an enduring one. In later years when John Dickinson journeyed down from Philadelphia to his lands in Kent, he would often meet Killen, then justice or still later chancellor of the state, living in Dover. When he failed to call, Killen in good humor would chide Dickinson over the omission.[16]

In 1750 John Dickinson was eighteen. His training, the long conversations with his father, and his study of Latin and history led directly to the law. Philadelphia was the court center for both Pennsylvania and the Lower Counties, as Delaware was known. John knew Penn's "Green Town" from previous visits to his relatives, the Cadwaladers and other kin. John Moland, who a decade before had come to Philadelphia as the king's attorney, was perhaps the most eminent member of the bar. His leadership attracted many students who read law with him. John Dickinson moved to the Quaker city and became one of them. Soon he and the other young men also in Moland's office, among them George Read of Delaware and Samuel Wharton, became warm and devoted friends.[17]

[15] L/HSP, XXIV, 62. See also a ledger in the Library Company of Philadelphia concerning Philemon and others; pp. 117ff. for Orr and Chew accounts.

[16] William Killen to JD, Item 18, R. R. Logan Collection of Dickinson Manuscripts, Library Company of Philadelphia (hereafter cited as L-D/LCP). On the basis of a "biographical account" of Dickinson by Deborah Logan it has always been declared that Killen was his tutor. The letter suggests this was not at least exclusively so.

[17] Charles J. Stillé, *The Life and Times of John Dickinson* (Philadelphia, 1891), p. 19.

Philadelphia was still a small town, its population expanding, yet not extending six blocks westward from the Delaware River. His kinship and close acquaintance with many prominent families eliminated any strangeness John might otherwise have known. The atmosphere of this comfortable Quaker society was one in which he felt at ease. John was advanced both in his sense of responsibility and, intellectually, in study. Friends in Kent had been few; the Wilsons had been neighbors and friendly,[18] the Rodneys neighbors but never close in personal association. Now in Philadelphia he found joy in meeting other young men pursuing the same interests. John entered this new life with enthusiasm.

The tasks of a law clerk ranged from assigned reading and research to being an amanuensis. The training was wholly pragmatic, based on the day-to-day experience of one's preceptor. The more advanced the mentor, the more likely the clerk was to enrich himself in legal action as well as in legal lore. But law in Pennsylvania and the colonies had its source in London, not alone because English law was the precedent for Penn's colony. Increasingly relations between Britain and the New World, as well as local mercantile associations with English agents, involved legal matters. Moland had studied at the Middle Temple. Americans, too, arrived yearly in London to pursue the study of law at the Temple, the Inns of Court, and Westminster.

For Samuel Dickinson it was not easy to forget the tragic loss of three sons who had been sent abroad and not returned. John's parents were also well aware of his alert and curious mind and his enthusiasm for his new intellectual mistress, the law. His expressed goal was to study abroad. The decision was finally made; they could not withstand their son's eagerness nor could they block his future career.

With excitement John wrote from Kent to his close friends Read and Wharton: "I am now preparing for my voyage to the other world not with the Common apparatus of coffin, winding sheet, etc., but with a cag of good spirits, a fine featherbed, gammons and fresh provisions—quantum sufficient—and I believe few

---

[18] In letters to his mother (L/HSP, L-D/LCP), the Wilsons are the only nonfamily to whom he sent greetings or usually mentioned.

Christians expect their departure with more resolution and alacrity."[19]

By mid-October the traveler set off at a gallop for the Chesapeake, accompanied by his black servant Cato. Waiting for the ship to collect its cargo, he dutifully called on his older half brother Henry at Croisadore. But John was anxious and doubtless nervous over the prospect that lay before him. He left almost at once to visit friends and neighbors in the county, promising to return. After a day or two, having sent Cato to Oxford to inquire about sailing, he learned he must be at the dock on Saturday. So on the last Saturday in October, young John Dickinson went on board, the anchor was weighed, and the vessel moved out into the bay. There had been no time to return again to Croisadore to say goodbye to Henry. Henry's early conflicts with his stepmother and the differing personality of the two sons had weakened familial ties.

The voyage lasted eight weeks and three days, beset at the beginning and the end by bad weather. John was a poor sailor, keeping to his cabin for five weeks. But Captain Hill was solicitous of his twenty-one-year-old passenger and even conducted him to the door of John Hanbury, the London merchant, who was to be Dickinson's mentor for the next three years.[20]

This was Hogarth's London. The bustle and the confusion, even the splendor of the great bridges across the Thames and of Wren's St. Paul's Cathedral, then less than a century old, failed to surprise the young visitor. The rush and tumble of the metropolis he perhaps expected, the architectural beauty he considered only "necessary and proper for the glory of so great a city." In all honesty he was bound to report that the city was more "troublesome than unkind." At first he found himself in a "social wilderness, as much at a loss amongst houses and men as in the strangest forest." Yet

[19] JD to Read and Wharton, Richard S. Rodney Collection, Historical Society of Delaware (hereafter cited as RSR/HSD).

[20] Trevor Colbourn, "A Pennsylvania Farmer at the Court of King George: John Dickinson's London Letters, 1754–1756," *PMHB* 86 (1962):241–86 and 417–53. The next pages are drawn from these published letters unless otherwise noted.

John Dickinson quickly wended his way amid the social and physical labyrinth of Britain's capital.

John Hanbury, the Dickinsons' London agent, greeted John warmly. Knowing the young man's kinship with the Goldsboroughs of Maryland, he at once sent him to the rooms of Robert Goldsborough, who lodged at the Temple where he had settled the year before. Dickinson moved in with his old friend until he found quarters for himself. Hanbury proved an unusually wise counselor, going at once into the matter of expenses. The family had expected £100 a year to be sufficient support for their son. Hanbury, however, pointed out that Goldsborough, living frugally, needed at least £120 and that beginning costs would certainly add £40 more.[21] This was an unhappy announcement for John to send his father but less so than the news that tobacco was currently a glut on the London market.

John's first few months in London were spent in getting settled. The Hanburys treated him as their son, and he frequently dropped in at their home unannounced for dinner, tea, or supper. Letters proved good introductions to many households. Mrs. William Anderson, who had been Rebecca Lloyd of Maryland's eastern shore, invited him for Christmas dinner; John Moland's sister welcomed him often; while Anthony Bacon and Elias Bland, the latter a former Philadelphia Quaker as well as an old family acquaintance, helped check any homesickness John may have felt.

Upon the advice of Charles Hopkins, subtreasurer of the Temple, Dickinson, four months after his arrival, took chambers in Essex Court[22] after they had been freshly painted and whitewashed. At the same time, on Hanbury's advice, he ordered mahogany furniture of the best quality which in the future he could ship home. As the new student observed, the young law students lived freely and without control, able to study quietly or to behave otherwise as they would.

Almost at once the young man met fellow Americans studying at the Temple: William Drayton of South Carolina, Charles Car-

---

[21] Colbourn (p. 251) points out that this figure is low.

[22] Account Book, 1754, L-D/LCP.

roll of Annapolis, William Hicks, son of Edward Hicks of Philadelphia, and John Hammond of Maryland, among others.[23] With
them he attended the theater and saw David Garrick and Hannah
Pritchard probably in a Shakespeare performance. He went skat-
ing on Rosamond's Pond for recreation and visited every monu-
ment of significance. The courts were adjourned until the end of
January, but when they finally reconvened the pleasures he enjoyed became less frequent.

Law, based on precedent, has an affinity with history. By March,
Dickinson found himself inspired by the thoughts that Coke and
Plowden had lived in the same Inns of Courts as he did, that the
halls where he daily heard cases debated once had witnessed the
defenses of Hampden and Holt against the tyranny of injustice.
The wisdom, knowledge, and intelligence of the barristers he
heard were more impressive than the grandeur and solemnity of
the courts of law themselves. Yet above all, assessing the most
learned of these judges, barristers, and solicitors, Dickinson noted
that knowledge needed the handmaid of clarity of expression to
be significant and that facts alone were insufficient for rendering
judgment.

Doors everywhere seemed to open wide upon one educational
experience or another, from the courts themselves to the House
of Lords. It was a surprise that members of that noble assemblage
were quite plain in appearance, "most ordinary men." The kalei-
doscope of London's streets, theaters, coffeehouses, and official sittings almost overwhelmed him, but, remembering the expecta-
tions his parents held for him, Dickinson asserted that the courts
were "the anchor that keeps the giddiness of youth from ship-
wreck."

John Dickinson had never been physically strong. Slight of
frame, he was easy prey to pulmonary attacks. This first son of a
second marriage at times was overprotected by love and thus beset
by exaggerated self-concern. He was frequently upset by changed
and changing conditions. The "fits" which he reported had preceded his voyage had been compounded by the rough voyage it-

[23] C. E. A. Bedwell, "American Middle Templers," *American Historial Review* 25 (1920):684.

self, making him fearfully seasick. The winter was damp and gloomy, and he was physically run-down. Early in February he drove four miles to Clapham, then a small village, where a month in clearer air restored him in health and spirit.

Thomas Cadwalader, his uncle, had sent him a letter of introduction to Thomas Penn from Richard Peters, a provincial secretary of Pennsylvania. Upon his return from the country, Dickinson took the introduction to Penn and was immediately received by the Pennsylvania proprietor. The visit was pleasant, the host inquiring about the fruits and products raised in the Lower Counties. Penn remembered Justice Dickinson, and in parting he invited the lad to dinner a few days afterwards. The proprietor opened many doors for the young Dickinson, who was appreciative of his many kindnesses and liked him personally. This hospitality, however, did not blind John, both then and in the future, to Penn's demands as proprietor and selfish attitudes toward his colony.

When the courts closed, Dickinson turned to reading; but this was no substitute for practical experience. He wrote, albeit with some self-consciousness:

> There is great variety & entertainment in the study of our profession, especially in England. We see how the courts of justice are crowded by people who know nothing of the law; how much more agreable then must it be to us who understand everything that is said. Here we are not always plodding over books: Westminster Hall is a school of law where we not only hear what we have read repeated, but disputed & sifted in the most curious & learned manner, nay frequently hear things quite new, have our doubts cleared up, & our errors corrected. The barr is a perfect comment upon the written law, & every great man at it is in some measure a master & instructor to these young students who have the wisdom to attend there.[24]

By May, Dickinson wrote his parents that a year and a half in England was insufficient for a proper grounding in the law there. He had lost the first four or five months to his poor health and ad-

[24] JD to his father, April 22, 1754, L-D/LCP.

justment. He reckoned that in two more years he would receive a degree as barrister. Coming home sooner would give the impression that he had completed his studies, which would not be the case. The elder Dickinsons were persuaded.

In his reassuring letters home, Dickinson wrote his father about the law and his experiences at the courts as well as any business of interest. To his mother he wrote accounts of his visits to friends, about the theater—to which he went a dozen times in the first six months—and his reflections on life and style. And in them all he was given to moralizing and often quoting historians, legal experts, and others. Much he wrote was self-conscious.

"As to the vicious pleasures of London," he assured his parents, "I know not what they are; I never hear of them; and never think of them. Good company is the bulwark of virtue. I was so happy as to get into a set of acquaintance who know their interest and are resolved to prosecute it." Another time he observed, "Virtuous company is the strongest guard to a person's morals." But his protests about his virtues often pall. Some eight years later, at the request of a concerned mother whose son was about to leave for similar study abroad, Dickinson reminisced and suggested the student would find it more agreeable to live with his uncle than in the Inns of Court, which were "more expensive, more inconvenient and more dangerous . . . dangerous to the morals of young gentlemen." To meet others engaged in the same study, the student should dine during term time in the Commons, as he had done. "It will be well worth your while to make very intimate connections with those you observe to be the most industrious. You will find conversation corrects a thousand errors that laborious reading may blunder into. It would be still better, after you have read sometime you cou'd form a little Society of 8 or 10 persons to meet at each other's apartments once a week; and argue points of law that were proposed the week before. I belonged to such a set in the Temple and am convinced that nothing would be of greater service to a young lawyer."[25]

The Westminster Courts, which Dickinson called a "school of law," were held at the far end of that great hall. The rest of the

[25] Draft of a letter, "Advice to a young man," n.d., Londoun Papers, HSP.

hall, lined with book stalls and shops, failed to compete very seriously with the notable barristers and justices of the courts themselves. The experience in Moland's office in Philadelphia proved valuable, for the young man commented that many of his fellow students at the Inns of Court began their studies without knowing anything of practice, believing "it sufficient to understand the difficult cases in the books while . . . ignorant of the law that is daily made use [of]." "A little practise," he asserted, "explains a great deal of reading—and many hours are often spent in discovering a point in one way that might be known in a few minutes in the other." While in that section of London, Dickinson often stopped at the "cockpit" in Whitehall to hear the Lords Commissioners for Appeals from the Plantations and hear the causes argued "by the best lawyers at the bar."

From time to time he would send notes of speeches in Westminster Hall to his father, or again notes of arguments such as those before the Lords of Trade on Pennsylvania laws to his Uncle Cadwalader. Young Dickinson by midsummer had resumed good health and settled down to a routine, rising at five, reading for nearly eight hours daily, dining at four o'clock, and early to bed. Having somehow discovered that to read standing up benefited his health, he had a reading stand built for the purpose.[26] He continued his study of the classics with Tacitus, Cicero, and Sallust, while Rapin and Bolingbroke gave him insights into the background of England and its laws. He purchased many books, legal and historical, and made appropriate marginal notes in their pages. He transcribed Servienti's *Doctrina Placitandi* and bound it with notes into three large volumes and studied the *Art of Reading*, which Coke had pronounced the "very life of the law." He continued with Coke's *Institutes* and the reports of Plowden, Ventris, and Salkend. But it was Bacon from whom Dickinson seemed to profit most and whom he admired for his brilliant use of language, phrase, and allusion.[27] When Dickinson went to St. Alban's

[26] The Library Company of Philadelphia has Dickinson's reading stand which authorities consider to be a music stand. No record of musical interest lies with the Dickinson family.

[27] William G. Soler, "Some Important Influences upon John Dickinson," Ph.D. diss., Temple University, 1953.

and there entered the little church of St. Michael's, where Bacon was buried, he was deeply affected, for he considered that writer "the greatest man that ever lived."

Early in March 1755 Dickinson again fell ill, and Hanbury suggested he see a doctor, who in turn advised him to "get into the country and use exercise," temporarily setting aside all study. Robert Goldsborough went with him, and together they took up lodgings in Kingston across the Thames from Hampton Court. Goldsborough, in a sudden decision, and without the consent of his father, married Sarah Yerbury late that month, a move that shocked Goldsborough's family in America and disturbed Dickinson's parents. John set forth as good a defense as he could of this marriage but assured his mother that "in an affair of so much importance, I should think oneself obliged to have the consent of my parents." His mother worried about her son's possible romantic inclinations and expressed her concern. John told her that he knew no one for whom he held a "single thought as a wife" and was free from "any engagement of affection."[28]

Residence in Kingston was a good tonic, and Dickinson remained there intermittently until October when, having fully recovered, he returned to town. To keep in shape, he engaged in fencing and shuttlecock and confidently looked forward to the last winter of his visit.

Many times his thoughts turned to his family and Kent. He worried about his mother's exhausting rounds of the plantations and the attendant care of the slaves and tenants. He urged her to find a white maid who could lighten her burden. His father had been ill with the gout. John pictured him sitting by a cheerful fire and strengthened by John's letters from London. New sights, too, contributed to new ideas for Poplar Hall, and John set forth possibilities for hedges and vistas and flower gardens to make it "a most delightful spot."[29]

The one year of London study extended to three. Admitted to the "Honorable Society of the Middle Temple" on December 21,

[28] JD to his mother, April 8, 1755, L-D/LCP.

[29] JD to his father, February 19, 1755, JD to his mother, October 29, 1754, L-D/LCP.

1753, John was called to the degree of the Utter Barr on February 8, 1757. The next day, all duties paid, the fact was published in the Common Dining Hall and finally inscribed on March 14, 1757.[30]

To his early interest in the law, John Dickinson had added experience and study, establishing a firm foundation as well as a breadth of understanding.

He reflected on all he heard and observed. The politics of England were disturbing yet engrossing. At one point he observed that public affairs were so badly managed that "it is disagreeable saying anything about them." The general elections in the spring of 1754 had been shocking, and to Dickinson the corruption and "decline of virtue" was clear. "It is astonishing," he wrote his father, "what imprudence and villainy are practised." Bribery (£1 million from London alone) and corruption were rampant, oaths were laughed off. When, following the death of Henry Pelham, other elections were held and the returns disputed, his earlier observations seemed confirmed. The election engravings of Hogarth were only too true. At one stage John declared the people licentious and without religion and observed that opportunities for the Wesleys abounded. Such a deplorable condition served only to strengthen his own sense of rectitude.

Yet he was not blind to the weakness of his native land and its institutions. Pennsylvania was rent by divisions over taxation, defense, and the authority of the Penns. Slavery, which he knew at first hand, he viewed as an evil which debased its sponsors. Factionalism, he found, led to party strife and was wasteful. He saw man influenced by "private passion" losing sight of the public good. He had learned his lessons well. Above all, the sense of individual liberty and the protection of it by law seemed paramount. England's impression upon him was immense. Now the time had come to sail westward and home.

[30] Certification, L-D/LCP.

☆ 2 ☆

Beginning a
Career

John Dickinson RETURNED HOME with greater understanding of the law and an affection for the mother country. But at heart and in manner he was unchanged. He had enjoyed the cosmopolitan life abroad, the theaters and entertainments of Vauxhall, the kaleidoscopic changes of London, yet soon they became far removed.

Wind and weather determined the exact time of his return to Kent in 1757. The eagerness to welcome him increased daily at Poplar Hall. Philemon, now eighteen, had recently gone to Philadelphia to live with his uncle Dr. Thomas Cadwalader. Judge Dickinson's health had grown progressively worse, and his bed had been brought down to the first-floor dining room. Mrs. Dickinson was tireless in her rounds of the plantation, with manifold tasks deflecting any anxious thoughts of her two absent sons.

When John's return was imminent, she sent word throughout the plantation. Violet, the daughter of Pompey, the personal servant of the old judge, never forgot the excitement. All the children were clothed in clean dresses and blouses. Then word came to assemble. "Like a flock of blackbirds," Violet recalled, they all came running to welcome the long absent heir. The chaise sent to meet him in Dover now clattered down the driveway. His parents' joy was unbounded, and the now silent and respectful servants and children gathered about. Old Pompey came forward and kissed his hand, and then the young barrister gently greeted the wide-eyed children. Cakes were passed to each of them in celebration.[1]

Early summer in Kent can be soft and compelling. Mixed with the emotion of seeing his parents once again was interest in the changes made to the mansion itself. John often in his homeward thoughts had pictured "the charming walk down to the wharf" and he was eager to see if his suggestions for landscaping in the English style had been implemented.

There were changes in the household. Judge Dickinson was now sixty-eight. Debilitating and constant attacks of gout limited his activities. From the south windows he could look across the field to the St. Jones River and watch the wagons being loaded and unloaded as the shallops lay along the wharf. From the north windows he could see the slave quarters and the work buildings of the plantation. Thus the squire could oversee much of the daily activity. The family gathered with him in the dining room, making it also a sitting room. Visitors could enter it from the outside by a separate door.[2]

John lingered long that summer, enjoying conversations with his father and recounting much that he had not reported in letters home. He had carried with him his major law books and other more particular notebooks. He reviewed his voluminous notes in the margins and interpages of the *Doctrina Placitandi*, written in a peculiar hodgepodge of French and English.[3] He also indexed his Commonplace Book.[4]

Other books arrived packed in chests: one containing volumes of Shakespeare, the *Odyssey*, Callimachus's *Hymn to Jupiter*, *Old Castle Remarks*, a work on the *Immortality of the Soul*, Plato's

[1] Notes by Sarah Norris Dickinson of a conversation with Violet, daughter of Pompey, L/HSP, IX, 65.

[2] Ibid.

[3] *Doctrina Placitandi on L'art & Science De Bon Pleading* . . . (London, 1677). See Dickinson copy, Logan Family Papers, HSP, with notes in vol. 1.

[4] Commonplace Book, L/HSP.

First Alabades, and Tacitus. The fine furniture he had purchased at the suggestion of Hanbury to furnish his Essex Court rooms also had been shipped, and much of it was forwarded directly to Philadelphia.[5]

There is little doubt that John Dickinson that summer had his attention drawn to the business of the plantations. When John was a boy in his teens his father had vested him with early responsibilities and specific duties. Now the twenty-five-year-old son, assisting his ailing father, was duty bound to look closer at the Dickinson holdings.

Mary Dickinson had her own responsibilities in seeing to the welfare of the slaves, who in men, women, and children numbered seventy-two in 1760. She made sure that they were all provided with shirts and shifts, supervised the labor of the house servants, and directed other household tasks.[6]

By the fall of 1757 the time had come for the young lawyer to practice all he had learned. On his return to Philadelphia, he reunited with friends and kin. John's maternal uncle, Dr. Thomas Cadwalader, in whose house he had lodged while first studying law, welcomed him once again. Dr. Cadwalader's three living children had grown. Lambert was now seventeen, John fifteen, and Margaret thirteen. There were also Morris relatives: his mother's sister Hannah, who had married the lawyer Samuel Morris, and their children, Cadwalader and Samuel, Jr. Still in their midteens, his cousins provided both warmth and liveliness. There was strong intellectual motivation in both families as well as involvement in current issues.

Philemon had come to the city to study at the College of Philadelphia. The sound, if somewhat nagging, "good advice" John had written his younger brother from London apparently had found a willing reception. Philemon left the college and now came directly under his brother's eye while he studied law in John's office.

John Dickinson took up residence in a house on South Second

[5] Ledger, 1758–59, L-D/LCP.

[6] Ibid.

Street. The city had spread both west and southward. Market Street continued as the busiest thoroughfare. A block to the east along Front Street, one looked down on the bristling wharves lining the riverbank. In this pleasant provincial capital one clearly sensed the dynamics of trade, the entrance both for ideas and for goods, the place of arrival for new people and often new notions. Westward and beyond lay the limitless future, the distance into which men and supplies moved to yet another kind of life, while eastward flowed their demands for governmental settlements and legal solutions.

John Dickinson rose quickly to the top of his profession, a preeminent position he held for the next fifteen years, during which he was active both as barrister and as solicitor.

The brilliance of the Philadelphia Bar in the mid-eighteenth century shone in retrospect for more than a century. William Allen was chief justice when Dickinson first came to court. Benjamin Chew, ten years John's senior, who had studied at the Middle Temple and first practiced in Dover, in 1754 moved to Philadelphia and the next year had been appointed attorney general of Pennsylvania. His relationship with Dickinson, however, was cool for the two families had disagreed over lands in Delaware. Joseph Galloway, son of a Delaware Quaker, a year younger than John, had practiced in Philadelphia since 1747. Already a brilliant lawyer and possessing a rich knowledge of history, he soon became a major political adversary of Dickinson. John Moland, John's former mentor, as well as Nicholas Waln, Edward Shippen, and James Tilghman became associates and often partners of Dickinson in court cases.[7]

His slightly more than average height accentuated Dickinson's slenderness. His clear eyes and a prominent aquiline nose dominated his face. There was an elegance in his carriage, a poise and confidence that were particularly notable. His professional approach was erudite and so markedly learned that his reputation

[7] A. J. Dallas, *Reports of Cases in the Courts of Pennsylvania*, 4th (Albany, N. Y., 1882), 1:3–5, 17, etc. See also John Dickinson, "Eastern Shore Lawyers at the Early Philadelphia Bar," *Pennsylvania Bar Association Quarterly* 13 (1942): 177–89.

grew easily. The hours he had spent at Westminster proved their value in the eloquent and persuasive manner in which the young lawyer pled his cases.

The cases Dickinson defended were less extraordinary than the serious and sincere approach to each which the young barrister took. Legal and historical precedent and above all a methodical presentation polished by his never-failing choice of expression won him quick acceptance—indeed, an unusually early reputation. Although Philemon had become his brother's clerk, the law was not to his taste. Other young men soon filled his place in Dickinson's office. Dickinson kept close record of every case undertaken. His continuance docket from the September term, 1760, to June 1772 was sedulously maintained. Moreover, the notebooks he had begun in London were extended.[8]

As a youth listening to his father, John had become instinctively aware of common law and its ethic. Property administration and all "rights, interests and perogatives" of landholders within the legal process had been the basis for his earliest understanding. Frequently involved with disputed land titles, Dickinson noted that many people with large tracts in the province had relied on deeds made from earlier patents.[9] In one case dealing with a land title in the estate of one C. Marshall, he wrote:

> If my opinion depended on the laws of England, it would be very clear. . . . But I cannot forbear entertaining some doubt what the decision would be here, under the customs of the Province. . . . I think upon the whole it may be justly observed that to consider the deeds of lease and release executed before the Proprietor set sail to take possession of his grant with his first Adventurers as *Declarations of Trust* is

[8] John Dickinson's Memorandum Book, 1762–72, L/HSP, and Manuscripts on the Practise of Law, L-D/LCP. See also Dickinson's Continuance Docket, 1760–72, L/HSP. For an account of legal fees received, see Lists, L/HSP, XXXIV, 135–51.

[9] Collections of Dickinson Papers in both the Historical Society of Pennsylvania and the Library Company of Philadelphia have innumerable notes, papers, and letters dealing with clearances of land titles and patents belonging both to Dickinson and to his clients.

to consider them in the same light as those adventurers did. Since the almost constant usage was on their arrival in America to take out patents of confirmation.[10]

Law for John Dickinson was an ennobling profession. Years later he declared "the law delights in certainty and quiet because, without these, there can be no liberty."[11] His practice was personally fulfilling. Not only did it satisfy him emotionally and intellectually; as a livelihood the law also was rewarding. Writing his mother in 1763, he happily reported: "Money flows in and my vanity has been very agreeably flattered of late."[12]

Returning to Philadelphia also meant renewing old friendships and establishing new ones. A certain precocity in John Dickinson's early years, accompanied by a somewhat dogmatic certainty about his actions and opinions, could be trying to those who knew him less intimately. Others admired him, and friendships ripened quickly.

To John Hall of Annapolis, an old friend, he wrote easily and with jocular analogy. By 1762 Dickinson had become involved in politics both in Delaware and Pennsylvania, and so had John Hall in his home state. Dickinson, reflecting on an earlier struggle between Pennsylvania's proprietors and the Assembly, wrote him, "Your patriots have taken deep draughts of our politics—We left some drops in the cup that might make another brewing; but your gentlemen have gone to the bottom—we drank a good deal—but it made us active—your dose was so strong that you have kept your beds these six years and the fumes of the liquor have not yet evaporated." Dickinson continued with other observations on the legislature, joked about horse racing, and then suggested that when the courts reconvened Hall would need to change his style. "However I think it will be proper both for you and me to remember old Cato's advice and mix pleasure with business—and innocence with pleasure—Application and fatigue may procure reputation

[10] JD to Marshall, February 9, 1764, L/HSP, XV, 4.

[11] Dallas, 4:viii.

[12] JD to his mother, September 14, 1763. Maria Dickinson Logan Collection, HSP (hereafter cited as MDL/HSP).

and wealth—but they destroy health and happiness." In spite of the levity of tone and comment, at the same time he returned with thanks a copy of Sterling's *Sermons*.[13]

The two lawyers Thomas McKean and George Read throughout their long lives proved to be steadfast and understanding friends of Dickinson. Read, short and stocky, left Philadelphia while Dickinson was in England and returned to his native Delaware. The two men were physically different yet temperamentally much alike. During the trying days of the Revolution and continuing into the period of Confederation, they were destined to act almost in tandem.

But it was Thomas McKean, who, two years younger than Dickinson, was not only a newfound colleague but a warm and affectionate friend, though the two often found themselves on opposite political sides. One of Francis Alison's most brilliant pupils, McKean at twenty had already been admitted to the Delaware Bar and in 1757 became clerk of the Assembly. The attraction was immediate, particularly for Dickinson. McKean was alert, abounding in ideas and enthusiastic in attitude. Intellectually he matched many of John's own qualities. In an early letter sent from Philadelphia to New Castle in the first few months after his return, Dickinson declared: "As I flatter myself that we are to look upon ourselves as friends to each other throughout life, I hope you will not expect any declaration of my esteem, but will be convinced by all my actions; the unaffected freedom of my behavior towards you, that it is very great: as an instance of this, I beg you will give yourself the trouble to take out a *capias* on the enclosed declaration against Hachett who lives at the Trap."[14]

When McKean was in Philadelphia it became occasion for reunion. In mid-June 1760, discovering that he had missed McKean, Dickinson wrote urging him to come up soon again: "If you have as much pleasure in being with me, as I have when with you, you will come up sooner than you mention. If you do not find this selfish motive sufficient to move you, let a more generous one pre-

[13] JD to Hall, May 3, 1762, Dreer Collection, Member of Congress (MOC), 32, HSP.

[14] JD to McKean, October 20, 1757, McKean Papers, 1, HSP.

vail; and come to make that addition to my happiness which it is in your power to make."[15]

The two lawyers frequently transacted business for one another at court. Dickinson cautioned McKean, however, that he should not overwork, teasing him about his activities in New Castle. "If you write with such application you will make yourself too weak to receive any benefits from your jaunt. Moderation in everything is the source of happiness—too much writing—too much reading—too much eating—too much drinking—too much exercise—too much idleness—too much loving—too much continence—too much law—physics—or religion—all equally throw us from the balance of real pleasure—this has been said a thousand times—always believed—and practiced against—this is still true."[16]

Legal matters carried both men to other courts, and they often traveled together. Dickinson promised that if McKean would come join him in Easton for a week in court, he would then follow him "to the Jerseys, to Thebes, to Athens or the Lord knows where."[17] McKean's interest in the Jerseys became evident when in the next year he married Mary Borden. The junkets together were thereafter less frequent, but the friendship forged was ironbound.

Philadelphia had three fishing clubs, social enclaves of prominent men, between the Upper Ferry and the Falls of the Schuylkill. Mount Regale Fishing Company in 1763 had forty-two members, including Justice William Allen, Benjamin Chew, Thomas Mifflin, and Edward Shippen. John and Philemon were both members. John also purchased a share in the Library Company from Abraham Taylor and bought a bond for the use and benefit of the Pennsylvania Hospital.[18] Acting upon one's responsibilities to the community, whether plantation, town, or colony, had been stressed by the Dickinson family. The young lawyer was to find many such opportunities.

[15] Ibid., June 16, 1760.

[16] Ibid., June 8, 1762.

[17] Ibid., June 14, 1762.

[18] Thomas W. Balch, *Letters and Papers Relating to the Provincial History of Pennsylvania* (Philadelphia, 1855), p. xx; *PMHB* 21 (1897):417; L/HSP, VIII, 63, 70.

Government service for colonial gentlemen of property was recognized as a duty and a trust. Although he practiced law in Philadelphia, young Dickinson's ties to his home acres in Delaware were strong. His friendship with both Read and McKean kept him abreast of politics in the Lower Counties. The residents of Pennsylvania and Delaware moved frequently between the two colonies and maintained close ties. The proprietary governor of Pennsylvania was also the governor of Delaware, though each colony had a separate legislative body.

In October 1759 John Dickinson was elected a member of Delaware's Assembly. Despite his residence and legal practice in Philadelphia, he had many interests, both familial and personal, in Delaware. The Assembly's sitting was a short one.[19] The following October, Dickinson was reelected representative from Kent County, as was Vincent Loockerman of Dover. The last week in October the governor convened the eighteen-man Assembly, and the twenty-eight-year-old John was chosen Speaker.[20] These two years of legislative experience proved to be a good test. Undergirded by the distinguished position his family held, the young barrister quickly grew in his new role.

Dickinson was not returned a third year. John was replaced by his neighbor Caesar Rodney, and Loockerman by John Vining, also from Dover. But Dickinson's interest in the affairs of the Lower Counties did not wane, though he was keenly aware that he had opponents. In October 1762 when asking Read to take over a law case, Dickinson proposed a law for Delaware similar to one passed in Pennsylvania. There was no personal involvement in the suggestions, but he commented, "I know some persons would industriously oppose it if they could find out that either my head or hand or even my little finger had been employed in framing it."[21] Dickinson already was supersensitive to criticism.

In the meantime, a major change occurred in the Dickinson family. Judge Samuel Dickinson early in July 1760 died at the age of seventy-one. The *Pennsylvania Gazette*, reporting his death, de-

[19] *Pennsylvania Gazette*, October 25, 1759.

[20] Ibid., October 9, 22, November 6, 1760.

[21] JD to Read, October 1, 1762, RSR/HSD.

clared him to be "a gentleman possessed of so many worthy and valuable qualities of disposition and understanding, that if justice only should be done to his merit, strangers to his person would imagine the character to be drawn by some near and afflicted mind; and to those who had any intimacy with him, nothing more than that is necessary to make them preserve the remembrance of his virtues and to render his memory ever dear to them."[22] He was buried in the family plot near Poplar Hall.

There was much to be done in settling the estate. Mary Dickinson and Philemon both renounced their executorship, turning over that responsibility to John. All three of them soon made their own wills: Philemon first, and six months later, their mother. "Sick and weak" in body, she made her own testament ordering that her "personal estate should not be appraised nor any account or inventory made thereof or filed in the Registers Office as my debts are very inconsiderable and entirely rely on the integrity of my sons."[23] This prohibition of an inventory and appraisal followed similar instructions given by the old judge and subsequently set forth by John in his turn.

Mrs. Dickinson chose to remain in Kent. Many affairs remained to be put in order. The slaves needed care and management. While John clearly regarded Philadelphia as his professional home, he was unwilling to cut his Kent County ties.

In 1761, the same year he was not returned to the Delaware Assembly, John Dickinson was proposed for the Pennsylvania House but lost the election.[24]

The next year, however, proved successful for him. Early in May 1762 Thomas Leech, member of the Assembly from Philadelphia County, died. A special election was held for his seat and John Dickinson was chosen.[25] By adjournment Dickinson had not yet appeared; his attendance was thus delayed until September 7,

[22] *Pennsylvania Gazette*, July 24, 1760.

[23] Wills and Papers, dated August 26, 1760, January 1, 1761, June 9, 1761, L/HSP, box 6.

[24] *Pennsylvania Archives*, 8th ser., Gertrude MacKinney, ed. (Philadelphia, 1931), 7:5669–70 (8th ser. hereafter cited as *Votes*).

[25] Ibid., 6:5343.

when the legislative body reconvened. When the regular October election was held, Dickinson became a formal candidate.

Early that month his mother had heard "many alarming accounts of the disorder which rages in town" and wrote her "dear Johnny" of her deep concern: "How can you answer to your own heart by running such an unnecessary risque—if you have no regard for yourself remember a mother who will be one of the most unhappy living if you should be too negligent about yourself till it is too late." She begged him to come down to Kent. But the election was more important. Dickinson won easily and became one of eight representatives from Philadelphia County.[26] The year before there had been a "candid manly declaration of reasons opposing" him, but now he had won, in his words, "the general approbation of good men." He wrote George Read after the election: "You may congratulate me on my salvation for I am certainly among the elect—and may enter into the assembly of righteous men—as I hope they all are. My pleasure is, that this happens without opposition, or the discontent of those I esteem—which I regard as a great happiness." A successful young man of thirty cannot be blamed for ambitious goals. The elated Dickinson happily added, "I confess I should like to make an immense bustle in the world if it could be by virtuous actions—But as there is no probability of that, I am content if I can live innocent and beloved by those I love."[27]

The Quakers may have endorsed Dickinson for this election, as they apparently did the year before. His mother was a staunch Friend, and so were many of his Philadelphia kin. The Quakers were espousing all the popular causes: taxation of proprietary estates, paper money, and voluntary military service. Nevertheless, his father's experience and his long discussions with his son regarding religious societies had turned the young man from even a hint of active membership, and John's predelictions came to place him opposite the Society.

On January 11, 1763, Dickinson took his seat in the Assembly. James Hamilton was governor. In his Council were Benjamin

[26] Dickinson's mother to JD, L/HSP, VIII, 62; *Votes*, 6:5367.

[27] JD to Read, October 1, 1762, RSR/HSD.

Chew, the attorney general, and Thomas Cadwalader, John's uncle. The thirty-six Assembly members included William Allen, chief justice, serving as an elected representative for Cumberland County, Joseph Galloway, elected by Philadelphia County, and Benjamin Franklin, representing the city.

In the first few months of the sessions, Dickinson served on committees charged with both colonial and city matters since the Assembly also regulated Philadelphia affairs. He assisted in the preparation of a "bill for regulating the Courts of Judicature" of the province, an "Act to regulate waggoners, carters, draymen and porters within the city," and the creation of a general law on the relief of the poor.[28] One bill erecting a lighthouse at or near Cape Henlopen at the mouth of the Delaware had a peculiar interest for the new legislator whose homeland was not far away.

At this time Penn's colony was enjoying a period of calm. William Allen, as leader of the Proprietary party, in 1761 had opposed Benjamin Franklin's continuation as Pennsylvania agent to England. Allen predicted that on Franklin's return, dissension would boil over once more.[29] Franklin returned to Philadelphia in the autumn of 1762, but did not take his seat until January 1763. In the meantime several matters became serious concerns for the Assembly, notably Indian trade, the raising of money for defense, and proper protection of frontier settlements.

Two factors stand forth concerning colonial Pennsylvania's Assembly. Defense costs were tied to taxation. The Charter of Liberties granted to the people of his province by William Penn in 1701 gave the unicameral legislature greater power than any other similar body in America with the exceptions of Connecticut and Rhode Island. Moreover, the king promised he would not tax the province "unless the same be with the consent of the proprietary or chief governor, or assembly, or by act of Parliament in England."[30]

A second and equally significant aspect of the Assembly lay in the early Quaker dominance of that body. As early as 1754, when

[28] *Votes*, 6:5383–84.

[29] Theodore G. Thayer, *Pennsylvania Politics and the Growth of Democracy* (Harrisburg, Pa., 1953), p. 79.

[30] Ibid., p. 3.

western frontier settlements were attacked, the proprietors, hoping for support for military budgets, found the German settlers siding with the Quakers, who were cool to the frequent defense needs. Robert Hunter Morris, newly appointed governor, in December 1754 sought to raise £20,000 in bills of credit for the king's troops and £20,000 in paper money to be added to the currency then in circulation. The question lay unsettled though an interim loan was obtained from the Loan Office. Meanwhile, the governor informed the Board of Trade of his dilemma. Finally, in July 1755, following Braddock's defeat, the Assembly voted £50,000 in bills of credit to be funded by a tax on all property, a bill which for the first time included the estates of the proprietors. Once more the proprietors objected to taxation of their lands. The demand set off a festering dispute that lasted a decade, with the proprietors on one side of the issue and the so-called Quaker party, of which Benjamin Franklin, a non-Quaker, was leader, on the other.

William Allen, representative for Cumberland County in the Assembly, had sent the Board of Trade petitions that protested the inadequate defensive measures established by the "Quaker Assembly." That Board in turn pointed out to the Privy Council the ineffective steps taken by the pacifists. Franklin had proposed a militia law, but it was declared inadequate, and Thomas Penn himself sought means to prevent its passage. The rising dissensions caused the Privy Council to consider prohibiting Quakers from holding office during a war.[31] Protection of the frontier superseded all other matters. John Dickinson, studying in London at the time, heard the disputes as they were argued in Westminster. He found himself torn between his friendship and understanding of the proprietor's interest and the case set forth in favor of the Assembly. He wrote to his mother, "Which side shall an honest man espouse, where both are in the wrong?"[32] A militia law seemed reasonable to him.

On January 28, 1763, following a report of the Commissioners on Indian Affairs on Indian trade in the province, a committee was appointed to prepare a bill to amend and continue the act to

[31] *Votes*, 1:xxxix.

[32] JD to his mother, August 2, 1756, L-D/LCP.

prevent abuses in the trade.[33] The measure as proposed and passed involved taxing proprietary estates in common with others. Governor Hamilton then vetoed it on the grounds that it would be contrary to the determination of the king in council. The House would not rescind its action. Philadelphia merchants feared that Indian trade would be disrupted, while the Indians were provoked and hostilities again broke out on the frontier. Writing his mother in the informative vein he had once used in correspondence with his father, Dickinson said: "I imagine there will be a good deal of opposition—as many people are more desirous of the trade being unrestrained—than they are afraid of the Indians—But I think both prudence and good faith require the continuance of the present Act which was calculated to preserve the Indians from the importations of the most infamous and extortionate rascals who trade amongst them."[34] The bill was resubmitted, again including the taxation of proprietary estates. After significant amendments, the act was passed.[35] Taxation of proprietary estates, however, was deleted from the bill and that demand continued as cause for future political division.

Frontiersmen, having endured a generation of wars with the Indians, found it easy to blame the Assembly for the lack of defenses. The Quaker and eastern county influences were significant, although the former exercised control more through their associates than as representatives to that body.[36] When, in 1763, a band of Indians at Conestoga, near Lancaster, were murdered by recalcitrant settlers, people in Philadelphia were incensed, and all manner of proposals for avenging the Indian villagers were proposed. In the meantime, over a hundred Indians were being fed and sheltered in the Quaker City. Angered at such protection and the failure to view frontier problems sympathetically, a group in Lancaster County known as the Paxton Boys began a march on Philadelphia to demand justice from the Assembly and threatened to

[33] *Votes*, 6:5396.

[34] JD to his mother, March 7, 1763, MDL/HSP.

[35] *Votes*, 6:5411–14.

[36] Richard Bauman, *For the Reputation of Truth* (Baltimore, 1971), pp. 19–33; for the unequal distribution of representations, see *Votes*.

kill the Indians held there. Anarchy was seen as inherent in the situation. Met by conciliators in Germantown, the Lancaster men agreed to send a small delegation into Philadelphia and petition the Assembly for redress of their grievances. Chief among the demands were additional representation for the western counties and an increased number of circuit courts.

In January 1764 the Assembly was faced with the necessity of raising £50,000 for military needs. Similar sums in 1763 had been met only after bitter attacks on the proprietors whose lands the Assembly again sought to tax. John Penn, who had succeeded Hamilton as governor, held strictly to the instructions of his uncle Thomas Penn forbidding paper currency and taxing their lands. Franklin, however, proposed once again that the notes be redeemed by taxes collected from proprietary holdings. The arguments were later coupled with a parlimentary enactment making bills of credit legal tender. Of the debate, in which Dickinson sided with Franklin, Samuel Foulke, an assemblyman, noted: "B. Franklin and John Dickinson greatly distinguished themselves: the first as a politician, the other as an orator."[37] Any amicable relationship between Franklin and Dickinson, however, was to be short-lived.

Nothing in Dickinson's words or performance at this juncture could be regarded as a deviation from a Quaker or provincial establishment position. On March 20 Dickinson was one of those who waited on the governor to explain the Assembly's view regarding taxation of the proprietor's reserved and uncultivated lands.[38] The governor's retort that he would be guided only by royal order led the Assembly in reaction to pass another bill adhering to the original proposal, which granted £55,000 for his Majesty from taxes on proprietary lands.

The governor's intransigence on taxation, coupled with his re-

---

[37] "Fragments of a Journal Kept by Samuel Foulke," *PMHB* 5 (1881):68. Both assemblymen later wrote remonstrances against the Currency Act imposed by Parliament in 1764. This act was one of the first that weakened colonial loyalty to England. In 1765 Dickinson published a pamphlet, *The Late Regulations Respecting the British Colonies Considered,* and the following year Franklin printed his *Remarks and Facts Concerning American Paper Money.*

[38] *Votes,* 7:5574.

fusal to prosecute those responsible for the Conestoga massacres, helped revive Franklin's hearty dislike of the proprietors. Writing the Quaker John Fothergill in London, Franklin asserted, "All hopes of happiness under a proprietary government are at an end."[39] His antipathy to the Penns was deep rooted. When agent in London, he had argued with Richard and Thomas Penn about guarantees of liberties contained in the colonial charter of which he thought they took too strict a legal interpretation. As Franklin told Isaac Norris, from that moment he felt "a more cordial and thorough contempt for him [Thomas Penn] than I ever felt for any living man."[40] The Penns reciprocated this feeling. Franklin had long believed Pennsylvania was shackled by proprietary interests and would benefit by coming directly under the crown. In addition he believed George III a virtuous young man who would triumph over factions and poor advisers.[41]

Angered by the governor's refusal to compromise, Franklin began an assault. There could be no agreement. The Assembly clearly recognized the need for the appropriation. On March 24 it sent the governor a message that verged on rudeness. It implied contempt for the proprietary family and their attitude, which was adding to the already recognizable "load of obliquy and guilt" the Penns bore. That same day the Assembly passed twenty-six resolves. The final one declared that during adjournment the members would consult their constituents "whether a humble addition should be drawn up and transmitted to His Majesty, praying that he would be graciously pleased to take the People of this Province under his immediate protection and government."[42]

The next month Franklin distributed a pamphlet entitled *Cool Thoughts on the Present Situation of Our Public Affairs*; in it he was hardly cool toward Governor Penn and the proprietors. The people of Pennsylvania split over the issue of substituting a royal government for that of the proprietors. The Governor's Council

[39] Franklin to Fothergill, March 14, 1764; Leonard W. Labaree, ed., *The Papers of Benjamin Franklin* (New Haven, 1967), 11:104.

[40] Ibid., 7:362; Franklin to Norris, January 14, 1758.

[41] Ibid., 10:406–7; Franklin to the earl of Straban, December 19, 1763.

[42] *Votes*, 7:5586–96.

and their friends found allies in the Presbyterians, who feared that the crown would bring the established church with its bishops and tithes to Pennsylvania. The Quakers, who favored the proposed change, had Moravians on their side, some Anglican clergy, and a divided German support.

When the Assembly reconvened on May 14, they received a letter from Isaac Norris, the aging and infirm but highly honored Speaker for fourteen years, declaring that for physical reasons he no longer could continue in that office. Dickinson drove out with two other members to Fairhill, the Norris estate, to ask him to continue if at all possible for the short session. Norris acceded to the request but with uneasy heart and mind.

Dickinson's every action up to March 1764 tended to ally him with the ruling antiproprietary majority. He and Franklin stood together in arguing for interest-bearing bills of credit. In the six-week interim between Assembly sessions, Richard Peters, proprietary secretary for the province, wrote Thomas Penn that Dickinson had "entered the lists" against the Penns.[43] What they did not know was that as the tide of criticism against the proprietors rose, Dickinson found himself seriously weighing alternatives. He had good reason now to consider the history of parliamentary and ministerial actions toward the various colonies. He also remembered his own criticisms during his London years when Parliament failed to enact a militia system that would avoid a standing army; he believed at the time that the king's ministers had connived to bring about the legislation's defeat. Slowly, he arrived on the side of the Proprietary party. William Smith, Anglican principal of the College of Philadelphia, Benjamin Chew of the Governor's Council, and William Allen were its recognized leaders.[44]

In the first week of the May session many petitions were received from diverse inhabitants of the province, asking for a change in the government. Franklin had seen to it that his proposal had sup-

[43] Peters to Penn, May 5, 1764, Penn Manuscripts, Official Correspondence, 9, p. 222, HSP.

[44] Oliver C. Kuntzleman, *Joseph Galloway, Loyalist* (Philadelphia, 1941), p. 43.

port. Consequently, on May 23 a committee including Joseph Galloway and Franklin was appointed to draw up a formal petition "to His Majesty for that purpose." That afternoon the committee presented its petition for a first reading. Dickinson was not present; such speedy action was unexpected. But he soon jumped into the fray. The storm now broke.

In retrospect the single-minded purpose of Franklin is disconcerting. By May it was known in Pennsylvania that Grenville, the king's minister, had proposed that certain taxes be levied on the colonists. The resulting Revenue Act of 1764 went so far as to suggest that if expenses were not met, it "may be proper to charge certain stamp duties in said colonies and plantations." An article in the *Pennsylvania Gazette* of May 10 discussed the new taxes at length, including those relative to trade, against which the writer felt it difficult to protest, and the proposed stamp tax, which he clearly saw as an "internal tax." William Allen had warned about the latter's illegality in talking with members of Parliament when he was in England. But Franklin held fast to the 1758 opinion of Richard Jackson. That London agent, whom he regarded almost with veneration, had convinced him that any change in government would mean no curtailment of charter privileges, one of the opponents' greatest fears.[45]

On May 24, the next day, Joseph Galloway led the fight in favor of the formal petition. When Dickinson rose to protest it, he was caustically criticized. Neither Franklin nor Galloway was accustomed to opposition on major issues. Dickinson, however, had carefully marshaled his criticisms, jotting down his thoughts in orderly fashion, and argued with apt and telling phrases.

Galloway pointed out that after any measure had been resolved by the legislature, it was contrary to "rule and order" to object to the measure itself. Only the mode of the resolution could be objected to. This rule, he asserted, was set aside because Dickinson was now permitted to object to the measure itself. Galloway further complained that the lateness of Dickinson's arguments was due either "to Mr. Dickinson's indolence in not [previously] at-

[45] Carl Van Doren, ed., *Letters and Papers of Benjamin Franklin and Richard Jackson, 1753–1785* (Philadelphia, 1947), pp. 68–85.

tending, or to his industry in forming his speech."[46] Dickinson, as a matter of fact, on May 23 was at home with "a severe attack of the fever and ague" and was still indisposed when he appeared on the twenty-fourth.[47]

First speaking from notes and interrupted at points by fellow members, Dickinson turned apologetically to his written arguments and read his closely reasoned brief. Galloway, on his part, hurriedly took notes during the long recital, rising to refute each ojection. Speaker Norris, suffering from the infirmities of age and from distress over the measure itself, adjourned the debate until the next day. Several members asked Dickinson to leave his speech "on the table for the perusal and consideration of the house." Norris supported the request. Dickinson, however, refused, declaring the speech was a rough copy and quite imperfect. Although Galloway later insisted that his colleague had promised to let him read the speech that evening as a guide for his own reply, when he called for it Dickinson demurred. Only after the third reading of the bill and its final passage did Dickinson lay his objections on the table, and then too briefly for others to read them.

In his speech Dickinson argued cogently though the odds lay heavily against him. He called for caution, noting that the passions of the moment "blind the understanding; they weaken the judgment." To him, this was "not the proper time to attempt the change in our government . . . [indeed] neither the proper season nor the proper method."[48] In addition, it seemed contradictory to him that although the king was requested to change the government, the Assembly at the same time could insist on the preservation of privileges. He feared the transfer of power from the Assembly, *"the proper guardian of the public liberties,* to *other* hands."

Pointing out that Pennsylvania was out of favor with the British

[46] *The Speech of Joseph Galloway, Esq* . . . (Philadelphia, 1764).

[47] *Last Tuesday Morning Mr. Galloway* . . . , (Philadelphia, 1764).

[48] Paul Leicester Ford, ed., *Writings of John Dickinson,* (Philadelphia, 1895), pp. 21–49. The quotations are from this version. Ford gives an extensive introduction to the *Speech of John Dickinson,* pp. 3–7.

government and that the ministerial position always was on the side of the proprietors, Dickinson asked how it was possible for much change to occur. He considered any confidence placed in the British unwarranted. Governing authority was in the hands of ministers rather than the king himself, and the ambition of men, he declared, seldom could be trusted. Moreover, he greatly feared the garrisoning of a permanent royal army in the colonies and thought it unwise for the petitioners to remark upon internal disorder within the province, which could only furnish reason to establish the military there.

Dickinson correctly believed that frontier representatives would support his view. For their benefit he turned to the enumeration of the particular rights Pennsylvania held under the Charter of Privileges of 1701. He also cited the restrictions, if not the harassment, of Quakers in neighboring royal colonies. It seemed to him absurd to demand a change in government in order to procure £400 or £500 in taxes yearly from the proprietors.

Galloway answered Dickinson, speaking from his own notes, taking up each point his adversary had made. The following day the petition was again the subject of discussion. Speaker Norris requested the right to express his own sentiments, a privilege to which the Assembly acceded. A few alterations were made to the text on a second reading. A vote was taken. The petition for a change in government was passed "by a great majority."[49] Isaac Norris resigned as Speaker the next day. Franklin was elected in his stead, and the first bill he signed was the petition to the king that he had so eagerly sponsored.

Four days later, on May 28, Dickinson made another motion in the Assembly. Having reduced his speech to its main points, which he called a "Protest," and joined by John Montgomery of Cumberland and Isaac Saunders of Lancaster, he asked that these objections be entered in the minutes. Not a single vote could be garnered in support of the request.[50] Franklin, with sound judgment, stated that there was no historical precedent for the record-

[49] *Votes*, 7:5610. The vote in all likelihood was 26 to 4.

[50] Ibid., 7:5615.

ing of such a protestation in the minutes either in England or in Pennsylvania.[51]

A week later the Assembly adjourned until September. The supply bill of £55,000 was finally passed. The House addressed an acrimonious message to the governor as an answer to the charges the governor had made against them and in defense of the Assembly's actions. Benjamin Franklin signed it as Speaker. The petition for a change in government would not be signed by the governor, but it was forwarded by the Assembly at once to its London agent.

The summer between sessions was marked by a pamphlet war. Dickinson could not rest happily. Decisively defeated by Franklin, Galloway, and the so-called Quaker party, he nevertheless felt assured that his position was a rightful one. He stubbornly refused to let the issue fade.

On June 29 his speech was published and put on sale at William Bradford's Book Store adjoining the London Coffee House. It sold well. Three weeks later a second edition was printed, and a German translation was published by Heinrich Miller. On the title page Dickinson included in both Latin and English this sentiment: "As for me, I will assuredly contend for that glorious plan of Liberty handed down to us from our ancestors; but whether my labours shall prove successful, or in vain, depends wholly on you, my dear Countrymen." An unsigned preface, reputedly written by the Reverend William Smith,[52] reviewed the long history of the petition for a change of government, going back as far as the supply bill of 1759. He stated that the speech was published at the behest of a great number of the principal gentlemen of Philadelphia, who believed the constitution was violated by such a petition. Dickinson also sent the editor of the *Pennsylvania Gazette* the protest that he had vainly asked the House to enter on its minutes. Then, with other opponents of a change in government, Dickinson wrote and circulated a broadside to be signed by "his Majesty's dutiful and loyal subjects" praying the king to ignore the Assembly's petition.[53]

[51] *The Speech of Joseph Galloway, Esq.*, Preface by Benjamin Franklin.

[52] *Papers of Benjamin Franklin*, 11:267–68.

[53] Ford, pp. 65–67.

Galloway's speech and his reply were published together by William Dunlap on August 11. It was introduced by a long, anonymous preface written by Franklin in answer to that of Smith because "a number of aspersions were thrown on our Assemblies, and their proceedings grossly misrepresented." Franklin's sarcasm was often heavy. He advised Dickinson "to preserve the Panegyrics" with which his admirers had "adorned" him and cuttingly observed that "Mr. Dickenson . . . though long hated by some, and disregarded by the rest of the Proprietary Faction, is at once, for the same reason as in Mr. Norris' Case become a *Sage* in the Law, and an *Oracle* in Matters relating to our Constitution."[54]

Dickinson, reading the preface to Galloway's speech and the advertisement of it, was furious. He was irked by Galloway's inferential charge that he failed to attend earlier sessions on the petition out of indolence and angered by the statement that he was influenced by "a restless thirst after promotion—a fondness to serve the purpose of power from an expectation of being rewarded with posts of honor and profit." He grew so angry over these accusations that it was reported he challenged Galloway to a duel with pistols.[55]

The day after the pamphlet's publication, on Friday, August 12, Dickinson left Philadelphia for a fortnight in Dover and New Castle to attend court. In his few moments of spare time, he attempted to write an answer. He returned to Pennsylvania for two days and then perforce had to spend four days at court in Chester. The Philadelphia County Court commenced September 3. There were few free hours between these various sessions to attend to nonlegal matters. Yet the mere thought of the Galloway pamphlet, the preface, and the accusations in appended notes made him smart. In less than four weeks Dickinson had not only attended to his legal duties but produced and published an extended reply to Galloway's speech.[56] The pamphlet bore no author's name, but the writer could not long remain anonymous.

[54] Reprint of *Preface, Papers of Benjamin Franklin*, 11:296.

[55] Benjamin F. Newcomb: *Franklin and Galloway: A Political Partnership* (New Haven, 1972), pp. 89–90.

[56] *A reply to a Piece called the Speech of Joseph Galloway, Esquire* (Philadelphia, 1764).

On the cover Dickinson quoted from Pope, his old favorite:

> Yes, the last pen for freedom let me draw,
> When truth stands trembling on the edge of law;
> Here, last of Britons! Let your names be read;
> Are none, none living? Let me praise the dead,
> And for that cause, which made your fathers shine,
> Fall by the votes of their unhappy line.

The elevated sentiment of the poet was lost in the diatribes describing Galloway as "writing confusedly and railing insolently" in what Dickinson called a "pretended speech," not delivered as published. It was a bitter and scornful rebuttal. An appendix revealed the frustrations of the young lawyer, who usually reflected benign reasonableness and an elegant manner. He detailed examples of Galloway's "continual breaches of the rules of grammar; his utter ignorance of the English language; the pompous obscurity and sputtering prolixity reigning through every part of his piece; and his innumerable and feeble tautologies."

Galloway's reaction to Dickinson's *Reply* was one of fury. On September 19, coming out of the House of Assembly, he caught up to Dickinson and demanded to know if he was the author of the piece. The author answered, "Yes, sir." The two men then came to blows. Stories of their encounter spread like wildfire. Galloway attempted to grab Dickinson's recognizably prominent nose and then struck out at him with his cane. Dickinson warded off the blow and gave his opponent a "fair knock on the head" with his stick. Several blows were exchanged for "about two minutes" until they were separated by others.[57]

When the Assembly reconvened on Monday, September 10, there was no quorum, and the House adjourned until the following day. William Allen, lately returned from England, where he had spent the previous year, and a leading proprietary supporter, took his seat, thereby swelling the number of "benchers" on that side. The unbridgeable chasm between Galloway and Dickinson

[57] Charles Pettit to Joseph Reed, September 20, 1764, Manuscript Division, New-York Historical Society (hereafter cited as NYHS); David Hall to William Strahan, June 12, 1767, American Philosophical Society (hereafter cited as APS).

deeply affected the relations between the opposing sides in most issues.

A letter received by the Speaker from Massachusetts Bay Province under date of June 13 was now read. The Assembly of that colony, having instructed its agent in London to work for a repeal of the Sugar Act and for the prevention of a stamp act or "any other impositions and taxes upon this and the other American Provinces," requested the other colonies to take like action.[58] A committee was appointed to draw up similar instructions for Richard Jackson, the Pennsylvania agent. In the meantime, efforts to secure a firm peace treaty with the Indians and support for the Indian commissioners in the west were taken up. Dickinson was appointed to a committee to draw up a bill to cover the latter. Now that dangers from marauding Indians had been quieted, the growing interior counties were petitioning for increased representation. This had significant bearing on the struggle for control of the Assembly, for the frontier tended strongly toward proprietary or, more exactly, anti-Philadelphia interests. The changing party alignments would become obvious in the fall elections.

Nevertheless, the Assembly itself remained clearly under the command of Franklin as Speaker. On August 16 the *Pennsylvania Journal* published an "Address of a Number of the Principal Freeholders of Lancaster County to Isaac Sanders, Esq.," their representative, and his answer "containing some reflections on the conduct" of the House. It asserted that the Assembly's petition for a change of government in no way "had the least tendency to deliver up, alter or change any one privilege now enjoyed" but had in fact asked for their continuation "under Royal care."[59] Within the walls of the State House the cauldron kept boiling, quite apart from the Dickinson-Galloway feud.

Dickinson was not content to let his battle with Galloway rest in an armistice. Galloway, not to be outdone in his turn, wrote a reply, offering it to a newspaper. He was refused space unless, said the editor, Dickinson could see it before publication. To this Galloway would not consent; he printed it himself as a broadside, *To*

[58] *Votes*, 7:5627–28.

[59] *Pennsylvania Journal*, August 16, 1794.

the Public, on September 29. Dickinson, now on the block for trying to prevent Galloway's publication, defended his action. Still another justification of his accusations against Galloway was printed without title or heading, beginning, "Last Tuesday morning Mr. Galloway carried a writing containing some reflections on me to a printer in this city." This flier appeared on October 2, Election Day. About the same time William Bradford, the printer, published a satire, "A receipt to make a speech" by J———— G————, Esquire, which also came from Dickinson's pen. The dispute had gone on too long. Nothing could be gained by further public notice.

The elections for the Assembly that fall were preceded by one of the bitterest campaigns the province had known. Dickinson's savage attacks on Galloway were more than matched by venomous letters, broadsides, and pamphlets regarding candidates and issues, particularly in the Philadelphia area. Samuel Powel of London wrote a friend, "In the name of goodness stop your Pamphleteer's mouths and shut up your presses. Such a torrent of low scurrility sure never came from any country as lately from Pennsylvania." [60] The Reverend William Smith led the pack. Dickinson had handled Galloway roughly enough, but Franklin was described by some as a lecher, a man of no moral fiber, and the illegitimacy of his children was revealed. Personalities came to dominate policy. [61]

Two parties now vied for seats in the Assembly: the "New Party," consisting of those favoring the proprietors or at least opposing the petition for a change in government, and the "Old Ticket," representing the majority, formerly the so-called Quaker party. Franklin ran, as was always the case, from the City of Philadelphia, but now also as a county candidate, a legal possibility. In the county one of his opponents was Dickinson.

Charles Pettit, a merchant, described election day in Philadelphia. The polls opened at about 9 o'clock in the morning. The steps leading up to the polling place in Philadelphia were filled with columns of voters that moved slowly until close to midnight.

[60] Powel to George Roberts, November 4, 1764, "Powel-Roberts Correspondence, 1761–1765," *PMHB* 18 (1894):40.

[61] *Papers of Benjamin Franklin,* 11:369–72, 390–94.

About three o'clock the next morning those favoring the New Ticket proposed closing, but the Old Ticket advocates, having a "reserve of the aged and lame" brought up in chairs and litters, protested, and 200 were voted between 3 and 6 o'clock. Watchers favoring the New Ticket by midmorning had rounded up additional supporters. Not until the next day were upwards of 3,900 votes tallied. Franklin and Galloway both lost. The New Ticket carried all but two of its candidates. Dickinson led, save for Isaac Norris and Joseph Richardson, all competitors in the county.[62] Franklin felt a twinge of humiliation. Writing his daughter Sarah a month later as he sailed for England, he commented ruefully that he had never given offense to any one in the private sector, but that many bitter enemies existed in the public arena, a fact she would also have to cope with.[63] Galloway, embittered by his loss, was now more determined than ever to avenge his defeat.

The new Assembly met on October 15. Isaac Norris was again elected Speaker, a position health did not permit him to retain. Dickinson had every right to feel a sense of political triumph as he looked about the House, but there was to be a limit to his influence. Instructions were sent to agent Jackson regarding English trade restrictions and impending taxation. A motion was then made to take up once again the consideration of the earlier instructions sent Jackson concerning the change in government, and a debate ensued with a "great Contrariety of opinions." Speaker Norris, as he had in a previous session, asked leave to deliver his own sentiments. He felt that the House had no right to delegate such an important matter to one man or set of men, and he favored "an entire prohibition on the Agent's presenting the said petitions."[64] Three votes were then taken, two as to whether the Pennsylvania instructions were to be recalled or delayed in their

[62] J. Philip Gleason, "A Scurrilous Colonial Election and Franklin's Reputation," *William and Mary Quarterly*, 3d ser., 18 (1961):68–84. James H. Hutson, in *Pennsylvania Politics, 1746–1790* (Princeton, 1972), suggests that other colonies, had they suffered such external demands as the Penns imposed, would have revolted earlier. The final outcome of the decision to favor royal government, he states, led to a realignment of political power in the colony.

[63] *Papers of Benjamin Franklin*, 11:448–49.

[64] *Votes*, 7:5682.

presentation. Both of these votes were negative. The third vote urged Jackson to proceed with caution, and if he believed any privileges were in danger of being abridged, he should so apprise the House and await further instructions. This motion was carried affirmatively, giving Dickinson and his New Ticket colleagues a partial victory. Once more the emotional strain of the issue proved too great, and Speaker Norris resigned his chair.

The third vote perhaps was a sop to the previous losers. On October 25 a motion was put whether to adjourn for a fortnight. The vote was negative. As in the partisan division of votes on the instructions to Jackson, the twelve supporters of the New Ticket, led by Dickinson, Allen, George Bryan, and Thomas Willing, were opposed by nearly twice their number. Therein lay the next move of the Old Guard. The House was asked to consider the ill consequences that might ensue if Jackson were to suffer some accident in disposition or even death. The basic question was whether the House should appoint another agent to assist him. Again the vote was in the affirmative.

The next day the question of selecting the second agent occupied the morning session. A remonstrance from a number of inhabitants of the city was presented expressing fear that Franklin would be so employed. Indeed, that afternoon Franklin was nominated, and his appointment carried 19 to 11. The opposition at once asked permission to enter reasons for their dissent. After debate the request was withdrawn. Franklin had won out without having to recover his seat in the Assembly.

Eight of the eleven in the opposition signed a protest which was printed with a prefatory note in the *Pennsylvania Journal* on November 1.[65] Dickinson was recognized as the author. The following year Isaac Hunt referred to it as a "rather infamous protest, considered as the Protest of Mr. A . . . n and the other subscribers, tho' tis well known to be drawn up by the pitiful Mr. D . . . . n, revised, corrected and amended by the Rev. Sentiment-dresser-general [William Smith] of the Pr . . . . ry Party." Franklin wrote his own reply to that sally, and Smith in his turn anonymously also gave answer.

---

[65] Ford, pp. 149–50. This pamphlet was also published in German.

Dickinson was wearying of the struggle. He had refused to sign the protest, and though he had written his own objections to the matter, he forbore publishing them. William Morris of Trenton, who had married John's aunt Rebecca Cadwalader, and other kin had discouraged him from doing so. Dickinson also considered he had been used by Norris and Pemberton to serve their own purposes. He decided not to run for reelection the next October. Samuel Wharton wrote Franklin that Dickinson's conduct was "clearly expressive of much folly and great want of either principle or firmness."[66]

Benjamin Franklin journeyed in happy triumph to Chester on November 7. Three hundred friends from Philadelphia accompanied him along the way. To the salutes of cannon, the shouts of his admirers, and a burst of song, he boarded ship for England. Franklin set sail with a feeling of satisfaction, limited only by the fact that he knew he had vengeful political foes. As for Pennsylvania politics, a temporary calm ensued. Galloway chose to bide his time until the following autumn, knowing that even without his presence his party continued as the Assembly majority.

Dickinson had proved no political match for Franklin. His pamphleteering against Galloway gained him no mark of distinction. When, years later, he was to select for publication those political writings he considered most significant, he included his perceptive speech setting forth reasons why Pennsylvania should not become a royal colony. Happily, he omitted the petty diatribes he had penned at the same time against Galloway.

[66] Wharton to Franklin, December 19, 1764, *Papers of Benjamin Franklin*, 11:525–28.

★ 3 ★

Reasonable
Protests

WHEN PARLIAMENT PASSED THE SUGAR ACT of 1764 lowering the duty on foreign molasses, what the colonies might have considered advantageous was instead viewed as alarming. The new tariff was regarded as a source of revenue rather than a mercantile regulation. Dickinson later called it the "first comet" of English restriction. Hitherto there had been little enforcement of trade measures and much smuggling and commerce with non-British islands in the Caribbean. The new act additionally laid restrictions on lumber exports and set new duties on wine and other imports. Jurisdiction of admiralty courts was also considerably extended and every means taken to tighten control. The threat of a stamp tax for additional revenue was also raised. Moreover, shortly after the Sugar Act was passed, a law previously applicable only to New England now prohibited the use of paper money throughout the colonies. The economic recession following the Indian wars already had caused a gloomy outlook.

Protest ensued. Colonial assemblies petitioned Britain for relief; merchants wrote their London agents to exert pressure on Parliament to rescind the acts; and societies were formed to promote colonial manufactures. Constitutional rights articulated during periods of past resistance to authority were now analyzed. James Otis of Massachusetts in his *Rights of the Colonies Asserted and Proved* found no justification for Parliament's levy of taxes, either internal or external. Governor Stephen Hopkins of Rhode Island, examining the rights of the colonies, was particularly alarmed by the suggestion of the proposed stamp tax. Even New York, usually always loyal to the crown, in October 1764 sent petitions to the king and both Houses of Parliament denying their right to impose the Sugar Act and claiming that any right to tax demanded the right of representation. Every colonial remonstrance "denying Parliament's right to tax the colonies was wholesale and unqualified."[1]

Lord Grenville suggested that the colonies might prefer to tax themselves. Yet so certain was he that they would not undertake such action that he set about to propose the stamp tax for parliamentary enactment. On February 13, 1765, the Stamp Act was introduced and after its third reading on March 22 became law. Pamphlets supporting the government's right to enact such tax measures appeared in England to answer rising colonial objections. Parliament's suggestion that "virtual Representation" of the colonies existed was viewed as "fantastical and frivolous."[2] Daniel Dulany of Maryland wrote the best defense of the colonial objections to the tax and such representations in his *Considerations on the Propriety of Imposing Taxes in the British Colonies*,[3] declaring that "taxation formed no part of the authority which Parliament enjoyed as the supreme power in the Empire"; rather, taxation was the function of representative bodies, which in America were the assemblies.

Agents of the colonies in London seemed powerless to prevent Parliament's passage of the Stamp Act. Most of them had received protests from their colonies for presentation to the ministry, but

[1] James Otis, *Rights of the Colonies Asserted and Proved* (Boston, 1764); Stephen Hopkins, *The Rights of Colonies Examined,* in John R. Bartlett, ed., *Records of the Colony of Rhode Island and Providence Plantation* (Providence, 1861), 6:416–427; Edmund S. Morgan and Helen M. Morgan, *The Stamp Act Congress* (Chapel Hill, N. C., 1953), p. 38.

[2] Morgan and Morgan, p. 78.

[3] Daniel Dulany, *Considerations on the Propriety of Imposing Taxes in the British Colonies* (Annapolis, 1765).

few forwarded them. Franklin as agent for Pennsylvania did little to arrest the act's passage.[4]

When news of the Stamp Act arrived in America, ringing protests were sounded from Virginia to Massachusetts. On June 8, 1765, the Massachusetts House of Representatives sent a circular letter to all colonial assemblies asking them to send delegates to a congress in New York in October. When the letter from Massachusetts arrived in Pennsylvania, the Assembly was in adjournment. Joseph Fox, the Speaker, asked those members from Philadelphia and nearby areas their informal opinion about the proposed congress. He found unanimous approval and promised it would receive first consideration when the House reconvened in September.

During the recess John Dickinson continued his legal practice with energy. Much Philadelphia business, both commercial and legal, involving land investment dealt with the interior areas, making it desirable to journey there. The first week in July he traveled to Bethlehem, Reading, Carlisle, York, and Lancaster, all county seats, transacting business at courts there. In Carlisle he saw John Montgomery, his good friend and supporter in the Assembly, and in Lancaster, Isaac Saunders. The summer was torrid and the earth parched, no rain having fallen for six or seven weeks except for a brief isolated shower. Dickinson stayed several days in the Carlisle area and was joined there by Lambert Cadwalader. En route from York to Lancaster, he wrote that he would visit "the Susquehannah Muse," Sarah Wright, a poet whose husband owned the area around Wright's Ferry across that river. The Wrights were Quakers and distant kin of his Philadelphia relatives. As he traveled through the frontier counties, Dickinson carefully gauged the political sentiment of the settlers whom he had met.

Dickinson had warned Pennsylvanians against arbitrary parliamentary action. He had opposed Franklin at every step in the petition for a change in government and later objected to his appointment as a London agent. Now events seemed to prove him correct. The newspapers were filled with letters inveighing against the hated stamp tax. Franklin was even accused of being a secret

[4] Thayer, pp. 113–15.

promoter of the act.[5] Believing that protests to Parliament would be useless, he went so far as to nominate his friend and supporter John Hughes as stamp collector for Pennsylvania, so certain was he that nothing would prevent enforcement of the tax law.

When the Pennsylvania Assembly met in September, Speaker Fox at the first sitting submitted the Massachusetts call for the proposed congress. It was resolved that "in duty to their constituents" a remonstrance should be made to the crown and a delegation appointed to go to New York.[6] An eight-man committee at once prepared a draft of instructions for the deputies to the congress. Dickinson, the first-named of the committee, served as chairman.

The following day four representatives were nominated to attend the congress: Speaker Fox, Dickinson, Bryan, and Morton. The appointment of these men was a distinct victory for the proprietary side. Galloway, although no longer a member of the Assembly, tried through his partisans to block any representation from Pennsylvania. But not only had proponents of resistance drafted instructions, three of them attended the congress. Only Fox absented himself. Galloway was left with the small consolation that the other three men might be out of the province at election time.[7]

Before adjournment the next week, the House voted to place resolutions in its minutes relative to the Stamp Act "by which their successors may be acquainted with the sentiments they entertain of those unconstitutional impossibilities."[8] Dickinson, not a member of the resolutions committee, nevertheless made a suggestive draft for the minutes.[9] These resolves were so close to those reported by the committee that he may have unofficially acted as scribe. Dickinson emphasized the right of the people to levy taxes upon themselves; any other manner, "being manifestly subversive

[5] Ibid., p. 112.

[6] *Votes*, 7:5767.

[7] Thayer, p. 118.

[8] *Votes*, 7:5778–79.

[9] Draft in L/HSP; printed also in Ford, pp. 173–77.

of public Liberty, must of necessary consequence be utterly destructive of public happiness." The constitution of the provincial government was founded on "the natural Rights of Mankind, and the noble principles of *English* Liberty." Dickinson also noted in his draft that the imposition of internal taxes was unconstitutional, but the committee failed to include this observation.

Neither neighboring New Jersey nor Delaware had official delegations at the New York congress. Delaware, nevertheless, had unofficial deputies present in Thomas McKean, Dickinson's warm friend, and Caesar Rodney, his near neighbor in Kent County, who wrote his brother that the twenty-seven delegates made up "an assembly of the greatest ability I ever yet saw."[10] For eleven days the debates ran vigorously.

John Dickinson arrived in New York on October 6, a day before the first meeting of the congress. He stayed with Pennsylvania cousins, the Jones family living on Wall Street, and met other kin as well. The gathering of colonial notables became occasion for festivities that included "solemn invitations" to dinner. Dickinson expressed his fear that the long convivial sittings afterwards would interfere with the goal he hoped for—a statement of American rights.[11] Yet what the congress accomplished was both remarkable and memorable. It wrote and agreed to a Declaration of Rights and Grievances; it adopted petitions addressed to the king, Lords, and Commons. Unanimity forged out of the diverse opinions held by the colonial delegates chartered a future course of action.

Dickinson now found himself on a larger stage. This clear-headed, analytical young man of thirty-three, slight physically, gentle in manner, impressed all who met him by his forceful arguments and his sincerity. Easily phrasing his thoughts by pen, he was soon offering pertinent drafts of statements to fellow delegates.[12] There were two possible courses of action that could be

[10] Caesar Rodney to Thomas Rodney, October 20, 1765, George W. Ryden, ed., *Letters to and from Caesar Rodney, 1756–1784* (Philadelphia, 1933), p. 26.

[11] JD to his mother, October 7, 1765, L/HSP.

[12] The Library Company of Philadelphia has two hand-written drafts with many interlinears in Dickinson's hand. The Historical Society of Pennsylvania has a printed copy with notes by Dickinson.

taken: either resist submission and protest or accede and simply argue against the unconstitutionality of the tax as laid down by Parliament. A simple insistence on a repeal of duties on trade was early laid aside. Internal taxation became a question of primary importance.[13] Dickinson stressed "the Rights and Liberties of the Colonists," which he later changed to read "the Principles of Freedom." Conservative deputies argued for these specifics, while others, more radical, wanted a broader and more general statement of the colonial position on acts of Parliament. Throughout the debates Dickinson echoed much that was in the Pennsylvania Assembly's resolutions upholding "the natural Rights of Mankind, and the noble Principles of English Liberty." The final resolutions, in the words and phrases adopted, were in large measure those of Dickinson, though rearranged by a committee.

An address to the king was prepared, assuring him of the loyalty of his American subjects who sought their rights as Englishmen. Dickinson was not a member of this committee, but here, too, suggested pertinent paragraphs. This petition to the crown was later altered "in the title and middle of it," but it was essentially Dickinson's thought, his handiwork.[14] Meanwhile, Dickinson left the meetings in New York before the Congress was adjourned, being called home on "urgent business." His contributions had been major. Unwavering in his opposition to the Stamp Act, he granted a few concessions to more hesitant colleagues. The resolves clearly set forth colonial distinctions between Parliament's authority to make laws rather than impose taxation. However no distinction was made between internal and external taxes.[15] The principle of taxation without representation became firmly implanted in the American mind.

Dickinson's experience at the Stamp Act Congress and his association with leaders of other colonies from Massachusetts to Virginia proved invaluable in later years. The united colonial appeal

[13] Robert R. Livingston to ———, November 2, 1765, quoted in Morgan and Morgan, p. 107.

[14] Ford, 1:191.

[15] Morgan and Morgan, pp. 112–15.

and the success of the petitions dominated Dickinson's subsequent approach to future British measures. If the year before he could have been called conservative in his support of the Pennsylvania proprietors, his stance toward the Stamp Act was bold and determined.

Dickinson returned to Philadelphia known to many of his peers from other colonies but no longer a member of the Pennsylvania Assembly. The fall election had taken place on October 1 before he left for New York. He had announced that he was not a candidate, a decision already made known the previous year, but his name nevertheless was submitted to the voters.[16] The Proprietary party was swamped by Galloway's legions, Galloway himself triumphing over Dickinson by 420 votes in Philadelphia County. Although crushingly defeated, the loser had now established his reputation in a wider sphere than Pennsylvania.

One of the mysteries of politics is who gets what and why. The campaign had been a bitter one, raging throughout the year following the previous election. Dickinson and Bryan, both leading Proprietary party representatives, had the backing of the growing "Presbyterian party," as it was pejoratively called, in opposition to the traditional Quaker party. Bryan had been returned to the Assembly. The dispute over the Stamp Tax seemed to have little influence upon the electorate's choices. Although Philadelphia was strong in its opposition to the act, Galloway, the victor at the polls, had been the defender of Parliament's right to impose it.

Dickinson had already left for New York when, four days after the election on October 5, word was received in Philadelphia that John Hughes's commission as stamp tax agent and some stamps as well had arrived on board a ship at New Castle, Delaware. The reaction was instantaneous. Several thousand protesting, angry people milled about the State House. Seven men were finally selected to visit Hughes and demand his resignation. Meeting with them, the agent-designate temporized; he agreed to postpone ac-

---

[16] *Pennsylvania Journal* and *Pennsylvania Gazette*, August 8, 1765; see also Samuel Wharton to Benjamin Franklin, December 19, 1764, *Papers of Benjamin Franklin*, 11:527.

tion until other colonial stamp agents began their sale. A "Union for the Preservation of Peace" was quickly organized by "sober men," and rioting was prevented.[17]

The law requiring stamps for newspapers, legal documents, and ship clearances was to go into effect November 1. By then Hughes had felt enough pressure and agreed not to enforce use of the stamps. The day before the act took effect, the *Pennsylvania Journal* mourned on the front page with black column borders, skulls, and other symbols, and editorialized "Adieu . . . to the Liberty of the Press." Newspapers continued their publication without purchasing the required stamps.

Lawyers in Philadelphia had met on October 16 to decide what position they should take about purchasing stamps for their documents. They were particularly conscious of the legal and constitutional aspects. After prolonged discussion, they decided to meet again, agreeing in the meantime not to take any precipitous action that might cause an imposition of penalties.[18] The final result was not so much formal opposition as it was an informal agreement to limit legal actions that would necessitate compliance. Accordingly, little litigation or recording of official papers took place until spring. Not until late April of the next year did the lawyers resume their regular business.

Merchants, on the other hand, could not delay action. Charles Thomson now assumed a prominent role and suggested a boycott similar to that already adopted in New York. In the first week of November leading merchants signed a nonimportation agreement. At the same time, they sent individual petitions to their agents in London, Bristol, and Liverpool asking for assistance in protesting the act. The following month the merchants continued their agreement to cease trade with Britain and defiantly engaged in illegal, stampless trade with other colonies and with Ireland. In mid-December, Governor Penn reported to his uncle Thomas

[17] David L. Jacobson, "John Dickinson and Joseph Galloway, 1764–1776: A Study in Contrasts," Ph.D. diss., Princeton Univ., 1959, pp. 72–73.

[18] Edward Shippen to his father, October 17, 1765, quoted in *PMHB* 24 (1900):419–20; see also L/HSP, xxxiv, 38.

Penn that the Stamp Act could not be enforced without "a great deal of bloodshed and mischief."[19]

Dickinson had been impressed by the united action of the Stamp Act Congress. Further reflecting on the historical and constitutional aspects of the act, he was increasingly concerned about the dangers to the colonies in their imperial relationships as a result of the parliamentary action. In his draft for the petition to the king written in New York, he had set forth certain fundamentals that he considered of utmost importance:

> ... that it is inseparably essential to the freedom of a people, that no taxes be laid upon them, but with their own consent given personally, or by their representatives.
> ... that the only representatives of the people of these colonies, are the persons chosen therein by themselves for that purpose . . .
> ... that trial by jury is the inherent and invaluable right of every free man in the colonies.
> ... [that the late acts] ... by extending the Jurisdiction of the Courts of Admiralty beyond its ancient limits, have a tendency to subvert the rights and liberties of the Colonists.[20]

Dickinson's intense feeling on the subject is clearly seen in a broadside addressed to "Friends and Countrymen" published in November 1765. This sheet asserted: "The critical time is now come" for "the future fortunes of yourselves, and of your posterity." It was necessary to "decide whether Pennsylvanians from henceforth shall be Freemen or Slaves." Compliance with the act and the use of stamped papers would "rivet perpetual chains upon your unhappy Country . . . and save future Ministers the Trouble of reasoning . . . and . . . free them from any kind of moderation, when they shall hereafter meditate any other taxation, upon you." Dickinson had a simple, cogent suggestion for his fellow colonists: "It appears to me the wisest and the safest course for you [is] to proceed in all business as usual, without taking the least notice of the Stamp Act. If you behave in this spirited manner, you may be

[19] John Penn to Thomas Penn, December 15, 1765, Penn Correspondence, X, HSP.

[20] L-D/LCP.

assured, that every colony on the Continent will follow the example of a Province so justly celebrated for its Liberty. Your conduct will convince *Great-Britain,* that the Stamp Act will never be carried into execution, but by force of arms; and this one moment's reflection must demonstrate, that she will never attempt."[21]

At this same time, Dickinson was preparing a pamphlet to be entitled *The Late Regulations Respecting the British Colonies.*[22] In it he sought to show that the trade regulations of Britain and the Stamp Act affected the prosperity both of the British Isles and the empire. Couched as a "Letter from a Gentleman in Philadelphia to his Friend in London," in the next year, 1766, the pamphlet was published in two London editions. One critic there noted: "Though the town has been, in a manner, glutted with pamphlets on American affairs, yet its sale has been very rapid. It is highly esteemed; has gained for the author much reputation, and most surely does him great honor."[23] The pamphlet was a temperate account, suggesting that colonial concern was "but the resentment of dutiful children, who have received unmerited blows from a beloved parent. Their obedience to *Great Britain* is secured by the best and strongest ties, *those of affection.*" Convinced that "the foundations of the power and glory of Great Britain are laid in America," Dickinson presented a closely argued brief.

Late in December, Dickinson boldly addressed a letter to William Pitt, stating that it was no exaggeration to declare "that an universal and unexampled jealousy, grief and indignation have been excited in the colonists." The "sudden and violent restrictions of their commerce were extremely disgusting and afflicting," and to have these followed by the equally odious Stamp Act was all the more deplorable. Dickinson did not limit his criticisms to the Stamp Act but pointed out that it was only the latest of a long series of repressive acts. His arguments for a just British policy

[21] Philadelphia, 1765; copy in Ford, 1:201–5.

[22] *The Late Regulations respecting the British Colonies on the continent of America considered, In a Letter from a Gentleman in Philadelphia to his Friend in London* (Philadelphia, 1765), reprinted in Ford, 1:213–45.

[23] *Philadelphia Gazette,* May 23, 1766; Ford, 1:209–10.

sought to gain Pitt's influence. Repeal, Dickinson wrote, would be a sign of wisdom, not defeat.[24]

Dickinson, in speech and in writing, carefully avoided suggesting any infringement of the prerogatives of either the king or Parliament. But at the same time he set forth the rights and privileges of the colonies. The right of the people's consent to the levying of taxes was essential to the "freedom of a people." Dickinson was determined to hold fast to all the "inherent Rights and Liberties" granted Englishmen. It was the constitutionality of the act that he always called into question. But he had no desire for separation from the mother country; this would never be the case "except it be by Great Britain herself; and the only way to do it is to make us frugal, ingenious, united and discontented."[25]

Belief in natural rights implied an obligation to resist arrogant assumption of political power. Dickinson embodied his thoughts in an *Address to the Committee of Correspondence in Barbados*, a pamphlet signed "by a North-American."[26] He hoped to put to rest the charge of rebellion that that island had made against the continental colonies in a letter to its London agent. Dickinson sought to get the pamphlet into print quickly, but news of the repeal of the Stamp Act arrived before it was distributed. In it he argued that the right of protest to king or parliament was derived from a yet higher source, "the King of Kings and Lord of all the earth." Earlier Dickinson had declared, "Man cannot be happy, without freedom; nor free without security of property; nor so secure, unless the sole power to dispose of it be lodged in themselves; therefore, no people can be free, but where taxes are imposed upon them with their own consent."[27] To that sentiment he held fast.

Although Dickinson had included a clause objecting to internal taxes in his first drafts for both the Pennsylvania Assembly and the

[24] JD to Lord Chatham, December 21, 1765, Chatham Papers, Public Record Office 30/8, bundle 97, Pt. I, 32–41.

[25] Drafts of Resolves by Dickinson, Item 151, L-D/LCP; see also drafts, box 1, L/HSP.

[26] Philadelphia 1766; reprinted in Ford, 1:241–42.

[27] *Friends and Countrymen*, in Ford, 1:202.

New York meeting, he had finally settled on the general assertion that "no taxes ever have been, or can be constitutionally imposed on them, except by their respective legislatures." Thus, the Stamp Act Congress had made no distinction between levying internal and external taxes. In his *Considerations* Daniel Dulany had emphasized the unconstitutionality of an internal tax and clearly set forth the distinction between taxes for revenue purposes and those for the regulation of trade. This popular thesis found echo in William Pitt's speech in Parliament in January 1770.

Philadelphia's protestations had been immediate, though Galloway, who in the midst of crisis in September 1765 had been elected to the Assembly, sought to temper the colony's response. His efforts were perforce limited. First word of the Stamp Act's repeal was heard in mid-April, and joy reigned in Philadelphia. A young Presbyterian parson, the first person to disembark from an arriving ship, found himself surrounded by eager interrogators and told the news at the London Coffee House. A barge with ten oars was immediately dispatched to fetch the captain, with his letters and newspapers. A great crowd and ringing huzzahs met him. But the cheer soon dampened. The accompanying London newspapers as late as February 22 told of the repeal's passage by the Commons but reported no subsequent action in the House of Lords. Mail was distributed. Two letters dated March 10 gave no further confirmation. Rejoicing was temporarily suspended.[28]

Finally, later that month the repeal was confirmed. Osgood Hanbury, the London merchant, wrote Isaac Norris that it had been "work of infinite labour and pains to those who had been engaged in obtaining it." James Pemberton, the Quaker leader and political representative, writing to Dr. Fothergill, minutely detailed the colonial response and his hope for further redress of grievances. The new whig party, as the Presbyterians preferred to be called, had shown their appreciation of Dickinson's aggressive support by running him for the Assembly in October 1766 in the place of their leader, George Bryan. But Dickinson lost the election once again. Pemberton, violently "anti-Presbyterian," was delighted

---

[28] William Logan to John Smith, April 15, 1766, John Smith Correspondence, p. 215, HSP.

that Dickinson had been defeated "after a smart struggle."[29] The Quaker party seemed endowed with new life.

Dickinson's constant physical complaints had diminished little as the years passed. Yet for all his woes there apparently was no slackening of either his private or his public interests. His brother Philemon, after their father's death, gave up managing the family estates, which now were leased to tenant farmers. He came up to Philadelphia once again, and their mother arrived soon afterwards to live with her sons. Philemon was the first of the brothers to marry. His choice was Mary Cadwalader, his first cousin, the daughter of Dr. Thomas Cadwalader. He then moved to an estate called Belleville near Trenton, and not long afterwards his mother joined him in New Jersey.

Mrs. Dickinson had lived in Kent County under what must have been difficult circumstances. Far from friends and responsible for the tenants and slaves on the large Delaware estate, she was uncomplaining about her duties and the rigors of the hot summers and damp winters in Kent. Her admirers were legion. Deborah Norris, the daughter of Charles Norris of Philadelphia, wrote a cousin that she would like "to be just of as much consequence as one Mrs. Dickinson, a lady of my acquaintance in Kent, is." Everyone inquired after her, Deborah reported, and sent love, "all with as much earnestness as if she was disposed of offices and pensions." William Killen, who had been a member of the Dickinson household, remembering Mrs. Dickinson's charm and gracious manner, wished he might send one of his daughters to her for guidance.[30]

Of all problems to be met, that of caring for the slaves was most perplexing. The Dickinsons took care to keep the Negro families together in any sale, and the character of prospective owners was also a consideration to them. For years to come John Dickinson at times paid for the support of slaves either too old to work or too young.[31]

---

[29] C. and O. Hanbury to Isaac Norris, June 13, L/HSP, XV, 20; Pemberton to Fothergill, November 14, 1766, Pemberton Papers, XXXIV, 147, HSP.

[30] Deborah Norris to a cousin, Norris Family Letters, II, 58, HSP; Killen to JD, June 6, 1770, L/HSP.

[31] Notes, L/HSP, XXXV, 110.

The Dickinson law office continued at full tilt. James Wilson, a young graduate of the University of Edinburgh, read law with Dickinson and became an active assistant, as did John MacPherson of Mount Pleasant, near Philadelphia. Each aided in legal research and sometimes acted as Dickinson's amanuensis. Their preceptor was exacting in detail and allowed no "slovenly" work to go out. Dickinson drove himself, triumphing over the frequent attacks of illness he so often referred to, illness that was reflected both in his pallor and his slender frame. His intelligence, determination, and self-drive were incentives for the law clerks, who could not do less than emulate their mentor. Dickinson practiced in the courts of Pennsylvania and Delaware, before the Supreme Court and the Courts of Common Pleas, as well as executing other legal business.[32] There was little free time for this lawyer, whose every concern was with the rule of law and liberty under it.

When Isaac Norris, so long an eminent political figure and for many years Speaker of the Pennsylvania Assembly, died in July 1766, he was survived by two daughters, Mary and Sarah. Mary, the elder, called Polly, was the more serious one. She and her sister Sally became, through their father's death, leading heiresses in the Quaker city. The Norris family was notable in the colony's history both politically and financially, and in family relationships they were kin to all the founding families whose descendants then dominated Philadelphia.

Norris had not completed his will at the time of his death, and his daughters by law were vested with powers and authority as heirs. James Pemberton, merchant and the leading Quaker of the colony, took over the administration of the estate. The girls promised to make an inventory, and Pemberton's power as attorney was forwarded to Capel and Osgood Hanbury, the London merchant-agents who had cared for Norris's English investments. Fairhill, valued at £20,000, was the single most valuable piece of property in the estate. Excluding Philadelphia real estate of £7,050, other real estate was assessed at £10,000. Rights to other land, bonds, and mortgages here and abroad were estimated at £23,350.[33]

[32] For examples of Dickinson's legal accounts, see L/HSP, XXXIV, 56.

[33] Item 169, L-D/LCP.

Dickinson was thirty-four years old in 1766. His every point of view was an intellectual one. His political approach was analytic and studied, never emotional. If his legal practice demanded research and reflection, those same scholarly concerns led him to protest against what he deemed Britain's unconstitutional colonial measures. There were no idle moments in his life. He was now being consulted about the Isaac Norris estate. This led to visits at Fairhill. The two sisters, alone save for their old aunt, were gracious to the young lawyer. Slowly, the early, perfunctory visits in the first year or two after their father's death were to become more frequent as the decade closed.

Dickinson was disturbed not only by Parliament's arbitrary and unconstitutional taxation in the Stamp Act but by its other recent acts designed to tighten the administration of customs, including a measure that set up a vice-admiralty court for America, denying violators a trial by jury. These measures all increased the uneasy reflection over the Quartering Act passed by Parliament in May 1765, under which the colonies were required to provide housing and supplies at the behest of British army commanders in America. The colonies reacted variously, Pennsylvania alone complying; it was "the only Province in which troops have been stationed that has not . . . openly refused to provide for them."[34] New York protested, asserting that the British Isles were under no such law. When the governor asked the Assembly to make requisition, it voted a niggardly sum. In retaliation Parliament then voted to suspend the New York Assembly unless all the articles were provided. But before news of this Restraining Act reached America, the legislature in another manner appropriated sufficient money for the governor to meet military demands, quieting the dispute.

The Townshend Acts, however, added more flames to the growing fires of colonial dissension. One of these acts, proposed in 1767 by the chancellor of the exchequer, laid certain external taxes on the colonies for administrative purposes. Galloway generally regretted the Townshend Acts as a hindrance to the campaign for royal government. The Pennsylvania Assembly seemed chiefly concerned with the matter of currency restrictions. While the As-

[34] General Gage, December 21, 1765, quoted in Jacobson, p. 108.

sembly voted to thank London merchants for their assistance in the Stamp Act repeal and asked its agents in Britain to inform it of any new threats to its liberties, it took no official notice either of the Townshend duties or of the Restraining Act applied to New York.[35] The issues were neither so clear nor so encompassing as the Stamp Act. Moreover, the duties established by the Townshend Acts were not heavy. Nor was the recent Declaratory Act affirming Parliament's authority to make laws for colonies inflammatory. Colonies had reacted in a halfhearted way to it. John Dickinson, however, alert to any restriction of liberty, could not rest as complacently as did most of the Pennsylvania legislators.

The Restraining Act suspending the New York legislature and its inherent threat to all the colonies first aroused Dickinson. Then the acts introduced by Townshend gave him equal alarm. Adept with pen, he sat down to warn of the new threat to American freedom. The result was a series of twelve letters published in the *Pennsylvania Chronicle* beginning December 2, 1767.

Dickinson's choice of the *Pennsylvania Chronicle*, of which William Goddard was publisher and editor, was a curious one. Joseph Galloway and Thomas Wharton were the original sponsors of Goddard, and though by agreement the publisher was to "keep a free press,"[36] their influence was evident. However, using Galloway's newspaper would help assure anonymity, and its circulation was considerable. The editor, unaware of the identity of the writer and observing that the letters were on "a subject of the utmost importance of the welfare of our common country," hastened to set them in type, printing the first one in a special supplement.

Dickinson's introduction to the letters was ingenious.

> *My dear Countrymen,*
>   I am a *Farmer*, settled, after a variety of fortunes, near the banks of the river *Delaware*, in the province of *Pennsylvania*. I received a liberal education, and have been engaged in the busy scenes of life; but am now convinced, that a man may be as happy without bustle, as with it. My

---

[35] *Votes*, 7:6069–72; Jacobson, pp. 59–60.

[36] Ward L. Miner, *William L. Goddard, Newspaper Man* (Durham, N.C., 1962), p. 66.

farm is small; my servants are few, and good; I have a little money at interest; I wish for no more; my employment in my own affairs is easy; and with a contented grateful mind, undisturbed by worldly hopes or fears, relating to myself, I am completing the number of days allotted to me by divine goodness.

. . . . .

From my infancy I was taught to love *humanity* and *liberty*.

. . . . .

These being my sentiments, I am encouraged to offer to you, my countrymen, my thoughts on some late transactions, that appear to me to be of the utmost importance to you.[37]

No setting could have intrigued his readers more. But from such a simple beginning, the writer moved with strength into his arguments. Dating his first letter November 5, 1767, the author noted that the day marked the seventy-ninth anniversary of William III's landing at Torbay, which occasion gave "Constitutional Liberty to all Englishmen." By constitutional arguments as well as by a historical overview, Dickinson buttressed his case.

The first letter chiefly concerned the Restraining Act. Was Parliament's order that the colonies furnish articles for troops on this continent, even though it did not stipulate how the money should be raised, still a question of taxation? Asserting he detested "inflammatory measures," the author believed "a firm, modest exertion of a free spirit should never be wanting on public occasions" and that when one colony is agitated, the rest ought to support its cause "with equal ardor."

The importance of this letter was immediately recognized by editors of other newspapers. Two days later the editors of both the *Pennsylvania Journal* and the *Pennsylvania Gazette* reprinted the letter. They continued to reprint the subsequent letters for eleven issues. Galloway, whose loyalty to British authorities was unquestioning, was furious about Goddard's printing the letter, terming it "damned ridiculous! mere stuff! fustian!" He suggested that

---

[37] All quotations are from the *Letters* reprinted in Ford.

it was a compilation by Dickinson and Charles Thomson,[38] though he did not know who the author was. As each letter was published, and the *Chronicle* found its way to newspaper offices in other colonies, editors throughout America clipped the columns and reset them for their own journals, until nineteen out of the twenty-three newspapers then in existence had printed all the *Farmer's Letters.*[39]

The enormous success of these letters was the result of several factors. First, of course, was the immediate charm of the signature "Farmer," which since Roman times had idyllic and reflective connotations. The publishing of John Pomfret's popular poem in 1700 called "The Choice" revived a hero called the Farmer and that figure remained an ideal throughout the century. In 1782 Crèvecoeur adopted the same pen name for his letters. Thus the signature called forth an image of sobriety, humility, and a sagacity that touched a common chord. Moreover, Dickinson's ideological approach was a crystallization of the whig theory that dominated the thinking of American leaders.[40] Throughout Dickinson's letters the threat to liberty, the loss of power over taxation, the dangers of a standing army, and the fear of political corruption were easily recognized notes. And, finally, the historical and constitutional approach in challenging the Townshend Acts, backed by the citation of Greek, Roman, and British authorities, gave peculiar strength to Dickinson's arguments.

Dickinson clarified the differences between internal and external taxation and regulation of trade versus taxation, a confusion that existed in Dulany's *Considerations.*[41] But from the beginning he emphasized that often the smaller the taxes levied, the bigger the trap, and he accused Parliament of seeking some precedent "the force of which shall be established by the tacit admission of the Colonies." He harked back to the Stamp Act, suggesting that

[38] William Goddard, *The Partnership* (Philadelphia, 1770).

[39] Carl F. Kaestle, "The Public Reaction to John Dickinson's Farmer's Letters," *Proceedings of the American Antiquarian Society* 78, Pt. 2 (1969):323–53.

[40] Ibid.

[41] See Bernard Bailyn, ed., *Pamphets of the American Revolution, 1750–1776* (Cambridge, Mass., 1965).

as it had been a law "that would be self-executing," so too, would the Townshend Acts be, and with the same limitation on American liberty. The dependence of the colonies upon the importation of both paper and glass was real. Moreover, this fact, added to restrictions on the manufacture of iron and steel, meant that in accepting taxation on these imported goods, the colonies would find themselves ensnared and lacking the power of protest. In short, he said, "the single question is, whether the parliament can legally impose duties to be paid *by the people of these colonies only,* FOR THE SOLE PURPOSE OF RAISING A REVENUE, *on commodities which she obliges us to take from her alone,* or, in other words, whether the parliament can legally take money out of our pockets, without our consent. If they can, our boasted liberty is but *Vox et praeterea nihil.*"

Dickinson's popular success in part lay in his ability to state and restate his opinions and arguments. In his third letter, he set forth in direct language the purpose of his writing: "I will now tell the gentlemen, what is 'the meaning of these letters.' The meaning of them is, to convince the people of these colonies that they are at this moment exposed to the utmost dangers; and to persuade them immediately, vigorously, and unanimously, to exert themselves in the most firm, but most peaceable manner, for obtaining relief."

Dickinson was aware that "a people does not reform with moderation." Thus he felt it necessary to caution against the use of force, stating that "the cause of liberty is a cause of too much dignity to be sullied by turbulence and tumult." It was liberty and freedom that concerned him. He decried any move toward separation, asking: "If once *we* are separated from our mother country, what new form of government shall we adopt, or where shall we find another *Britain* to supply our loss?"

Dickinson then set forth suggestions for redress of grievances:

> The constitutional modes of obtaining relief are those which I wish to see pursued on the present occasion; that is, by petitions of our assemblies, or where they are not permitted to meet, of the people, to the powers that can afford us relief.
>
> If however, it shall happen, by an unfortunate course of affairs, that our applications to his Majesty and the parlia-

ment for redress, prove ineffectual, let us then take *another step*, by withholding from *Great Britain* all the advantages she has been used to receive from us. Then let us try, if our ingenuity, industry, and frugality, will not give weight to our remonstrances. Let us all be united with one spirit, in one cause.

Three days after the publication of the first letter, Dickinson wrote James Otis of Boston, whom he had met at the Stamp Act Congress, with a wish that Boston would "first kindle the Sacred Flame" of liberty. He enclosed manuscript copies of the first four letters, partly out of personal admiration for Otis and because of his regard for the "indefatigable zeal and undaunted courage" Massachusetts Bay had shown in the Stamp Act controversy. Then Dickinson turned to the new issue at hand, reiterating the opinion he voiced in the published letters: "Our cause is a cause of the highest dignity. Is it nothing less, than to maintain the Liberty with which heav'n itself hath made us free? I hope it will not be disgrac'd in any Colony, by a simple rash step. We have constitutional methods of seeking redress: and they are the best methods."[42] Two and a half weeks later the Boston *Evening Post* began publication of the letters, although with certain omissions.[43]

For the first few months Dickinson was successful in maintaining anonymity as author. Before publication he had shown his manuscript to three friends for their approval. They had kept silent, as did Otis, about the writer. John MacPherson, Dickinson's law clerk responsible for copying the manuscript, in his turn pleaded ignorance as to the author's identity when writing friends. "This, however, is certain," MacPherson wrote; "he is a friend to his country and has contributed (not barely his mite) towards the delivery of America from slavery."[44] In February, remarking that

[42] JD to Otis, December 5, 1767, Massachusetts Historical Society, hereafter cited as MaHS.

[43] These omissions make it probable that the *Letters* were published without any prompting by Otis. On the other hand, certain letters were published before Philadelphia papers had time to arrive in Boston.

[44] MacPherson to William Patterson, March 11, 1768, W. H. Horner Collection, HSP.

a number of "Sons of Liberty—in particular those of a neighboring Province" had expressed a desire to know who the author was, the *Gazette* boldly concluded: "It is said, and believed, to be wrote by J--n D-ck-n, Esq. of this City." Not until mid-May was the secret confirmed.[45]

The popularity of the letters surpassed any possible expectation. The title the "Farmer" first meant the author of the letters and later became the common pseudonym of John Dickinson. From Massachusetts to Georgia toasts and tributes were raised to him. There was no precedent for such enthusiasm. An official Declaration of Praise by Boston, suggested by Samuel Adams, praised this "friend of Americans, and the common benefactor of mankind"; grand juries of Cumberland County, Pennsylvania, and of Cecil County, Maryland, each hailed him, and more than once he was dubbed an "AMERICAN Pitt."[46] Newspapers from Boston to Savannah even incorrectly informed their readers that a grateful gentleman of Virginia had willed the Farmer a fortune.

A published account of a private event honoring the Farmer proved embarrassing to Dickinson. It occasioned charges of vanity and criticism that wounded him. He later described it as "the private act of a Club of Friends."[47] It was then that Dickinson was publicly revealed as the author. The *Pennsylvania Chronicle* published a tribute by the Society of Fort St. David's on May 19, 1768. Fourteen gentlemen of the club, a fishing society, had presented Dickinson with a box of heart of oak, finely decorated on top with an inscription and representation of the Cap of Liberty on a sphere which rested upon a cipher of the letters *J.D.* Within it was the notation:

THE LIBERTIES OF
THE BRITISH COLONIES IN AMERICA
ASSERTED,
WITH ATTICK ELOQUENCE,
AND ROMAN SPIRIT,

---

[45] *Pennsylvania Gazette*, February 6, 1766; Kaestle, pp. 333–34.

[46] Kaestle, p. 327.

[47] JD to Matthew Carey, n.d. [1789?], L-D/LCP.

BY
JOHN DICKINSON, ESQ.
BARRISTER AT LAW.[48]

Dickinson's simple and engaging introduction to the letters and the clearly stated reasons for protest, whether the use of duties for revenue or other insidious British measures against the colonies, appealed at once to those liberty-loving men whose common experiences were beginning to set them apart from the mother country. He had well expressed their unspoken fears; moreover, the extensive quotations and the reasoning so well anchored in a wealth of footnotes gave the letters authority. Until Thomas Paine's *Common Sense* was published early in 1776, no other document earned the acclaim given the *Farmer's Letters*; none reached a wider public. Until the year of Independence, John Dickinson, apart from Benjamin Franklin, was probably the American known to more colonists than any other. He was indeed, to the convening of the Second Continental Congress, recognized as the chief spokesman for American rights and liberty. The very human confession Dickinson had made to George Read half dozen years before, that he would "enjoy making a bustle in this world," had happily come true.

Less than a month after the newspaper publication of the letters, they appeared in pamphlet form.[49] A second edition came out in June, and William and Thomas Bradford printed a third. Two Boston editions included that town's resolutions to the Farmer and Dickinson's response, and Richard Henry Lee wrote a preface to a printing in Williamsburg combining the *Farmer's Letters* and Arthur Lee's *Monitor's Letters*. Benjamin Franklin in London wrote a preface for publications both in London and Paris. His attitude, however, was cautious. Writing his son, he confessed that he did not know the Farmer would "draw the lines between duties for regulation and those for revenue; and if the Parliament

---

[48] See also C. V. Hagner, *A History of the Falls of the Schuylkill* (Philadelphia, 1809) and *American Museum*, December 1788, 4:546–47.

[49] *Letters From a Farmer in Pennsylvania to the Inhabitants of the British Colonies* (Philadelphia, 1768). For all the printings see bibliography.

is to be the judge, it seems to me that establishing such principles of distinction will amount to little."[50]

Yet for all the acclaim Dickinson received, the words of admiration expressed in England by the liberty-loving John Wilkes and in France by Voltaire, who compared him with Cicero, there was a heavy artillery of negative comment aimed at the writer, both against his person and against his arguments. That he should be taunted for vanity was unfair. Years before, in his commonplace book he had recorded the words of Tacitus: "To despite Fame is to despite the Virtues by which it is acquir'd."[51] His intent had been wholly commendable. Galloway, as Speaker of the Assembly, inspired much of the criticism leveled at the Farmer. Both officially and unofficially, he still controlled Philadelphia mercantile leadership. All efforts toward colonial unity being urged by Massachusetts Bay and those attempted by the "popular party" of Philadelphia were blocked by Quaker merchants, Galloway, and their allies.

The stronger currents that ran throughout the colonies were favorable to Dickinson's stance. Encomiums kept coming in; praise continued; and R. Bell, publisher, issued a primitive engraving of "J--n D--ks-n, Esq.," against a background inspired by the presentation by the Society of Fort St. David. Paul Revere in 1772, taking the Bell print as his model, engraved a portrait plate of Dickinson for *Nathaniel Ames' Almanac*.[52]

In April 1768 Dickinson again wrote Otis.[53] He expressed his particular affection for Boston. This time his words were written on "the best made Pennsylvania paper" he could get. The writer continued his pleasant correspondence with the Boston patriot. Remembering that Cardinal de Retz enforced his political points with song, and always himself enjoying attempts at rhyme, if not poetry, Dickinson composed what he called "a song for American

[50] Benjamin Franklin to William Franklin, March 13, 1768, *Papers of Benjamin Franklin*, 15:74.

[51] Commonplace Book, p. 69, L-D/LCP.

[52] Clarence S. Brigham, *Paul Revere's Engravings* (New York, 1969), pp. 202–3 and plate 71.

[53] JD to Otis, April 11, 1788, MaHS.

freedom." He showed it first to Arthur Lee, who was en route to study law in England. Lee wrote eight lines of the eight-stanza total with chorus. On July 4 the author forwarded to Otis this first American patriotic song, set to "Hearts of Oak," an English tune composed a decade earlier by William Boyce.[54] The most notable phrase was "By uniting we stand, by dividing we fall," while the refrain ran:

> In FREEDOM we're born, in FREEDOM we'll live,
>   Our Purses are ready,
>   Steady, Friends, steady.
> Not as SLAVES, but as FREEMEN our Money we'll give.

Two days after sending the manuscript to Boston, Dickinson sent an additional stanza and corrected copy, feeling the first had been "too bold." Otis forwarded the song to the *Boston Gazette*. In the meantime it was printed in Philadelphia as a broadside and appeared in both the *Pennsylvania Gazette* and *Pennsylvania Journal*, from which it was reprinted in New York and Massachusetts newspapers. It proved immensely popular. In Boston it was also circulated as a broadside, and words and music were later reproduced in two Boston almanacs.[55] The song's popularity found a parody, and this in turn begat a parody parodized either by Mercy Warren, the sister of James Otis, or by Dr. Benjamin Church.

In the third letter Dickinson urged colonial assemblies to protest the Townshend Acts by petition. Should that not move the crown and Parliament, he suggested "withholding from Great-Britain all the advantages she has been used to receive from them." As Dickinson hoped, Massachusetts kindled the fire. On February 11, 1768, before the weekly letters had all been published in Boston, the Massachusetts Assembly sent a circular letter to other colonial assemblies noting that it had petitioned Britain concerning "the several acts of Parliament imposing Duties and Taxes." The Assembly expressed its hope for a harmonious response from all the colonies, and a sharing of their concerns. The Pennsylvania House, under Galloway's control, ignored the letter. Boston free-

[54] JD to Otis, July 4, 1768, MaHS.

[55] Ford, 1:421–29.

holders as early as October 28, 1767, resolved to boycott British goods and to encourage American manufactures. But Franklin sided with Galloway and thought such action harmful to the cause of repeal.[56]

Announcement in Philadelphia of the freeholder resolutions resulted in a meeting of city merchants in November. A timid expression of sympathy was the only response, much to the chagrin of the sponsors. The Bostonians sought more affirmative support. They announced a suspension of imported goods from England beginning December 31, 1768, provided New York, Pennsylvania, and other colonies would fall in line with similar agreements. Another Philadelphia meeting was held March 28, 1768. Once again no action resulted. Suspicious that Boston would continue to smuggle goods in and out, the merchants refused to move, declaring that Pennsylvania would only suffer from such compliance. Hard-liners or tories feared Boston radicals and suggested that a next step might be the "importation of town meetings," which they referred to as an American bedlam. New York merchants for their part supported their Boston brethren.

Charles Thomson, Joseph Reed, and Thomas Mifflin united in efforts to obtain some sort of nonimportation agreement, voluntary if not compulsory. Since Dickinson's appearance would be a trump card, he was importuned to address another group meeting on April 25. Reading an appeal first published in the *Pennsylvania Journal*, and later reprinted as a broadside, Dickinson not only restated his objections to the recent taxation but listed eight other regulations he considered grievous, from the restriction of manufacturing and double taxation due to the control of the shipment of certain goods to emptying jails and "making the Colonies a receptacle for their rogues and villains." He concluded with the stricture "Let us never forget that our strength depends on our Union, and our Liberty on our strength," adding that advice so often quoted, "United we conquer, divided we die."[57]

Though seeking power through protest "in a peaceable and con-

[56] *Votes*, 7:6181–84; *Papers of Benjamin Franklin*, letters to Galloway, especially January 9, 1769, 16:18.

[57] *Pennsylvania Journal*, April 28, 1768; Ford, 1:411–17.

stitutional way," neither the meeting's sponsors nor Dickinson's temperate words swayed the mercantile interests. Signatories were few. The activists were irked, and Thomson was particularly furious. In May he wrote a letter to the *Pennsylvania Gazette*, signing it "A Freeborn American," to which Galloway disguised as a "Chester County Farmer" responded.[58] They continued to spar anonymously in the *Gazette* throughout the summer.

Arthur Lee, that summer in Philadelphia, had not only added stanzas to Dickinson's *Liberty Song* but spent many hours with him discussing the problems confronting the colonies. Although Dickinson was unremitting in his demands for freedom, he feared that there was a limit to the personal impact of his appeals. Once more he took up paper and pen, this time for a piece published as a broadside and entitled *A Copy of a Letter from a Gentleman of Virginia to a Merchant in Philadelphia*. Lee copied it for the printer, so the authorship would remain secret.[59]

A July meeting was held at the State House. There was renewed stress on the need for colonial cooperation against England's tyrannical actions. Yet the only action was a declaration of sympathy with the more active measures taken by Boston and New York to be sent to the London agents. In September for a fourth time merchants of Philadelphia were entreated to show resistance through nonimportation, but in vain. New York was especially angry over their failure to cooperate. Finally, at its September meeting the Pennsylvania Assembly, perhaps goaded by a letter sent in May from the House of Burgesses in Virginia, approved sending petitions to the king, Lords, and Commons praying for a relief of grievances.[60]

The beginning of 1769 again saw a determination on the part of the "popular party" to obtain voluntary resistance. Neither Parliament nor king showed signs of answering the colonial petitions. London agents and merchants were not encouraging in

[58] *Pennsylvania Gazette*, May 12 and June 24, 1768.

[59] Broadside [1768], reprinted in Ford, 1:435-37.

[60] *Pennsylvania Gazette*, July 27, August 4 and 11, 1768; R. L. Brunhouse, "The Effect of the Townshend Acts in Pennsylvania," *PMHB* 54 (1936):363; *Votes*, 7:6271-73.

their responses, suggesting the time was not ripe to press for any remedy. Franklin, as Pennsylvania's agent, declared in February that matters were growing worse daily and foresaw the trend "more and more to a breach and final separation."[61] The time had come to order goods for autumn delivery, a propitious point at which to move.

The people of Philadelphia took the lead themselves. Efforts at home manufactures were proceeding. Freeholders of Philadelphia, joined by four fire companies, pledged not to eat lamb in the year to come, in the hope of increasing woolen manufactures in the colony. Some people even agreed to wear leather jackets, thus disregarding English fashion.[62] Thomson and Mifflin led another effort to enlist the merchants in a nonimportation agreement. This time, due to such pressures, the response was successful. Excepting some twenty-two necessary articles, merchants and traders agreed to suspend trade with England until either repeal had been achieved or the subscribers might meet again for reconsideration. Merchants who had held back now joined the others. Thus in April, Philadelphia joined Boston and New York.

Dickinson, who had so long hoped for such firm action, saw a certain irony in the end. As he wrote Arthur Lee, "Can you believe it, my dear sir, that there are *Americans*, who discouraged to the utmost of their power the first struggles against the oppression of their country, yet afterwards being forced from their subterfuge, pretend to act the part of Catos?"[63] The English ministers might make "twists and turns" that would serve their private interests, but he questioned the certainty of their adherence "to the grand principles of government." Unable to invest faith in the rulers of Great Britain, Dickinson came to believe that "we must take care of ourselves."[64] Satisfaction to him meant total repeal of

---

[61] Arthur M. Schlesinger, *Colonial Merchants in the American Revolution* (New York, 1917), pp. 128–29; Franklin to Lord Kames, February 21, 1769, *Papers of Benjamin Franklin*, 16:48.

[62] Brunhouse, p. 365.

[63] JD to Lee, April 20, 1769, Richard Henry Lee, *Life of Arthur Lee* (Boston, 1829) 2:294.

[64] JD to Lee, November 25, 1769, ibid., 2:298.

all revenue acts, not only the Townshend Acts but the Sugar Act and all other duties of similar nature. Then only should resistance end.

On April 12, 1770, the House of Commons removed all taxation save that on tea. In the fall the Philadelphia merchants met to lift their nonimportation agreement except for that of tea.[65] Any gratification Dickinson may have experienced was limited in observing the rush of the merchants to end their embargo. He reflected unhappily that his countrymen had not been provoked enough to eliminate future oppression. He castigated the failure of the mercantile class on this score, but he also rejoiced in seeing that "there is a spirit and a strength in the land-holders of this continent sufficient to check the insolence of any infamously corrupt minister."[66]

The toast of the American colonies from Boston to Virginia, John Dickinson was relied upon to encourage the cause of liberty and freedom. He refused to take public office as a member of the Assembly. Continuing to be the antagonist of Galloway, however, Dickinson was a champion of both the Presbyterian party and the "popular front" of Thomson, Mifflin, and others.

[65] *Pennsylvania Gazette*, September 27, 1770.

[66] JD to Lee, September 21 and October 31, 1770, *Life of Arthur Lee*, 2:302–3.

★ 4 ★

A Change
of Pace

THE EXTRAORDINARY SUCCESS OF THE *Farmer's Letters* was reflected in many ways. Patience Wright had even added his
figure to her famous waxworks. Saved from a fire in Boston, the
collection was brought to the Quaker City for exhibition, where
the "beloved farmer of Philadelphia" was declared the "living
image of John Dickinson, Esq."[1] Later a ship's figurehead with his
likeness ornamented a vessel named for him.

John Dickinson at thirty-six was a middle-aged bachelor, firmly
established in his points of view. Born into a devoted Quaker
household, he acquired by his father's defection from that persuasion a lasting suspicion of all formally organized religious
bodies. Yet an abiding moral sense was embedded in his mind and
conscience. He developed a peculiar personal certainty and reli-
ance on conscience, or "inner light," and one result was an often
vexing rigidity in his makeup. But whatever criticisms might be
hurled at him, no one could ever fault him for a lack of integrity.

Dickinson's lonely fight in the Assembly against the petition
seeking royal government had found weak support and that exclusively from frontier Scotch-Irish Presbyterians. This growing,
articulate group became the foundation for the Popular party opposing the eastern establishment still dominated by the Quakers

[1] *Pennsylvania Chronicle*, June 10 and 17 and September 9, 1771.

[76]

and by Franklin through Galloway. The alliance contributed to Dickinson's reputation as a liberal.

Some who objected to Pennsylvania's becoming a crown colony feared that the Church of England would become officially established. Franklin seemed to suggest that possibility in his pamphlet *Cool Thoughts* in support of the king's intervention. Rumors abounded that members of other denominations might even be disqualified by law to fill important governmental posts.[2] On March 28, 1768, a series of weekly articles entitled "The Centinel" appeared in the *Pennsylvania Journal* and the *Weekly Advertiser* opposing plans for an American episcopate as proposed by the Anglican church. Dickinson was said to be the author of many of these essays, though subsequent research concludes that he wrote only the three signed "A.B."[3] The belief at the time regarding his contributions was so strong that a series in the *New York Gazette* affirmed: "even that Whig, that champion for liberty, the FARMER himself, is one of the best writers against an American Episcopate."[4]

Dickinson's visits to Fairhill to call on Mary and Sarah Norris were resumed. The sisters were pleasant company. He had detoured along any road to matrimony by filling his days with politics and the law. John's free time was consumed by the challenge of writing arguments in protest to Great Britain's curtailing of American liberties. Dickinson had discovered a power of persuasion by pen. He enjoyed the marshaling of arguments. Thus the *Letters from a Farmer*, essays against the establishment of bishops, and the *Address on Non-Importation*, appearing in rapid succession in the spring of 1768, were all satisfying in a creative way as well as winning him favor and renown.

Polly and Sally, as their family and friends called them, came into town for extended periods and stayed with their aunt Mrs. Charles Norris, known as the Widow Norris. The imposing house

[2] Francis Alison to Ezra Stiles, May 27, 1759, March 29 and May 7, 1768, Manuscript Division, YU.

[3] Richard J. Hooker, "John Dickinson on Church and State," *American Literature* 16 (1944–45):82–98.

[4] *New York Gazette or the Weekly Post Boy*, June 6, 1768.

with its surrounding gardens where she lived with her children Deborah, then seven years old, and Charles was on the southeast corner of Chestnut and Fifth streets. She had long acted as confidante to her nieces. On one of the sisters' visits, their path crossed that of Dickinson. Friendly ties begun when he had visited them after their father's death were renewed.

The visits soon turned to an affair of the heart. It was the elder sister, the twenty-eight-year-old Mary Norris, who became the object of John's affections. The three were often together and made a congenial trio. But there were also misunderstandings. Dickinson, like his father, did not attend Quaker meetings. Moreover, he held strong views on the subject. The Norrises were devoted Friends. On one particular visit the conversation turned to religion. John stated his definite opinions, and Mary took umbrage at what she thought were critical references to the Society of Friends. The suitor was considerably shaken over the misinterpretation of his viewpoint. Arriving home and almost in desperation, he wrote and rewrote a clarification of his intent. This he addressed to Sally in a letter begging her to intercede with her sister on his behalf. He assured her that his remarks had been general and had been aimed against all organized religious denominations.[5] The matter was happily settled. But a far greater blunder, in turn, was to be made.

Sometime after Dickinson and Polly Norris had agreed on marriage, talk turned on the question of property and the Norris estate. Dickinson was a man of property and wealth in his own right. His father's lands in Maryland and Delaware had been divided between him and his brother Philemon. Though the Norris sisters were among the richest heiresses in the Middle Colonies, John Dickinson by any standard was a proper prospective husband. His distinguished family background, his Philadelphia standing, and his personal fortune were notable.

Fairhill, the Norris estate, had been well named. On a height, well set back from the Germantown road and some six miles from Philadelphia, it was the handsome country seat built by the first

[5] This letter and those dealing with other disputes, particularly during the period Dickinson courted Polly, are in drafts only (L/HSP). These are difficult to decipher as to date or the persons addressed.

Isaac Norris in 1717. From the house set above well-designed parterres, one could see in the distance the tall-masted ships lying at anchor in the Delaware. As a country retreat it possessed serenity and beauty, both natural and cultivated. A few days after Dickinson proposed marriage, he learned that Fairhill had been entailed to the son of Charles Norris, a cousin of Mary and Sarah. Though Dickinson realized that the bequest struck off half the fortune to which he believed Mary entitled, he said little; his behavior was circumspect. Nevertheless, he frankly questioned the advisability of turning over the property to Charles while he was still a minor.[6]

Sometime later Mary mentioned that she intended to lend the money that was invested in England to her widowed aunt for her children's education. Dickinson commented that considering the difficulty the family would meet in paying any interest during their minority or afterwards, he viewed it "a gift under another name."[7] As he later remarked, "These Dispositions reduced Miss N's Fortune in my opinion to a very moderate one." Dickinson's interest primarily concerned the girls and their future comfort. His gratuitous advice led to strained relations.[8] Dickinson again took up his pen and addressed Sally. It was a tortured, much revised letter. He drafted it painfully and then carefully rewrote it. Sally proved herself an understanding intermediary. She was also touched by Dickinson's faith in her and by being called "truly my friend," as well as his assurance that "if Miss N. had thought proper to settle her whole Estate on her Cousin, and then would have favored me with her hand I should have instantly accepted it knowing that my Life and Fortune could not be better." The storm clouds passed by; the sun shone once more at Fairhill.

John's advice, however, was spurned. Between May and mid-September 1769, Mary Norris in six installments loaned her aunt Mrs. Charles Norris a total of £6,400 which was to be paid back in 1789. Although her father died intestate, he intended Fairhill to descend in the male line. Following her father's wishes, in Au-

---

[6] JD to Sally Norris, letter draft, n.d., L/HSP.

[7] Ibid.

[8] JD to Hannah Harrison (later Mrs. Charles Thomson), August 24, 1769, Thomson Papers, X, Library of Congress (hereafter cited as DLC).

gust 1769 Mary conveyed the property in trust to young Isaac Norris, her Uncle Charles's eldest son, preserving the right of tenancy for twenty-one years. On that young man's death several years later the trust was revoked, and, then acting in concert with her husband, Mary conveyed the property to Isaac's brother Joseph Parker Norris.[9]

Next, John's religious position became the cause of disharmony. In discussing their marriage, Dickinson told his fiancée that he had no intention of going to Meeting even for the wedding. Mary was a dedicated Friend whose whole deportment could be cited as a model.[10] John was distraught, saying he felt as if he were on "the Brink of a Precipice." The visit ended unhappily. The suitor yet another time sought Sally's intervention. He wrote her that "if Miss Norris resolves never to marry but before the Meeting, she resolves to make me the most unhappy man on the face of the earth."[11] Sally calmed the waters in her gentle way, and for awhile discussion of the marriage rites was avoided.

A sudden and almost overwhelming loss to the Fairhill family occurred on June 24, 1769. Sally Norris died after a short illness. She was, of the two sisters, the liveliest, the most sympathetic, and ever an enthusiastic friend and companion. She had contracted smallpox and continued fairly "easy and sensible" until nearly the end. The day following her death she was buried from the townhouse of the Widow Norris.[12]

John Dickinson had loved both sisters, if in different ways. He once referred to Sally in a letter to her cousin Hannah Harrison as "my valuable, my beloved, my sincere Friend—for such she affectionately and generously declared herself to me."[13] John was deeply devoted to the bereft Mary, and his every act was testimony

[9] Indentures of May 19, August 5, 10, 24, September 1 and 14, 1769, L-D/LCP.

[10] As one of her kinsmen wrote in deploring her marriage. William Logan to John Smith, July 20, 1770, John Smith Papers, LCP.

[11] JD to Sally Norris, n.d., L/HSP.

[12] L-D/LCP, XV, 78.

[13] JD to Hannah Harrison, August 24, 1769. Thomson Papers, X, DLC.

to the fact. Any wounds of misunderstanding that now remained were healed. Love proved restorative. In the weeks that followed Mary spent most of her time with her aunt, with Dickinson in constant attention. He was almost too solicitous. One Saturday he sent her a note saying he looked forward to seeing her the next evening but begged her not to go to Meeting the next day, "for the ground will be so damp and from that cause the air will be so moist, that I am sure there must be great danger of catching cold by going."[14] While at court in Chester, he sent a few hurried lines to Mrs. Norris saying how uneasy he had been over Mary's indisposition the last time he had seen her. Because of the severe February weather he worried about a proposed trip to Fairhill. He requested return word by way of his servant Cato, who would be riding down to Chester the next day.[15]

Marriage plans were once again discussed, Dickinson urging a decision, his fiancée giving many reasons for delay. He now sought her aunt's influence, drafting an appeal that was touching:

> The reasons she urges for delay will not bear examination. She appears to be sensible of this and therefore seems to aim at enforcing them by the decisive manner in which they are given. . . . Madame, I do not mean to hurry the dear lady. Her health is mending daily. What I desire at present is, that we should put it into our own power, to take the last step when we please which cannot be done till a month after we have signed a Declaration of our Intentions. The law may be sufficiently complied with, without publishing this declaration.[16]

His concerns, he said, were "the anxieties of a distressed friend." Promising that he would avoid "the least appearance of a shew" out of respect for Sally, "the dear Saint in Heaven," he begged help in resolving this unexpected problem. So at last the wedding

[14] JD to [?], n.d. ("Saturday Evening"), letter draft, Norris Family Papers, II, 72, L-D/LCP.

[15] Ibid., 73.

[16] JD to Mary Norris [?], February 25, 1770, letter draft, Norris Family Papers, II, 71, LCP. It is possible that he was addressing Polly's Aunt Elizabeth, who was likewise known as Aunt Norris and lived at Fairhill.

day was set. It was even agreed that the ceremony would be a civil one.

The marriage took place on Thursday evening, July 19, 1770, in the home of "Aunt Norris." Both Mary and John kept the proposed wedding as secret as possible. The previous Sunday, when James Logan called at Fairhill, Polly invited him and his wife to attend but asked him to keep the matter confidential. James Pemberton, another kinsman of the Norris family, was told of the event only the day before. As strict Quakers, they were appalled by a civil marriage. William Logan, of Stenton, writing to his brother-in-law, John Smith of Burlington, declared, "I am grately concerned for the example Polly has set by this her outgoing in marriage. I fear she has slipped from the Top of the Hill of the reputation she has gained in the Society and among her Friends and that it will be a long time before she gains it again if ever. I wish she may not repent it."[17]

Logan reported that very few were present—only Dickinson's mother and his brother Philemon, Dr. Cadwalader, his wife and son Lambert, Hannah Harrison, Mary's cousin, some of Samuel Morris's children, and the Norris household. He commented sardonically on the date of the wedding, saying that it was "exactly four years since Isaac Norris died—a Day that Polly was always to keep with the greatest Solemnity. Perhaps she may think she has made herself whole by taking Husband and Father in one."[18] Logan erred in his statement concerning the anniversary; Norris had died on July 12.

The marriage, "solemnized according to the Laws of the Province," was performed by George Bryan, Dickinson's friend from Assembly days, then justice of the peace and of the Court of Common Pleas in Philadelphia. The union was later recorded before Thomas Willing, one of the judges of the Supreme Court.[19] Dickinson had held firm to his decision that the occasion should be devoid of any religious aspect. Love for her prospective husband and

[17] Logan to Smith, July 20, 1770, John Smith Papers, LCP.

[18] Ibid.

[19] L-D/LCP, XV, 78.

recollection of her sister Sally's sympathetic interventions softened Mary's own judgment. Her decision did not lessen the shock of her actions, and stern relatives found reason to decline invitations to be present. The day was hot and humid, and that provided sufficient excuse for some to be absent.[20]

Dickinson sent carefully worded letters to local newspaper editors on the following Monday requesting that as "a favor of great weight" they would not insert

> any other account of my Marriage than this—
> "Last Thursday John Dickinson Esquire was married to Miss Mary Norris"—
> Your mentioning it in any manner whatever different from this, or giving in any part of your paper an account of the expressions of joy shown on the occasion, will give inexpressible pain to me, and very great uneasiness to a number of very worthy relations—
> Your compliance with my request will oblige, more than you can imagine.[21]

Both English-language newspapers in Philadelphia complied exactly. The *German Weekly* did also though it identified both the bride and groom in respectful fashion.

John MacPherson, serving in Dickinson's law office, announced the marriage of his mentor in an imaginary newspaper account when he wrote his friend Will Patterson in New Jersey: "Last Thursday evening was married John Dickinson, Esq. of this city, author of the Farmer's Letters, to the amiable Miss Polly Norris of Fairhill, only surviving daughter of the late Isaac Norris, Esq. deceased. She is a young lady endowed with every qualification requisite to make the marriage state happy, with a fortune of £50,000 (some say £80,000)."[22]

Old friends and new forwarded congratulations to the newly-weds. George Read of Delaware sent affectionate felicitations, and

[20] Samuel Morris to JD, July 20, 1770, L-D/LCP.

[21] JD to William and Tho. Bradford, Monday . . . , Collection of Letters of Members of the Pennsylvania Provincial Congress, IV, 29, HSP.

[22] Macpherson to Patterson, July 24, 1770, W. M. Horner Collection, HSP.

the printers of Philadelphia in a letter poetically and imaginatively wrote of the bells that rang on that occasion.[23]

In spite of the rejoicing, Mary Norris Dickinson had a conscience to be put at rest. In late December she presented an apology to the Philadelphia Monthly Meeting regretting the breach of discipline in the manner in which her marriage was conducted.[24] She was excused, and never again did she depart from strict adherence to the Society's rules.

A postwedding journey was projected into the western counties as far as Carlisle by way of Reading. A party of six set out by horse and by carriage, Mary with her cousin Hannah Harrison as companion, Charles Thomson and Dickinson and Thomas Mifflin and his wife. They looked forward to seeing old friends. For the newlyweds these included James Wilson, Dickinson's former law student, just then beginning his practice in Carlisle, and some of Mary Dickinson's distant Quaker kin, the charming Wright family who lived on the banks of the Susquehanna. Dickinson, now having a determining voice in the Norris estate as Mary's husband, would have an opportunity to look over landholdings and other investments in Berks County and elsewhere.

In addition, the gentlemen of the party were concerned with political developments in the province and in imperial relations. Dissatisfactions over Assembly matters controlled by the eastern counties were severe in the frontier regions where the population was growing fast. The political ideas of the Pennsylvania Germans and, even more, the opinion of the Scotch-Irish settled west of the Susquehanna were of great significance to the future of Pennsylvania.

Dickinson's bride was a good traveler, he reported to Aunt Norris.[25] He had covered the same areas before, but it was the first such excursion for Mary. And the others proved congenial com-

[23] Read to JD, August 10, 1770, L-D/LCP; Printers of Philadelphia to JD, L/HSP.

[24] "Early Minutes of Philadelphia Meeting," *Publication of the Genealogical Society of Pennsylvania* 14 (October 1942):43.

[25] JD to Mary Norris, September 20, 1770, Stillé, pp. 320–21.

panions, cementing ties of friendships that were to continue strong and enduring throughout the years ahead.

Fairhill, to be the Dickinsons' home for the next six years, was an exceedingly comfortable country seat. Sixty feet square, the mansion had an English basement, one main floor, and a hip roof broken by dormer windows. Its recessed center entrance doors led into transverse halls dividing the interior into four large rooms. The hilltop location and the surrounding orchards, meadows, and groves of trees were an especial delight. The first Isaac Norris had sought plant specimens from both Europe and the southern colonies, and the estate was further enriched by the country's first willow trees, a sprout of which Benjamin Franklin had presented to Norris's granddaughter Debby. Fields and forests stretched from the Delaware River to the Frankford Road and westward to the Germantown Road. These tracts, lying in what was known as the Liberties, were three: one called Sepviva, of some 155 acres, between the Delaware River and the Frankford Road; Fairhill, the largest, of 530 acres, extending northwest to the Germantown Road; and across the road Somerville, of about 200 acres. Isaac Norris II intended to reserve the latter estate for his two daughters on his death.[26]

Dickinson and his wife were among the wealthiest couples in the prosperous Quaker City. John's own inheritance was substantial, his legal practice enriching, though a professional income less than that earned by Philadelphia merchants. In aristocratic fashion when a member of the Pennsylvania Assembly, he had turned over his per diem to charitable causes.[27] He had, moreover, frequently subscribed to demands of the needy both in Philadelphia and Delaware. Though he had lived comfortably in Philadelphia with Cato as his personal servant, Dickinson as a married man now shared another fortune and could indulge his personal taste.

Fairhill as originally built, although handsome, exhibited no extravagance in its interior, either in detail or furnishing. The

[26] Stillé, pp. 314, 320–21; Thompson Westcott, *The Historic Mansions and Buildings of Philadelphia* (Philadelphia, 1877), pp. 481–83.

[27] JD to the Rev. Dr. Alison, January 10, 1766, Society Collections, HSP.

highly polished oak and cedar wainscoting and the spacious, livable quality of the rooms were its charms. Isaac Norris II had constructed two flanking dependencies, one of which housed his library, second only in the colony to that of James Logan, his father-in-law. Many of the books were in Latin, all of them showing Norris's wide-ranging studies.

Dickinson now launched an ambitious building program, first changes to Fairhill and then the construction of a townhouse in Philadelphia. David Evans, a cousin of the Norris family, was the carpenter-contractor for both. At Fairhill he rebuilt chimneys, reframed both the front and back doors with arches, added seventeen new window sills and trusses, constructed a new staircase, and trimmed the interior with mahogany. Benjamin Randolph had imported twenty-one logs of mahogany in June 1771, which Evans approved for Dickinson's projects. As boards they added up to 4,244 feet. The restyling changed the general character of the house from its earlier Jacobean aspect to more classic Georgian lines. The outbuildings flanking the central house were also renovated, including a bathing house and an improved library-study. The work consumed many hours and much labor, as the 103 gallons of Jamaica spirit bought of Anthony Benezet for the workmen indicated.[28]

Remembering the handsome gardens of England that had so impressed him, Dickinson provided a new setting for the Fairhill mansion. Fencing was built, and 526 yards of paving were laid. The improvements warranted writing an English friend to find a "proper gardiner" to help with the task of maintaining the grounds. But in this search he met with no success. When Josiah Quincy, Jr., came through Philadelphia in 1773 en route home to New England, having visited many great houses of the South, he went out to Fairhill, and declared it superior to all he had seen. He observed that Dickinson should be the happiest of men considering "the antique look of his house, his gardens, green house, bathing house, grotto, study, fishpond, fields, meadows, vista, through which there is a pleasant prospect of Delaware River, his paintings, an-

[28] L-D/LCP, XXX, 25–31.

tiquities, improvements, etc., in short his whole life." Thus, as Deborah Logan noted, John and Mary lived "in great elegance."[29]

Philadelphians had been building houses of extraordinary beauty. Continuing the Georgian style, the 1760s witnessed the erection of the country seat of Captain John MacPherson called Mount Pleasant; Benjamin Chew's Cliveden; and, in town, John Stamper's house and that of Charles Stedman, later known as the Powel House. Dickinson's first cousin John Cadwalader in 1768 had married Elizabeth Lloyd of Wye House, Talbot County, Maryland, whose family also possessed a large plantation in Kent County, Delaware.[30] Cadwalader's marriage to this heiress enriched his own fortune as his cousin John was to do two years later on his marriage. Purchasing the property of Samuel Rhoads on the west side of Second Street between Spruce and Pine, Cadwalader had bought neighboring lots and beginning in 1769 set about making extensive alterations and improvements to the already large house. Gradually the Cadwalader house developed into a mansion of unsurpassed elegance. Dickinson, then living in Second Street in the block above, watched the reconstruction with great interest.

Fairhill, though extensively redesigned, was, after all, a Norris house and entailed to that family. Dickinson thought in terms of a house that could be his own. Early in 1771 he purchased two lots between Sixth and Seventh streets on the north side of Chestnut. David Evans, who was working at Fairhill, was one of the property owners in the block. Dickinson sought his aid in obtaining the adjoining properties. Already word had spread that Dickinson was "going to build a house [with a] 70 foot front."[31] But before he could do so his first problem was to dislodge the tenants from houses on the land he had purchased. This action disturbed his

[29] Edward Cottrell to JD, June 6, 1771, XII, 11, L-D/LCP; "Journal of Josiah Quincy, January 1773," *Proceedings of the Massachusetts Historical Society* 49 (1916):473. Deborah Logan as quoted in Stillé, p. 313.

[30] Nicholas B. Wainwright, *Colonial Grandeur in Philadelphia* (Philadelphia, 1964), p. 3. The paragraphs which follow, unless otherwise noted, are indebted to this book.

[31] William Logan to John Smith, February 23, 1771, Smith Collection, LCP.

wife Polly, in part perhaps because of her reservations about the general plans.[32] She knew that her husband's designs for a new house were elaborate ones, and she was hesitant about the proposals being made.

The Dickinson house on Chestnut Street took nearly four years to complete. The major building on the property between Sixth and Seventh streets was a sturdy house that had been built by Joshua Carpenter in 1722.[33] To this house, set well back from the street, Dickinson planned a front addition in which a central hall would connect with the original stairhall of the old house. The earlier building was also to be completely restyled to match the new portion.

Bids were asked for and then accepted. Dickinson was not sparing in his intentions to make his house a notable one. The ceilings were elegantly decorated in stucco designs and all mantels and room cornices equally elaborate.[34] The doors and staircase were of mahogany. Hercules Courtney provided the carvings for the wood paneling in a variety of patterns.[35] The finest marble outlined the fireplaces and floored the hearths, white downstairs and gray above.[36]

While the construction of Dickinson's house slowly progressed, all Philadelphia watched with interest. Catercornered from the square on which the State House stood, its central location vied with that of the three-storied Charles Norris house at Fifth and Chestnut. But Mrs. Dickinson, attached to Fairhill and disturbed by the unabashed show of luxury, was unhappy. Her husband kept hoping he could persuade her that they should move into town as soon as the residence was completed. At one point he disavowed any intention of occupying it, but as the building progressed, Dickinson became more encouraged and, to ward off speculation, began to talk of moving to town.

[32] Ibid., February 27, 1771.

[33] George B. Tatum, *Penn's Great Town* (Philadelphia, 1961), p. 153.

[34] List dated October 22, 1771, L/HSP, XXX, 74.

[35] Wainwright, pp. 142–50.

[36] Instructions to Peter Biggs, May 26, 1774, L/HSP, XXX, 85.

John Penn's wife, having heard various descriptions of the mansion, thought of it as a possible governor's residence and wrote to Joseph Shippen, Jr., asking for particulars. His answer in March 1773 was explicit:

> The Building is two stories high, 62 feet in front and 30 deep, it adjoins the old house and is placed exactly in the front of it, leaving a space of about 25 feet between the new house and the line of the Street—The ceilings of both stories are 14 feet high;—the lower one contains two Rooms of 27 feet by 24 each, and an entry of —— feet;—each room has 4 windows the East room having 2 south & 2 east windows, and the other has 2 looking to the South also, & two to the west;—both of these rooms will be pleasant & handsome—But the upper story is divided into 4 chambers ill shaped and ugly, each of them being 24 feet long and only 13 wide. The old stairs are to serve both houses, which will be very inconvenient, as the floors in the new house are considerably higher than those in the other.—This building has too low an appearance for a town house; it would have been greatly to its beauty if it had been raised higher by an attick story. Mr. Dickinson is universally blamed for connecting it with so ugly and ill contrived a pile of building as the old one is.

He also reported on Samuel Powel's future plans and noted that the house he then occupied on Second Street had cost him £5,500, continuing: "When Mr. Dickinson's house is completely finished & accomodated with coach house & stables, I reckon the whole cost of houses & lot will amount to a sum about equal to Mr. Powel's without including in the estimate the 80 feet corner Lot which Mr. D. bought of Mr. James Allen [along Sixth Street]."[37] Actually, Dickinson even before completion reckoned the total cost of house and land at £8,000.

Dickinson finally faced the fact that Mary would never consent to live there. He considered selling it to Governor Penn. A cash transaction was practically impossible for anyone to consider. The

[37] Shippen to John Penn, March 15, 1773, Edward Shippen Papers, 1727–83, LCP.

rent he sought was £400 to £500 annually.[38] But Dickinson never lived in his elegant mansion. It first served as a hospital in the early days of the Revolution. The French ambassador afterwards became a tenant.

Dickinson's interest in restoration and building was a pleasant diversion. There was, however, more pressing business to be done. As manager and now legal controller of the Norris estate, he wrote Osgood, Hanbury and Company in England sending notices of Sarah's death, of Mary's marriage, and of his own responsibility in holding power of attorney for his wife. The London agents needed these documents for proper administration of Norris bonds and investments in England. The following year they sold £7,100 of stock held there, and Dickinson immediately withdrew £3,000 from the cash account.[39] The rents, ground rents, bonds, and mortgages held by the Norris estate needed to be gathered in. These netted about £1,000.[40] Certain lands lying to the west around Reading and in York County needed clarification of titles, always a difficult problem.[41]

Both his flourishing law practice and investments were demanding. William Henry Stiegel, a German immigrant familiarly known as Baron Stiegel, living near Manheim, engaged Dickinson's attention, both as Stiegel's lawyer and as a part mortgage holder on one of the properties. Along with Charles and Alexander Stedman, Stiegel had purchased several tracts of land on which the Elizabeth Iron Furnace and Charming Forge were located. To these were later added what became known as the Manheim Tract. Glasshouses were added to the iron furnaces. Dickinson was one of several who had taken a mortgage on the Charming Forge land of the Stedmans in 1767.[42] That same year Mary and Sarah Norris had

---

[38] JD to Mr. Physick, September 4, 1773, L/HSP, XII, 78.

[39] JD to Osgood, Hanbury, October 11, 1770, February 16 and May 17, 1771, L/HSP, XXXIV, 48.

[40] Estate holdings, L/HSP, 79–80.

[41] Ibid., XXXIV, 95, 107.

[42] Frederick W. Hunter, *Stiegel Glass* (New York, 1950), pp. 26–93; L/HSP, XXI.

invested £2,120 of Pennsylvania currency in a second mortgage on the Elizabeth Furnace and on 10,124 acres of land. Two years later, after her sister's death, Mary transferred this mortgage to her aunt Mrs. Charles Norris.

Dickinson's relationship to Stiegel was on several planes: a desire to have Stiegel succeed in his glassmaking projects in an effort to achieve colonial industrial independence, as an investor, and as legal adviser. Stiegel's optimism was winning, and Dickinson was a sympathetic friend, even suggesting that Stiegel hold a lottery to help raise funds for his endeavor. Dickinson generously supported the scheme, drawing £282.2.7½ in winnings. But Stiegel found it necessary to seek mortgage after mortgage until the sheriff finally knocked. The fatal blow came in October 1775. Deserting Manheim and moving to Elizabeth Furnace, the baron failed to recover his losses, but his ambition never flagged.[43] Dickinson finally cooled to Stiegel's continuing enthusiasms.

Legal matters asserted themselves; some routine, other cases challenging, and a few involving personal considerations, such as that concerning the romantic Elizabeth Graeme, the daughter of Dr. Thomas Graeme and granddaughter of Sir William Keith. She had fallen in love with a Scotsman, Henry Hugh Fergusson, ten years her junior. Her father had vehemently opposed the marriage. They were secretly married in April 1772, with only a few friends such as Dickinson privy to it.[44] In the fall of that year her father died, and Lady Fergusson, as she came to be called, asked the lawyer for legal advice, at the same time happily declaring that her husband was her "second self" and enclosing a manuscript she had written. Elizabeth Fergusson's spirit was blithe, yet her life continued to be an endless series of mishaps and complications.

There was a voluminous personal correspondence to be dealt with. Jacob Rush wrote from London describing his study of law there; Lucretia Bozman, distant kinswoman who lived in Kent County, planned to send her son to Philadelphia to study and asked for advice. Dickinson consented to supervise the boy while there.

[43] L/HSP, XXXVIII, 72, 78, 81–82; Hunter, p. 82.

[44] Elizabeth Graeme Fergusson to JD, Sept. 21, Oct. 4 and 15, 1772, L-D/ LCP.

Catharine Macaulay, the English historian and advocate of the American cause, to whom Dickinson had sent a piece of American-made silk, wrote thanking this "man of the most Dignified Character" for the gift and expressing her hopes for America's future.[45]

Dickinson was deeply devoted to and considerate of friends. None was older or dearer than Thomas Willson, his childhood playmate, whom he called Tommy. Willson died in 1763, leaving two very young children, Sally and John, whose guardian Dickinson had become.[46] Settlement of the estate extended over ten years. Dickinson's concern for the children lasted as long as they lived. But no greater evidence existed of his kindness of heart than in Dickinson's assistance to the orphaned children of William Hicks of New York. He had engaged in unhappy correspondence with Hicks at the time the *Letters from a Pennsylvania Farmer* were being published. The temporary misunderstanding, however, had been bridged before Hicks's death in the autumn of 1772. He left five sons and a daughter, whose interests Dickinson oversaw for many years, seeking aid from New York friends concerning Hicks's property on Long Island and engaging in lengthy correspondence in support of the children.[47] Much of his charity, too, considered the welfare of children for whose schooling he was paying, a favorite benevolence often repeated.[48]

Dickinson properties held in common with his brother Philemon were time-consuming responsibilities. In February 1771 Dickinson had sold 600 acres of inherited land in Dorchester County, Maryland, and 778 acres in neighboring Queen Anne County for £1,400, but, as was so often the case, final execution of the sale

[45] Jacob Rush to JD, Feb. 8, 1772, JD to Lucretia Bozman, October 12, 1772 [draft], March 20, August 8, 1773, John Leeds to JD, Oct. 1, 1772, June 30, 1773, Catherine Macauley to JD, July 18, 1771, L/HSP.

[46] Account of the Thomas Willson Estate and Settlement, May 16, 1766, L/HSP, XXXIX, 96.

[47] E. Hicks to JD, B. Hicks to JD, June 28, 1783, L/HSP; Jacob Hicks indenture, Dec. 20, 1788, William Hicks to JD, Sept. 12, 1771, William Hicks [Jr.] to JD, June 18, 1798, Jan. 21, 1799, L-D/LCP.

[48] There are innumerable receipts for such items in the Dickinson and Logan Papers, HSP.

and recording did not take place until late in 1778. Philemon gradually sold his Delaware holdings, such as the tract near Duck Creek and other acreage adjoining the Kent County plantation, to his brother John. John reinvested some of the proceeds from his own sales in Philadelphia's Northern Liberties.[49]

Most important of all, the Dickinson marriage proved a blessed one. John's affection was returned by an adoring wife who while clinging to him was often the winner in family decisions. He was content with his lot. Dickinson wrote James Wilson on his marriage in 1771 wishing him and Mrs. Wilson "the blest delights of the best state," and happily announced that "on the 10th of this month Mrs. Dickinson presented me with a little girl as hearty as if she had been born in the Highlands of Scotland. I hope in a few months you will know how much more truth there is than you ever thought in the expression In est sua gratia parvis [Small things have their own reward.]"[50] The daughter was named Sarah.

Dickinson was too intellectually involved in the critical political affairs of the colonies to remain a spectator. He had been incensed at the Pennsylvania Assembly's permitting "the vilest acts of despotism . . . and daring outrages against the liberty of themselves [to go] uncensured and unnoticed."[51] His own approach to proper protest lay in the peaceful if forceful path of nonimportation agreements. But the fire of enthusiasm which had been difficult enough to kindle turned to ashes. On hearing that New York had ended its embargo in July 1770, Philadelphia merchants sought an end to their own agreement. But at a meeting on July 14 Philadelphia reaffirmed its support for the cause. Popular clamor forced their acceptance this time, yet the merchants would not be deflected from their demands. In September they temporarily succeeded in abolishing import restrictions.

Dickinson's name at the last minute had been added to the Philadelphia ticket for the Assembly in October 1770. He was in Lancaster returning from his trip to the western counties when he

[49] L/HSP, XXIII, 65, XXXIV, 67–68, XXV, 36.

[50] JD to Wilson, Dec. 28, 1771, Gratz Collection, HSP.

[51] JD to Richard Henry Lee, June 22, 1769, Richard H. Lee, *Memoir of the life of Richard Henry Lee*, 2 vols. (Philadelphia, 1825) 1:77, 2:77.

received word from his cousin Joseph Morris, Jr., that he had lost by only six votes. Morris reported that had Dickinson's name been formally placed on the list, he would undoubtedly have won. Consequently, the next day his friends had added it to the "Burgess ticket," and Dickinson received an almost unanimous vote. Some, Morris reported, asserted they feared he would not serve, but, he added, "if you don't you will disoblige every friend you have and very particularly one who loves you and who got wet to the shins yesterday in your service and who is also Your Very Affect., J. Morris, Jr."[52]

Dickinson hesitated to heed the call to service. His wife, although the daughter of a former Speaker, viewed her husband's politics with mixed emotions, if not timidity. He had been disgusted with the Old Ticket and had written and spoken for the advocates of resistance. He was clearly a supporter and member of the Popular party. But entering the political arena was another matter. Yet progressively he grew more and more irked by the Assembly and its hesitant, if not reactionary, positions in support of what he viewed as fundamental rights. Following the October victory at the polls, Dickinson commented to Arthur Lee with some acidity on the rejection of his opponents, "Our mercenaries have been defeated."[53]

On October 17, 1770, Dickinson took his seat. Galloway, elected from Bucks County, still commanded majority support, though by slimmer margins. Thus, when it wrote the provincial agents in London, the House failed to add instructions relative to "the general Rights and Liberties of America."[54] The session was short; the Assembly adjourned in mid-October until January 7. During the intervening months new propositions were advanced.

Except for a letter asking its agents to act jointly with those of other colonies in seeking a repeal of the Revenue Acts, a measure it could hardly avoid after a mass protest meeting in April of that

[52] Morris to JD, Oct. 3, 1770, Item 183, L-D/LCP.

[53] JD to Lee, Oct. 31, 1770, Richard H. Lee, *Life of Arthur Lee,* 2 vols. (Boston, 1829) 2:302–3.

[54] *Votes,* 7:6589–90.

year, the Assembly had avoided criticism of any parliamentary restrictions. It ignored urgent communications from Massachusetts and Virginia. But on February 4, 1771, a committee which included Dickinson was appointed to bring in a "Draught of a Petition to his Majesty in Council" asking the king to intercede with Parliament in obtaining "a Repeal of the Duty remaining on Tea, etc., imported into the American colonies."[55] Dickinson had gone so far as to think an address to the people of Britain also might have value. Arthur Lee, with whom he regularly corresponded, agreed. He also supported Dickinson's continuing call for nonimportation, writing, "If our Liberties are not worth, in the estimation of the people, the difference between a homespun and a broad cloth coat, between a worsted and silk stocking, how are we to found a hope of any exertion to retrieve our rights."[56]

The petition protesting the tea tax was not an easy document to write; it would have to satisfy both the timid and the bold. The first draft was referred back to the committee for future consideration.[57] His colleagues' cautious and soft attitude disheartened Dickinson. For his own part, he would have inserted stronger words, not weaker, amending it to read:

> Slaves *who have nothing but a miserable Life to lose and whose minds must be infected by their condition* are influenced *only* by their feelings. Freemen *possessed of the blessing that gives a value to life, ever attentive to its preservation, believe they have a right to consider their situation, the dangers that threaten them, and respectfully to express their apprehensions on all proper occasions.* The importance of this their most reasonable of *inestimable privileges,* is demonstrated by the blessings it has procured.

He would have stated that "Innocence was no protection; and our Reason became a Misfortune" when faced with the imposition of taxation while lacking representation. The petition as finally

---

[55] Ibid., 7:6628.

[56] Arthur Lee to JD, January 18, 1771, L-D/LCP.

[57] *Votes*, 8:6638. For the final document see ibid., 8:6658–59.

passed, however, did contain the primary point of protest, "the fear of a precedent in the retention of the tea tax, small as it was."[58]

The threepence duty on tea was so small that most colonists thought it inconsequential. Even the Boston Massacre and colonial incidents elsewhere did not arouse indignation in other provinces. For nearly three years, British-American relations had seemed on the mend. Dickinson found he could not generate much enthusiasm for principle, important though that was. There seemed no use to run against the tide. In 1771 he refused to run for the Assembly.

Any temporary calm that lay upon the colonies soon broke. But another objection on top of the tea tax came in granting a monopoly of all tea exported to the colonies which in turn gave its agents exclusive sale rights. This meant elimination of local merchants.

Some hotheaded protestors in Rhode Island, angered by Britain's customs men who interfered with the smuggling of certain goods into that colony (including much tea), in 1772 set fire to a revenue cutter, the *Gaspee*. Lord Dartmouth threatened to order the culprits to England for trial should they be discovered, declaring the destruction of a "deeper dye" than a simple act of piracy.

Samuel Adams in Massachusetts, where passions were most easily kept alive, organized committees of correspondence, first in New England, then extending to west of the Hudson and to the southern colonies. Thus a network which kept leaders of each province in touch with others was effected and infringements on rights and liberties became quickly known.

Four Rhode Island leaders wrote Dickinson in January that Dartmouth's proposal of a trial in England for the *Gaspee* attackers was "shocking to humanity." They asked Dickinson how they could proceed in stopping such inroads upon their liberties. Richard Henry Lee too sought Dickinson's sentiments in the matter

[58] Notes and Corrections by Dickinson to a manuscript of the 1771 Petition to the King, Item 356, L-D/LCP; Ford, pp. 451–52, the petition as finally adopted.

and urged the adoption of correspondence committees by all the colonies.[59]

In Pennsylvania the Assembly had considered no act of protest after the petition sent to the king in March 1771. It had read and filed letters from other colonies, but it gave no official support to the protesting provinces until May 1773, just before adjournment, when it appointed a committee of correspondence. Josiah Quincy, Jr., considered "the political state of Pennsylvania" more calm than that of other colonies, but the temper of the people of Philadelphia was undergoing a major change. Fear and necessity were to unite merchants, mechanics, and professional men into a growing popular movement.[60]

The Tea Act of 1773 became the rallying cry. Parliament, having granted the ailing East India Company a monopoly, at the same time retained the threepence import duty. Ironically, the Philadelphia merchant Thomas Wharton was advisor to the company. Was the retention of the import duty a trick of the ministry? The colonists had no reason to think otherwise.

A town meeting in Philadelphia on October 16, 1773, brought more than eight thousand people together to protest the duty on tea, the first such meeting in any of the colonies. Importers did not fail to recognize the growing discontent. The merchants were irked because the company had limited its export agents. As a result, Wharton resigned as tea commissioner and the selected importers agreed to refuse tea consignments.[61] Yet a few recalcitrants remained, among them Abel James and Henry Drinker.

Dickinson did not rest content. He sent an anonymous "Extract of a Letter" to Bradford's *Journal* on October 30 and it was printed in the issue of November 3. The brief column was a paragraph-by-paragraph analysis of the parliamentary measure setting forth the

[59] Darius Sessions, Stephen Hopkins, and Moses Brown to JD, January 1773, Item 25, L-D/LCP.

[60] Richard Henry Lee to JD, April 4, 1773, L-D/LCP; Arthur L. Jensen, *The Maritime Commerce of Colonial Philadelphia* (Madison, 1963), p. 197.

[61] *Pennsylvania Gazette*, October 20, 1773; *Pennsylvania Chronicle*, September 20, 1773.

monopolistic features that aided the East India Company and the indirect tax on tea. A second letter, signed "Rusticus," more exciting in its phraseology, was published first as a broadside in Philadelphia and then in New York by the Association of the Sons of Liberty, who in a prefatory note suggested that from the style and other characteristics, it was from the pen of the "celebrated Pennsylvania Farmer."[62] As "Rusticus," Dickinson pointed out that "*five ships* loaded with TEA, [were] on their Way to *America*, and this with a View not only to *enforce* the *Revenue Act*, but to *establish* a *Monopoly* for the East-India Company, who have espoused the Cause of the Ministry; and hope to repair their broken Fortunes by the Ruin of *American* Freedom and Liberty." He urged action against the British effort but called for moderation, noting that "it is not only the cause, but our Manner of conducting it, that will establish Character." Sensible to the feelings of some that the issue was slight, Dickinson suggested that "it is something of Consolation to be overcome by a Lion, but to be devoured by Rats is intolerable." He asked that no man permit the ships to land or the tea to be unloaded or give any other assistance to those who would receive the goods sent them. Dickinson concluded with the half-jocular proposal "that your Watchmen be instructed as they go their Rounds to call out every night, *past Twelve o-Clock, beware of the East-India Company.*"

New York, Charleston, and Boston were now confronted with the issue of the landing of the tea. All were to see to its final refusal; the action of Boston on December 16 was the most lively, with its "Tea Party" and the tea's destruction.

Philadelphia was well prepared and distributed letters to all river pilots addressed to the captain of the approaching *Polly Ayres*, which warned him of the citizens' determination to prevent his cargo from being received. When news of the ship's arrival reached Chester on December 25, a call for a town meeting on the twenty-seventh was given. Impressed with the vociferous attitude of the people, which indeed horrified some of the citizenry themselves, the captain consented to return to England without unloading his cargo. Even the new coach of Thomas Wharton was not

[62] *A Letter from the Country To a Gentleman in Philadelphia* [Philadelphia, 1773], broadside.

delivered.[63] Philadelphia had succeeded in preventing the landing of the tea, and by peaceful means.

Marriage limited John Dickinson's activity a bit, but it did not lessen his deep conviction that serious inroads were being made on colonial rights and liberties. He did not permit private pursuits to override public demands. He had not refrained from warning of the dangers of the duty on tea. Charles Thomson was courting Hannah Harrison, Mary's cousin, and the two men met more frequently and discussed matters of common concern. Mary Dickinson, gentle by nature, did not hide her feelings and her perturbation over her husband's energetic protests. Thomson understandably did not press his friend into active, personal involvement in the meetings which protested the importation of tea. When news of the Boston Port Bill, which closed that city to all sea-going traffic, was received, however, it was time for Dickinson actively to go on stage.

[63] Lincoln, pp. 158–59; Thayer, p. 154.

☆ 5 ☆

Dickinson as
a Radical

By 1773 John Dickinson was recognized as the leading champion of American liberty throughout the colonies.[1] His writings and his every declaration earned him that place. His objectives were clear and specific. That he abhorred violence had proved well known. His distaste and even fear of it he expressed frequently. Yet he did not shrink from active participation: Dickinson was a man engagé but at the same time a man of peace.

A historian and an heir of the best that England stood for constitutionally, Dickinson had now arrived at firm conclusions. Following the English whig tradition, he believed in petition and united action as guarantees of redress. Such acts proved successful in the repeal of the Stamp Act. Nonimportation and nonexportation he regarded as a subsequent step if the first means of protest proved unavailing. At the same time Dickinson encouraged American manufactures—silk, wool cloth, and paper—which would help free the colonies from dependence upon Britain. Dickinson had

---

[1] His position was recognized equally by Charles Thomson and Joseph Reed. The early part of this chapter owes much to the written memoirs of these two men. See "Early Days of the Revolution," Charles Thomson's account of the Boston Port Bill, *PMHB* 2 (1878):411–23, and William B. Reed, *The Life and Correspondence of Joseph Reed* (Philadelphia, 1847), 1:61–68. Thomson's interpretation is the one here most relied upon. Reed's has overtones of his later political outlook; that of Thomson seems freer from any such cast. Also see *New-York Historical Society Collections* XI (1873), 269–73.

been less vocal after 1770 when the Townshend Acts had been partially repealed, but the general mood of America was also less restive. In 1771, looking to the future, Dickinson had written Arthur Lee:

> The more I observe of what passes among us . . . the more I am induced to think we must wait for a cure till the waters are disturbed.
>
> We may be provoked some other way, than by renewing the attempt to tax us; or if no fresh cause of discontent be afforded, a better opportunity may open for obtaining redress. One thing I am convinced of, that we ought never to intermit our applications for relief. We should convince our oppressors that the injury *manet alta mente repositum* [remains set deeply back in my mind].
>
> There is a strong spirit of liberty subsisting among us. . . . We must trust to that spirit for favorable circumstances, and a prudent use of them for success in our designs. As to our British friends, we ought to expect everything from them but—assistance. I confide in Providence that we shall not want it.[2]

The predicted provocation came with the passage of the Boston Port Bill in the spring of 1774. John Dickinson once again assumed the mantle of a leading actor.

The severity of England's response to Boston's destruction of the cargo of tea caused tremors of concern to shake the American seaboard. Philadelphians, although deploring the destructive measures of the Bostonians, nevertheless believed that the closing of the port was an extreme, inflammatory measure. Other parliamentary acts regarding Massachusetts were equally alarming. Committees of correspondence already established in many towns throughout Pennsylvania were quickly aroused by the Philadelphia "radicals," much to the dismay of many of that city's Quaker merchants and conservatives. But, as "A Philadelphian" reflecting the popular temper wrote in the *Pennsylvania Gazette*, since other cities could not expect to escape the fate of Boston, active concern was justified.[3]

[2] JD to Lee, September 21, 1771, *Life of Arthur Lee*, 2:303–4.

[3] *Pennsylvania Gazette*, May 18, 1774.

On May 19 Paul Revere arrived in Philadelphia carrying a letter authorized by a Boston town meeting. It appealed for help and support. Most important was the proposal for a "solemn League and Covenant" to obtain unity of action from all the colonies. But Philadelphians found no unanimity concerning this suggestion. Even the sympathizers hesitated to give active support for such a move. These men included those whigs labeled radical as well as merchants and craftsmen living by their own handiwork. The artisans had little to lose and increasingly demanded political rights. They willingly followed leaders who took both political and intellectual positions on the issue. Their day was soon at hand and their support now sought.

Charles Thomson was the most prominent of these radical leaders. He was a friend of those holding more moderate views, such as John Dickinson, Joseph Reed, a lawyer active in the Presbyterian party and advancing in radical leadership, and Thomas Mifflin, both aristocrat and merchant. These men were sympathetic to Thomson's views; they agreed that there should be some kind of colonial action in support of the Bostonians. Yet most Quakers and perhaps a preponderant number of merchants in the city were truly conservative, insisting that Boston by the precipitous action of its citizens had courted the strong British response.

Dickinson certainly did not condone the destruction of tea in Boston, but he was alert to the increasingly severe restrictions of Britain. Thomson knew the great influence Dickinson wielded. The propitious moment had arrived for him to come to the fore.

A mass meeting was called for Friday evening, May 20, 1774, in the Long Room of the City Tavern on Second Street near Walnut. Thomson, Reed, and Mifflin drove out to Fairhill, where they dined with Dickinson at midday, and the four of them discussed every aspect of that evening's proposed meeting. Their host agreed to attend and to speak, being assured that he might hold to a moderate stance. Such a stand would be likely to appeal to those Quakers and merchants who were resolute in their conservative attitudes. Having settled on the agenda and determined all the views to be expressed, even to radical sentiments, Mifflin and Reed returned to the city, while Thomson sometime later accompanied Dickinson into town. Years later the meeting at Fairhill was to become an important, and contradictory, recollection: Thomson was sympathetic to Dickinson; Joseph Reed, a political enemy and rival of Dickinson, considered him the timid captive of a fearful wife and mother.

The meeting at the City Tavern was large; perhaps two to three hundred persons were present. Reed reported: "The proprietary party had sent its representatives. Many of the leading men among the Friends and the sons of nearly all officers of the government were present, and all awaited with great apparent excitement the opening of the meeting." Reed spoke first as chairman and attempted to humor the heterogeneous assembly. The Boston letter was read, and the chairman in a moderate tone pointed out Pennsylvania's common cause with Massachusetts and asked that the governor be urged to call the Assembly into session so that the province could discuss legal steps that might be taken to seek redress for the sister colony and its chief city. Mifflin followed as speaker, increased the emotional fervor, and urged more immediate action. Thomson next stepped up to the podium. The crowded room was warm and oppressive. Thomson in his speech rose in almost violent crescendo. He fainted, thus adding to the mounting confusion. Revived, he continued to urge aggressive action. Alexander Wilcox and Dr. William Smith of the College of Philadelphia then spoke for the conservatives.

Both sides had presented their extremists. Dickinson, according to plan, then rose to address the meeting. He spoke "with great coolness, calmness, moderation and good sense"[4] and set forth two proposals based on previously stated suggestions: one, that the governor be requested to call a special session of the Assembly, and another, that a committee of correspondence be appointed to send an answer to Boston. Reed noted that Dickinson's position was "a great relief," in marked contrast to the violence of Thomson's demands, and as a consequence Dickinson's recommendations were approved. A committee of nineteen was appointed, including Dickinson. And letter of sympathy was ordered sent to the people of Boston to serve until another, more general meeting of citizens might be called.

---

[4] Stillé, pp. 107–8, quoting Edward Tilghman.

The City Tavern meeting was highly significant. Town meetings of political nature were discountenanced by both the Quakers and many conservative merchants. Though a moderate position had been taken, the action itself favored the radical. The gathering consisted of unelected representatives who lacked a legal base; although it called on the governor to convene the Assembly, the committee it appointed became a public body of sorts empowered to plan a future course of action. The Committee of Nineteen was the first of a series of such committees which were to foster a new, more radical movement, involving new leadership and extending opportunities to mechanics and others not hitherto represented in Pennsylvania's protest movements.[5]

The letter to Boston did not give the solace and comfort that the beleaguered port had expected from the City of Brotherly Love. It did, however, clearly reflect the divided opinions of Philadelphia citizens, a condition that would inhibit revolutionary actions during the next two years. While urging Boston to act with "Firmness, Prudence and Moderation," the letter failed to subscribe to any proposal for a continental nonimportation agreement. Sympathetic to Boston's suffering, which Philadelphia recognized as a "common cause," the letter promised only to seek suggestions from other colonies on how they might together render further aid. Mifflin privately explained to Sam Adams that it had been necessary to take an "oblique view" since any stronger position would disunite and "ruin the cause of America" (at least in Philadelphia).[6]

Dickinson was more at home writing in his library or sitting in earnest conference with his friends than on a public platform. Since newspaper columns were significant channels of influence, he addressed four anonymous letters to the "Inhabitants of the British Colonies" that appeared weekly in the *Philadelphia Jour-*

[5] *Pennsylvania Gazette*, May 25, June 8, 1774; Richard Alan Ryerson, *The Revolution Is Now Begun: The Radical Committees of Philadelphia, 1765–1776* (Philadelphia, 1978).

[6] July 30, 1774, Samuel Adams Papers, New York Public Library (hereafter cited as NYPL).

nal beginning May 25.[7] In his second letter, Dickinson wrote that he sought to prove "that a plan has been deliberately framed, as pertinaciously adhered to, unchanged even by frequent changes of Ministers, unchecked by any intervening gleam of humanity, to sacrifice to a passion for arbitrary dominion the universal property, liberty, safety, honor, happiness and prosperity of us unoffending, yet devoted Americans.—And that every man of us is deeply interested in the fate of our brethren of Boston."[8] His final letter suggested that Parliament was in the act of changing the chartered constitution of the province of Massachusetts Bay into a military government while yet another proposed act empowered the administration to send for and to try persons in England for actions committed in the colony. Both required protest. Observing that resolutions of some town meetings in Massachusetts might better have been suppressed, he did not fault the towns otherwise. Dickinson urged unity, asserting that "the man who fears difficulties arising in the defense of freedom is unworthy of freedom." In his letter of June 15 he called for a general congress of representatives of all colonies.

To many Philadelphians a colonial assembly was considered more "moderate and prudent" than an immediate nonimportation agreement.[9] Approval for such a call gained almost unanimous support. After all, the Stamp Act Congress in 1765 had proved successful. Meanwhile, the Committee of Nineteen was active. A petition to Governor Penn asking him to convene the Assembly was circulated and signed by nearly nine hundred inhabitants. The leaders also continued to move in extralegal directions, yet ever sensitive to the critical hesitations of merchants and leading Friends. The committee, in charge of all steps furthering support of Boston, met May 30 together with some forty representatives of different Philadelphia organizations.[10] For ten to twelve hours the men wrangled over resolves which had previously been written

[7] Ford, reprinted in 1:467–501.

[8] Ibid., 1:474–75.

[9] Thomas Mifflin to Sam Adams, May 26, 1774, Samuel Adams Papers, NYPL.

[10] Thomas Wharton to his brother, July 5, 1774, *PMHB* 33 (1909):436.

and submitted by Dickinson. Thomas Wharton, who had been the conservative agent of the East India Company, disapproved of many of them and was glad that certain acrimonious parts "had been deleted." Little decisive action resulted. It was agreed that June 1 should be a day of mourning, although even this proposal was opposed by representatives of the Society of Friends and a few Anglicans. When the bells of Christ Church pealed their muffled sound two days later, Philadelphia's mood was described as one of "sorrow, mixed with indignation." The "pause" of that day hastened the pace of the resistance movement.[11]

On June 8 the committee's petition was formally presented to the governor. Although he was not expected to comply with the request to convene a special session of the Assembly, it was a necessary first step in order to gain support from hesitant dissenters. The committee then turned to calls both for a provincial convention in Pennsylvania and a continental congress for united colonial action. Few objections were raised. The manner of choosing delegates was less certain. The reaction of Joseph Galloway, the Speaker, was a matter of some concern. The committee discussed the question from every angle. Joseph Reed hoped the Assembly would officially support whig actions and argued that any such convention should await that body's action.

Dickinson thought otherwise. He favored a special convention of delegates equitably representing all sections of Pennsylvania. Such a convention would assure whig sentiment, particularly as the frontier areas would have a determining voice.[12] The result would also be quicker action. The leaders met again in Philosophical Hall on June 10 and 11 to thrash out the question. Assembly action remained uncertain. A provincial convention was called for, and if the Assembly did not act by the time it was convened, the committee agreed to authorize the convention's appointing delegates to a general congress. Little did Dickinson realize that his proposed convention would become "the dominant

[11] William Duane, ed., *Extracts from the Diary of Christopher Marshall, 1774–1781* (Albany, N. Y., 1877). Also see Ryerson, 43–44.

[12] Charles Thomson, Memorandum Book, Gratz Collection, HSP.

strategy of revolutionary mobilization."[13] Those matters settled, the committee considered what should be accomplished at a general meeting.

Support for both convention and congress increased in many areas. The mechanics in Philadelphia and the surrounding areas were in correspondence with the mechanics of New York. They had appointed two of their number to cooperate with and encourage merchant action and otherwise to work toward convincing "the world [that] Americans were born and are determined to live free."[14]

On June 18 a meeting of an estimated eight thousand freeholders and freemen of the Philadelphia area was held in the yard of the State House. Only those who had the right to vote were in attendance. Wharton had predicted that it would be the greatest number "ever known on any occasion" to meet together.[15] John Dickinson and Thomas Willing, a prominent merchant, jointly presided. Resolutions were passed denouncing the Boston Port Bill as unconstitutional and again calling for a continental congress. It was an impressive assemblage, indeed an almost overwhelming one. An enlarged Committee of Forty-three was appointed to continue correspondence with other colonies as well as with other parts of Pennsylvania, to "unite in promoting and endeavoring to attain the great and valuable ends."[16] Many of the moderates on the old committee who had forestalled action were replaced by so-called radicals.

Dickinson was made chairman of the new committee. In accepting this post, he did not equivocate. The extralegal aspects of committee action by which members were to consult and to speak for the colony of Pennsylvania were shunted aside as unimportant.

---

[13] Ibid., pp. 278–79; see also Ryerson, p. 47.

[14] *Pennsylvania Gazette*, June 15, 1774.

[15] To a friend, June 10, 1774, *PMHB* 33 (1909):432.

[16] Quoted in Lincoln, p. 173. See also, Charles S. Olten, *Artisans for Independence: Philadelphia Mechanics and the Revolution* (Syracuse, N. Y., 1975), pp. 62–63.

The question was liberty, and that was a larger consideration than simple legalities.

The committee met June 27 in Carpenters' Hall and drew up resolutions to be sent to each county requesting each to urge the Speaker to call the Assembly into session as soon as possible. The counties were also asked to appoint representatives to meet in Philadelphia at the same time as the Assembly and to advise on the best way to appoint deputies to a general congress.[17] Thus in answer to the appeal of the Philadelphia committee, on July 15 Pennsylvania county representatives joined those of Philadelphia in a provincial convention. The actions of the town meetings and the Philadelphia committee had no legal justification. In both instances these departures from statutory procedures and the charter were radical. The committee was to assure the dominance of liberal whigs of Philadelphia and the back counties in future action.

Speaker Galloway saw the radicalism of these steps and as leader of the conservative opposition proposed to summon the Assembly on his own. But Governor Penn was also fully aware of the committee plans. On June 28, citing Indian uprisings instead, he issued writs asking the Assembly to meet in Philadelphia on July 18.[18] The call in no way dampened plans for the proposed provincial convention. Preparations had been carefully laid for the convention to convene on Friday, July 15. Advisory suggestions and encouragement in the appointment of deputies to a general congress were high on the agenda. To underscore the unity such a situation demanded, the leaders reported that "all the colonies from South Carolina to New Hampshire seem animated with one spirit in the common cause."

Dickinson's actions somewhat disguised his fundamental thought concerning eventual conciliation with Britain, which at this date he took for granted. In May, writing Charles Morrison, Dickinson begged his correspondent to make sure Bostonians would avoid "Blood or tumults." "Nothing can ruin us but our violence," he declared. "Reason teaches this." Dickinson wrote Josiah Quincy,

[17] *Pennsylvania Gazette,* July 6, 1774.

[18] *Votes,* 8:7085.

Jr., of Pennsylvania's wide-ranging sympathy for Massachusetts's distress yet cautioned, "Nothing can possibly throw us into a pernicious confusion but one colony's breaking the line of opposition by advancing too hastily before the rest."[19] Dickinson believed control of Pennsylvania and Philadelphia protests would be most easily achieved if the provincial convention elected deputies to the proposed congress. Dr. William Smith and Attorney General Allen had objected to this proposition, saying it was the responsibility of the Assembly. This opinion, Charles Thomson believed, had little support in the public meetings held to that date.[20]

As time drew nearer for Pennsylvania's convention, "the Mechanics" of Philadelphia sent a petition to Dickinson imploring him to take a stern position, citing attempts to intimidate his committee members in an effort to baffle strong actions. The petitioners expressed fear that the appointment of men "obnoxious to the people" to the coming congress would certainly produce a riot and perhaps endanger their safety. "Our intelligence is good," they said. "You we revere and you we depend upon. Your love of the cause will readily pardon our Freedom and Fears."[21]

Some seventy-five provincial delegates gathered in Carpenters' Hall on July 15 at 4 P.M. Their mission was clear: to set forth principles for guidance, a general plan of conduct to be followed by the forthcoming continental congress, and future action to counter repressive parliamentary acts. Thomas Willing was chairman of the convention and Charles Thomson secretary. John Dickinson, chairman of the Philadelphia committee, presented the major address. He had spent the previous two weeks preparing a closely reasoned argument on Great Britain's powers and the constitutional rights of the colonies and their inhabitants as Englishmen. Following his address, proposals for sending delegates to a continental congress were made. The proceedings of the Provincial Convention, including the resolutions, the instructions, and the arguments explaining the purposeful work of that body, were col-

---

[19] JD to Morrison, May [1774], NYPL; JD to Quincy, June 20, 1774, MaHS.

[20] Thomson, Memorandum Book, Gratz Collection, HSP.

[21] Address of the Mechanics to John Dickinson, June 27, 1774, with postscript of July 4, Item 156, L-D/LCP.

lected by Dickinson and printed within a fortnight.[22] In an *Essay on the Constitutional Power of Great Britain*, setting aside any contrary legal precedents, Dickinson asserted that the end of government (i.e., the constitution) was "the happiness of the people" and that anything that mitigated against their welfare was illegal. The unanimity of the convention was limited only in respect to nonimportation and nonexportation agreements, but even these passed by a "great majority." The opposition here was largely over a desire to have other means of protest tried first. In sum the convention acted with unanimous voice.

The convention also suggested means that would be the basis for the resumption of peaceful relations between the mother country and the colonies. It resolved that there was an absolute necessity for a congress of deputies to assemble immediately to consult and to determine a plan of action for the relief of our "suffering Brethren [and] obtaining redress of our grievances . . . firmly establishing our rights and restoring harmony between Great Britain and her colonies on a constitutional foundation."[23] Although resistance to any parliamentary right of taxation was as clearly expressed as was insistence on constitutional justice, respect for the crown was carefully indicated.

The convention appreciated Dickinson's preparatory work that had lightened the burden of delegates, unanimously agreeing "that the thanks of this committee be given from the chair to John Dickinson, Esq. for the great assistance they have derived from the laudable application of his eminent abilities to the service of his country." Chairman Willing "in a very obliging manner" delivered this testimony to Dickinson, who was absent at a family funeral the day the motion was passed. In response, Dickinson declared, "I will try, during the remainder of my life, to remember my duty to our common country, and if it be possible, to render

[22] *An essay on the constitutional power of Great Britain over the colonies in America; with the resolves of the Committee for the province of Pennsylvania, and their instructions to their representatives in Assembly* (Philadelphia, 1774). This was reprinted in London.

[23] *Votes*, 8:7093; see also *Pennsylvania Journal*, July 23, 1774, and *Pennsylvania Gazette*, July 27, 1774.

myself worthy of the honor for which I now stand so deeply indebted."

The earlier decision to have the Provincial Convention appoint delegates to a continental congress was abandoned after the Assembly itself on July 22 approved the idea. In agreeing to let the Assembly appoint the delegates, the convention took a calculated risk in an effort to win larger support, particularly among Philadelphia's conservatives. The Provincial Convention and its leaders had their own strong opinions as to the proper choice of delegates.[24] Their choices lay with Dickinson, James Wilson of Cumberland County, Thomas Willing, and perhaps Thomson and Reed, the last two with Dickinson making up a committee of three to present the completed resolves to the legislature. The calculated risk turned out unhappily. Galloway determined that delegates should be chosen from the Assembly itself, a proper source if the congress was to have any legality. Dickinson and Thomson were thus cleverly eliminated. Those chosen by the Speaker, with the exception of Thomas Mifflin, had not been notably active whigs.[25] Galloway himself joined Mifflin, Samuel Rhoads, Charles Humphreys, John Morton, George Ross, and Edward Biddle as delegates and later claimed authorship of the instructions to the appointed committee from the Assembly.[26]

On September 1 delegates from the various colonies began arriving in Philadelphia for the First Continental Congress. On Monday morning, the fifth, at ten o'clock, the representatives assembled at the City Tavern. A meeting hall had not been chosen. Joseph Galloway offered the State House for the purpose. However, Carpenters' Hall had also been proffered, and the gentlemen walked the few blocks west on Chestnut Street to look the hall over.[27] The first floor provided a commodious assembly room; the

[24] Cf. Charles Thomson, "Early Days of the Revolution," p. 418 n. 3.

[25] Jacobson, p. 80.

[26] *Votes*, 7098–99.

[27] Lyman H. Butterfield, ed., *Diary and Autobiography of John Adams* (Cambridge, Mass., 1961), 2:122.

second housed the Library Company of Philadelphia. The decision to meet in the hall removed the Congress from any obligation to the Pennsylvania Assembly and Galloway's influence. Sessions were immediately opened, and the delegates settled down at once to decide upon rules of conduct, matters for debate, and committee structure.

For a week Philadelphia greeted the incoming delegates, who found rooms in various taverns and boarding houses of the city. John Dickinson's name was the only one universally known to the visitors. He was forever to be the Farmer. The delegates also were well aware of his continuous and determined resistance to British restrictions. Some knew him through correspondence.

In August, Dickinson's propensity toward ill-health again came to the fore. His maladies were now complicated by gout. Yet he planned and plotted, knowing full well that although ignored by Galloway in the selection of delegates, he would be consulted by many of them. Moreover, he looked forward to seeing old friends first met at the Stamp Act Congress or known even earlier when he was a student in London.

On the last day of August, in his impressive coach drawn by four handsome horses, Dickinson drove into town to call on the assembling representatives. At the lodgings of Governor Samuel Ward of Rhode Island he met, among others, John Adams. That evening the Massachusetts delegate wrote his impression of Dickinson: "He is a shadow-tall, but slender as a reed—pale as ashes. One would think at first sight that he could not live a month. Yet upon a more attentive inspection, he looks as if the springs of life were strong enough to last many years."[28] On September 12, Adams, with other delegates including Robert Treat Paine, went out to dine at Fairhill with the Dickinsons and other guests. Paine was impressed:

> Mr. Dickinson has a fine seat, a beautiful prospect of the City, the river and the country—fine gardens, and a very grand library. The most of his books were collected by Mr. Norris, once Speaker of the House here, father of Mrs. Dickinson. Mr. Dickinson is a very modest man, and very in-

[28] Ibid., 2:117.

genious, as well as agreeable. He has an excellent heart, and the cause of his country lies near it. He is full and clear for allowing to Parliament, the regulation of trade upon principles of necessity and the mutual interest of both countries.[29]

In Congress there was no unanimity of approach toward a solution. There existed only a consensus on the need to stand firm. New Englanders, notably led by both John and Sam Adams, were particularly rigid in their positions. Representatives of the colony which had received the harsh penalties imposed by Britain, they favored radical moves, stern measures, and the suspension of all trade, import and export, with Great Britain. The southerners, though favoring nonimportation, feared they could not economically endure such a provision. Instead, they limited their arguments to the support of a strong statement of grievances and a petition for redress. New York and Pennsylvania delegates were even more cautious, indeed conservative in their positions, as reflected in a petition presented by New Yorker James Duane and one by Joseph Galloway, who on September 28 proposed a conciliatory plan for a union between the colonies and Britain. The latter temporarily triumphed over the general feeling of suspicion toward him and got his proposal laid on the table for later consideration. (Subsequently even the introduction of the plan was expunged from the minutes of the Congress.)

Charles Thomson and Dickinson both influenced the Pennsylvania contingent and, even more, the Congress without having seats in that body. Thomson had recently married Hannah Harrison. A few days later, coming into town to pay a courtesy call on his wife's Aunt Norris, he was hailed by a delegate who told him he had been chosen secretary. This action thus placed him at the center of the Congress. By the end of the week, on Saturday, September 10, Thomson assumed that position.

The radicals in Philadelphia began to exert their influence. Galloway was threatened, and a halter and coffin were placed on his doorstep. Then on October 1 the regular fall election for the Pennsylvania Assembly was held. The results more clearly indicated the people's will. John Dickinson was almost unanimously

[29] Robert Treat Paine, Diary, entry for September 12, 1774, MaHS.

elected to the Assembly from the county of Philadelphia and Charles Thomson by the city. Thomas Mifflin was reelected. John Adams reflected that "the Change in the elections for this City and County is no small Event. Mr. Dickinson and Mr. Thomson, now joined to Mr. Mifflin, will make a great weight in favour of the American Cause."[30]

Dickinson, with his rich knowledge of constitutional history and deep respect for the unity embodied in the adoption of the Stamp Act Congress resolves, contemplated success through similar joint action. His general plan for the Congress entailed the enumerations of colonial grievances and a petition to the king asking for redress. On Tuesday, September 6, the first business of the Congress after receiving credentials of the delegates had been the appointment of a committee "to State the rights of the Colonies in general, the several instances in which these rights are violated or infringed, and the means . . . for obtaining a restoration of them."[31] Then on Friday, September 15, Paul Revere arrived with the Suffolk Resolves for the Massachusetts delegates. They were read to the Congress the next day. The assembled delegates moved unanimously to adopt a resolution approving the "wisdom and fortitude of the resolves," recommending "perseverence in the same firm and temperate conduct as expressed in the resolutions." They further resolved that all the colonies should continue their contributions in "alleviating the distresses of our brethren at Boston."

Meanwhile, delegates encountered each other frequently, both informally and at dinner. John and Sam Adams dined with the Charles Thomsons later in September. The Dickinsons were the only other guests. Delegates were honor-bound not to divulge congressional discussion, but there never was avoidance of common interest. "A most delightful afternoon we had," John Adams wrote of that occasion. "Sweet Communion indeed we had—Mr. Dickinson gave us his thoughts and his correspondence very freely."[32]

---

[30] Adams, *Diary*, 2:147.

[31] Worthington, C. Ford, ed., *Journals of the Continental Congress* (Washington, D. C., 1904–6), 1:26 (hereafter cited as *JCC*).

[32] Adams, *Diary*, 2:137.

Sam Adams was equally enthusiastic, calling the Farmer "a True Bostonian."

On September 8 and 9 the designated committee had already met to consider a statement regarding the rights of the colonies. The committee seemed unable to agree on a statement involving such rights. Plans for "non-importation, non-consumption and non-exportation" were also discussed. Finally, on October 1 a committee was appointed to prepare an address to the king. The delegates continued their discussions about means to be employed for a restoration of rights. Paul Revere once again rode into the town, this time carrying an urgent letter from Boston asking Congress for recommendations. Their appeal to the governor of Massachusetts had been ignored; more fortifications had been built; and the General Court had been prevented from meeting.

Specific actions affecting trade were not resolved, and discussion lingered on into mid-October. Nor had the Congress yet settled on resolutions concerning rights and grievances. Major John Sullivan of New Hampshire had been chairman of the subcommittee, and that committee, in conjunction with another larger one, haggled over the document for nearly three weeks.[33] Any reference to a "law of nature" was quickly eliminated. As a declaration of rights it would follow English precedent.

John Dickinson's pen could not be stayed. It was a certainty that he would be added to the state's delegation when the Pennsylvania Assembly met on October 15, and he was. But even before appointment, he had apparently written a draft of colonial rights and grievances which he thought applicable. Thomas Mifflin, a close friend and member of the committee, among others, had kept him abreast of their problems. The suggestive manuscript written by Dickinson was passed to John Adams, who in turn passed it along to Sullivan. Modified by the committee, the Dickinson manuscript was retained by Adams in final form.[34] A year and a half later,

---

[33] See *JCC*, 1:63 nn.

[34] The so-called Sullivan Draught (Adams Papers, MaHS) "in a script somewhat resembling that of Major Sullivan," is actually in the hand of Dickinson. See Paul H. Smith, ed., *Letters of Delegates to Congress, 1774–1789* (Washington, D. C., 1976), 1:193–4.

when the Declaration of Independence was written, Jefferson's list of grievances echoed those of Dickinson as adopted by the First Congress.

John Jay, Richard Henry Lee, and William Livingston were appointed to draft a memorial to the people of British America and an address to the people of Great Britain. Lee was to prepare the memorial, Jay the proposed address. The next week, after discussions of the drafts, the address was recommitted and the memorial laid on the table for future consideration.[35] The address to the people of Great Britain was finally approved. The memorial, however, proved troublesome. Though Lee has been credited with drafting it, Dickinson not only transcribed the document but carefully edited it. When finally printed in the *Journal of Congress* it contained revisions of the first draft, notably Dickinson's additions to it and other emendations.[36]

The same day that the Address to the People of Great Britain and the Memorial to the Inhabitants of the British Colonies were ordered printed, Congress ordered that an address to the people of Quebec, seeking their support, be prepared. Thomas Cushing, Lee, and Dickinson were appointed as a committee. That same day, the address to the king, which had been proposed much earlier, was read, debated, and recommitted. Dickinson was now added as a member to the committee. This was Friday. Both committees brought in reports on the following Monday. The address to the people of Quebec, after some "nibbling and quibbling," was recommitted. The hesitations and tedious criticisms of the Congress infuriated John Adams. Finally it won congressional approval. The address to the king was also debated paragraph by paragraph until it earned acceptance. This Address to the King, which had been revised by Dickinson, was more temperate than Lee's rejected draft, but it was nonetheless firm and clear in pur-

[35] JCC, 1:75.

[36] The R. R. Logan Papers in the Historical Society of Pennsylvania contain a much-worked-over manuscript of the memorial in Dickinson's hand. It is possible that, approved in substance, this Dickinson manuscript represents his preparation of it for final consideration and publication.

pose, setting forth all claims to constitutional liberty yet couched in respectful tone.[37] John Adams now watered down his assessment of Dickinson to "very moderate, delicate and timid." New Englanders who were directly under British siege and increasing pressures found expressions in the petition that they thought too solicitous. But balance was sought and evident in that final address:

> Yielding to no British subjects, in affectionate attachment to your majesty's person, family and government; we too dearly prize the privilege of expressing that attachment by those proofs, that are honorable to the prince who receives them, and to the people who give them, ever to resign it to any body of men on earth. . . . We ask but for peace, liberty and safety. We wish not a diminution of the perogative, nor do we solicit the grant of any new right in our favor. Your royal authority over us, and our connection with Great Britain, we shall always carefully and zealously endeavor to support and maintain.

Dickinson, as he put it, had attempted to bring the address into harmony with the "conciliatory disposition of Congress." The work of the Congress had been accomplished. Shortly before adjourning on October 26, the colonial delegates resolved to meet on the following May 10 if the grievances were not resolved. Adams, like the other delegates, left "the happy, peaceful, the elegant, the hospitable, and polite city of Philadelphia" expecting it unlikely he "would ever see this part of the world again." Thomson and Dickinson were less sanguine. The secretary wrote to Franklin: "Even yet the wound may be healed and peace and love restored. But we are on the very edge of the precipice."[38] Dickinson, pleased that the Congress had acted decisively, felt that a civil war was inevitable unless there was a quick change of British measures.[39] He saw a "determined and unanimous resolution animating the con-

[37] See Edwin Wolf, 2nd, "The Authorship of the 1774 Address to the King Restudied," *William and Mary Quarterly*, 3d ser. 22 (1965):189–224.

[38] Adams, *Diary*, 2:157; Thompson to Franklin, November 1, 1774, *JCC*, 1:122–23.

[39] JD to Josiah Quincy, Jr., October 28, 1774, MaHS.

tinent . . . in the great struggle for the Blessings of Liberty that alone can render Life worth holding."[40]

Obtaining unanimity in the Congress had been difficult. Differences were compromised. Dickinson knew the extremes on both sides. The wish of some New Englanders "to shake off all dependence or connection with Great Britain" was generally considered "wild and absurd." But Dickinson knew that realization of that desire would be more likely if the British ministry did not read the temper of the people correctly.[41]

Dickinson's committee appointments in the October session of the Pennsylvania Assembly had been limited by the Speaker. Thomson was similarly given light responsibilities. Both were preoccupied with their work in the Congress. Indeed, the Assembly itself had become diminished in importance; Galloway was dethroned as leader; and Edward Biddle, who had been a delegate to the Congress, was elected Speaker in Galloway's stead.

During the brief hiatus between meetings in late 1774, Dickinson continued to improve Fairhill, that "convenient, decent, elegant Philosophical Rural Retreat" as Robert Treat Paine found it, enlarging the greenhouse and adding new hotbeds. The house being constructed on Chestnut Street had encountered many delays. After more than three years, it was still uninhabitable. Now in addition to these projects Dickinson took a personal hand in the remodeling of Somerville, where Charles Thomson and his bride were to live.

The Assembly, which had adjourned until December, obtained a quorum on the eighth. The governor reported he had no business to lay before them but certain members did. Five of the six delegates presented the *Resolutions and Proceedings of the Continental Congress*, together with a written report requesting its consideration by the House.[42] Galloway was in New York and had not signed the request. Dickinson, taking advantage of Galloway's absence, at once sought to gain Pennsylvania's approval of the im-

---

[40] JD to Arthur Lee, October 27, 1774, Edmund C. Burnett, ed., *Letters of Members of the Continental Congress* (Washingfton, D. C., 1921–36), 1:83.

[41] Dr. John Jones to JD, October 15, 1774, Item 25, L-D/LCP.

[42] *Votes*, 8:7148–58.

portant and significant Continental Association and all the actions of the Congress. After two days of debate, the Assembly recommended that all Pennsylvanians pay "strict attention to and inviolable attention to those matters printed in the Journal of the Congress." This was unanimously approved. Dickinson had got his way; as one commentator wrote, his "politicks turned the scale, and caused the vote to pass as it did."[43]

The unanimous action of the Assembly, however, did not end dissension. Many Philadelphians were as determined in their opposition to protests as the Massachusetts delegates had been radical in their demands for action. Public criticism mounted, spurred by Quaker meetings. Leaders of the Society urged their members to submit to all official English demands and to forbear under penalty of excommunication attending county committees. Daily meetings of members of the Friends continued. On January 24 a *Testimony* was published setting forth Quaker views. Christopher Marshall, himself a Quaker, thought it contained "gross abuse" against those who opposed British laws or other restrictions.[44]

The *Testimony* appeared the day after a Conference of Provincial County Committeemen, or Second Provincial Convention, met in the State House January 23, 1775. Many leaders had opposed calling the convention, believing that it might antagonize some moderates and add to polarization. Dickinson believed the time called for "great delicacy" and that nothing should be done to risk upsetting the successful proceedings to date. But the new Committee of Sixty-Six of Philadelphia city and county, established in December 1774, insisted that the conference be held. Joseph Reed had accepted the chairmanship only because he did not want to show any break in the ranks of the party. And Dickinson's name led the list of delegates. He did not appear, however, until January 27, the day before adjournment, and then in considerable fury, to contradict what were called "notorious lies" in *Rivington's New York Gazette*. This article dealt with supposed positions taken by the Pennsylvania Assembly and its leaders. The

[43] Thomas Wharton to Samuel Wharton, January 31, 1775, "Extracts from the Letter Book of Thomas Wharton," *PMHB* 34 (1910):43.

[44] Marshall, *Diary*, p. 15.

Gazette's correspondent reported that Philadelphia whigs were abandoning the cause daily and that "the Pennsylvania Farmer, a gentleman of great discernment and possessed of a very large estate, has deserted them. He has declared he will not meet them any more, and he does not declare alone." This charge Dickinson strongly refuted by his presence and by his address.[45]

The day after the convention's adjournment Dickinson wrote Samuel Ward of the great necessity "*at present* to keep up the appearances of an unbroken harmony," fearing that otherwise Britain might be encouraged toward further hostilities.[46] Only Bucks County had failed to send delegates to the meeting, and that perhaps was the result of Galloway's influence. Outwardly at least the resolutions of the convention showed a united front. Actions there lay in the encouragement of home manufactures, a determination to resist any force if the address to the King was disregarded, and a declaration pledging "at every hazard to defend the rights and liberties of America." The conference also agreed that if hostile action was taken against the City and Liberties of Philadelphia, all Pennsylvania counties would join in their relief. In an unexpected move it recommended that future importation of slaves to the province be prohibited.[47] A suggestion to organize and arm military associations for defense was turned down because such action might be considered armed rebellion.[48]

The convention once again had acted as an extralegal body. It put its own seal of agreement on the resolutions of the Congress, as the Assembly had already done. The Philadelphia committees, and particularly the one now numbering sixty-six, exercised significant functions.[49] In short the colony had organized a revolutionary governing body, although any such intention would have been denied.

[45] Frank Moore, *Diary of the American Revolution* (New York, 1859), 1:13, quoting *Rivington's Gazette*, no. 91. See also Ryerson, pp. 100–102.

[46] JD to Ward, January 29, 1775, Gratz Collection, HSP.

[47] *Pennsylvania Gazette*, February 1, 1775.

[48] *Pennyslvania Packet*, January 30, 1775.

[49] Lincoln, p. 191.

At the winter session of the Assembly, Dickinson had been ordered to prepare a draft of instructions for the delegates appointed to the next session of the Continental Congress. When the Assembly reconvened in February 1775, Governor Penn sent a message coolly suggesting that separate petitions by the several assemblies of the colonies were the only proper and constitutional modes to obtain redress from Britain. He urged the Assembly to adopt such a procedure. His message, however, was ignored. A committee was appointed to draft a reply and Dickinson made chairman, with Mifflin and Galloway as the other members. When the proposed answer was brought in, a motion was made to recommit. Debate ensued, and after considerable argument the motion was turned down. The whigs triumphed. United action, which Dickinson always considered paramount, was maintained. It was generally believed that the governor's message had been Galloway's inspiration. The defeat now marked his final eclipse. Although Galloway was appointed delegate to the Second Continental Congress, that action seems a studied attempt to reflect varied opinion. At his request, he was excused from serving. The Assembly adjourned March 18. The events that transpired before it reconvened on May 1 changed the course of history.

Galloway in January had published a pamphlet entitled *A Candid Examination of the Mutual Claims of Great Britain*, in which he suggested that the whigs were on "the high road of sedition and rebellion." It was, in fact, a matter that plagued his old friend Benjamin Franklin.[50] Dickinson answered in an essay entitled *To the Author of the Pamphlet. . . .*[51] Defending the Congress, he reiterated his belief that Parliament's authority in relation to trade and other matters was limited. Legislative power, he asserted, belonged to the colonies within defined areas, and only the king had authority over them. Galloway, his power dissipated, could only resort to another reply in April. His intemperate diatribes revealed a recognition that the tides of his influence had run out.

Dickinson was determined on the need for moderation. The di-

---

[50] *A Candid Examination . . .* (New York, 1775); also see Newcombe, pp. 272–74.

[51] *Pennsylvania Journal*, March 8, 1775.

vision of public opinion in Philadelphia was growing more acute. The mechanics opposed the Quaker merchants; the supporters of the Continental Association were matched by those who viewed nonimportation and nonexportation as a mark of belligerancy; and the Society of Friends increased its efforts to thwart whig measures. Presbyterians, advocating radical protest, were also politically active. Dickinson's own hope—indeed expectation—was that the king would directly involve himself and bridge the chasm between Parliament's unconstitutional measures and the colonial claims.

In December 1774, writing Thomas Cushing about the Assembly's approval of the *Resolves and Proceedings of the Congress,* Dickinson recorded the factors that ruled his actions then and for the future.

> Procrastination is Preservation. States acting on the defensive should study for delays. It is a melancholy employment to peruse those various instances recorded in history in which the best causes have been ruin'd by an excess of virtuous zeal, too hastily to promote them. I ever thought, and think still, that a just reverence for the lives of our countrymen should determine us at all events, to wait for a turn of European affairs, and of British statements [sentiments?]. Either of these may save us without an effusion of blood. If at last, the choice must be the sword, or submission, America cannot hesitate.[52]

Dickinson's moderation was founded upon his observations and knowledge of the deep political discord that existed in Philadelphia, both the city and the county. With the now aggressive rise of laboring groups allied with new leadership from the merchant and professional class there was a danger of civil strife. Dickinson found no reason to change the statement he had so eloquently written in *The Farmer's Letters*: "The Cause of Liberty is a cause of too much dignity to be sullied by turbulence and tumult." But he did not flinch from recognizing the possibility, even probability, of an increasing use of British force.

The whole climate of opinion changed on Monday evening, April 24, 1775, when news arrived of the encounter at Lexington.

[52] JD to Cushing, December 11, 1774, P.R.O., CO5/118–80006.

The next day eight thousand people gathered in the yard of the State House. In unison they approved a resolution to associate and "to defend with arms their property, liberty and lives." Volunteer companies were organized. Even many Quakers now had second thoughts. James Pemberton went so far as to approve raising money for the beleaguered Bostonians, while others, setting aside a doctrine of nonbelligerency, joined military companies. One company formed was known as the Quaker Blues, rivals of John Cadwalader's "Greens." Reports that New York's port had been closed and that Philadelphia would next feel British wrath caused consternation and panic.[53]

On May 1 the Pennsylvania Assembly met again. The atmosphere was charged in a way it had not been before Lexington and Concord. Governor Penn on May 2 sent the February 20 *Resolution* of the House of Commons and prayed the members of the Assembly to consider it. The *Resolution* was tempting, offering exemption from all taxes save those on trade to all colonies whose legislatures would agree to contribute proportionate shares toward their own defense and civil government.

The members had already read the Parliamentary resolutions, just as they had read the published *Address of the Lords and Commons* in which Massachusetts Bay had been declared in a state of rebellion and all those who signed protests declared guilty of high treason. The divisive intent of the proposal was clear. Dickinson was appointed chairman of an Assembly committee to bring in an answer. The next afternoon the committee reported its answer. This British plan, "offered by the Parent to her Children," it refused, stating that "for a single Colony to adopt a Measure, so extensive in Consequence, without the Advice and Consent of those Colonies engaged with us by solemn Ties in the same Common Cause," would be "a dishonourable Desertion."[54]

A petition from certain inhabitants of the City and Liberties of Philadelphia was then introduced, setting forth a need for some £50,000 to put the province into "a State of Defense." The question was debated at length. Finally, a standing committee was ap-

[53] Thayer, p. 166.

[54] *Votes*, 8:7224–25.

pointed, including Dickinson, to provide necessary military stores, although the sum was not to exceed £5,000.[55]

The Second Continental Congress was to convene May 10. Benjamin Franklin, back from England after an absence of a half-dozen years, and James Wilson of Carlisle were appointed to join other Pennsylvania delegates. Joseph Galloway, who had repeatedly asked to be excused from serving, was now relieved of that responsibility.

[55] Ibid., 8:7228–29, 7234.

☆ 6 ☆

Dickinson as
a Moderate

AT THE CONCLUSION OF the First Continental Congress, Dickinson observed to Josiah Quincy, Jr.: "The most peaceable
provinces are now animated; and a civil war is unavoidable, unless
there be a quick change of British measures."[1] His correspondence
was enormous with friends in other colonies and in England. He
continued optimistic, but some of his friends were less sanguine.
Samuel Chase of Annapolis, for one, thought the *Resolves* were of
no consequence; if the colonies agreed to resist, military force was
a necessity. In his opinion that step should have been taken to
begin with.[2]

But Dickinson was not to be converted so easily. Arthur Lee,
then in England, had forwarded the Petition of the Merchants,
Traders and Others of the City of London dealing with North
American Commerce to the House of Commerce on January 23,
1775. As Dickinson noted in the margin of a copy, "This petition
was signed by near 400 houses, the most considerable in North
American Trade."[3] The next month, Lee remarked to him, "If
you can escape the disuniting effects of treachery and corruption
and the Congress continues firm, cool and determined as before

[1] JD to Quincy, October 28, 1774, MaHS.

[2] Chase to JD, February 6, 1775, Item 25, L-D/LCP.

[3] *Petition . . .* , L-D/LCP.

your success is sure."[4] That was exactly Dickinson's thought. If Britain's choice should be unfriendly, then he hoped "every man of Sense and Virtue in America will draw his sword, without any regard for the yet respectable doctrine of discussion." But, he prayed, "may infinite goodness avert the occasion."[5]

However, the winds of opinion were shifting slowly. Thomas Cushing pointed out that although Massachusetts had avoided open belligerency, "it is an arduous piece of work to keep a numerous, brave and free people who are daily injured and insulted, quietly waiting the event of peaceable applications for a restoration of their rights." This was even more difficult, he declared, since that colony was "without law, without courts, without the administration of justice." It was not a wholly comforting reply to Dickinson's expression of pain over the rumors that Massachusetts planned to resume its old charter and to choose a governor.[6]

Family concerns intervened in Dickinson's life. A second daughter, Mary, born in the preceding May, died almost exactly one year later, on May 5.[7] The father had the activities of state in which to immerse himself—member of the Assembly, delegate once again to the Continental Congress, and actively corresponding with friends in other colonies. And as determined by the May Assembly there were the exigencies of defense to be considered. Mary Dickinson happily was blessed with an abundance of concerned relatives.

The Second Continental Congress was to assemble on May 10. A few days before, delegates began coming to town. At Bristol, six miles north of Philadelphia, New England representatives were met by officers of the militia and a large company of gentlemen on horseback and then, two miles from the city's outskirts, by a company of riflemen and infantry attended by a band of music. Some

[4] Lee to JD, April 7, 1775, L-D/LCP.

[5] JD to Samuel Ward, January 29, 1775, Gratz Collection, HSP.

[6] Cushing to JD, February 13, 1775, Miscellaneous Small Collections, HSP; JD to Cushing, January 26, 1775, P.R.O., CO5/118, 8006.

[7] Family Bible, L/HSP.

five hundred in all, this goodly company must have raised the spirits of the newcomers.[8]

Dickinson had framed the Pennsylvania instructions to its delegates. The precise orders advised the representatives to "consult together . . . exert your utmost endeavors to agree upon and recommend such measures, as you shall judge to afford the best prospect of obtaining redress of American grievances and restoring that union of harmony between Great Britain and the Colonies necessary to the welfare and happiness of both countries." They were, moreover, enjoined to take special care to avoid any proceedings that might tend to destroy hopes for reconciliation and to "utterly reject" any proposition leading toward separation.[9]

Unity was the keynote for the Second Continental Congress as it had been for the first. Equally important was the sworn agreement of each delegate to keep the proceedings secret. The concern for joint action that from the beginning Dickinson had felt so necessary was adhered to by all the representatives no matter how much they might personally object to both the ideas and the actions approved by the majority. At the outset the delegates agreed to avoid those decisions that would disrupt.[10]

Achieving outward unanimity was no small task. The New Englanders, having suffered longer than other areas and now having experienced a bloody baptism at Lexington and at Concord, were unsympathetic to soft words and conciliatory attitudes. They found understanding and support from the Virginians. Pennsylvania's political atmosphere had changed considerably since the confrontations in Massachusetts, yet dominant Quaker opinion still shackled the leadership. New York and Delaware became the natural allies of the host colony. James Duane of New York, conservative and legalistic, was a particularly congenial colleague for Dickinson, who, though he had not changed his point of view by an iota, now appeared more moderate than radical.

Dickinson was not only a leader in the Congress. He had a pro-

[8] Marshall, *Diary*, p. 25.

[9] "Instructions to Delegates," n.d., Gratz Collection, 3/14, HSP.

[10] George Bancroft, *History of the United States* (New York, 1898), 4:192.

gram. He believed both in defense and in reconciliation. There were three possible positions that could be taken, he asserted. "1st, We may prepare with the utmost diligence for war, without petitioning or sending agents to England to treat of accommodation. 2nd, We may prepare in the manner that is mentioned, and also petition, but without sending agents. 3rd, We may take all three measures." [11] He declared that the first wish of his soul was for the liberty of America, the second for constitutional reconciliation with Great Britain. If these were not obtainable, then "let us seek a new establishment as the Pius Aeneas did." Dickinson reiterated what he deemed the "Blessings of Liberty" yet warned that "no people can be free who are governed by laws made by others." [12]

The first major actions of the Second Congress dealt with the news of the successful attack on Fort Ticonderoga and New York's request for advice on its further defense. The greater part of the first fortnight, however, was spent in considering the "State of America," during which time the members sat as a committee of the whole.

Silas Deane wrote his wife of the canvassing and manipulating that went on within the Congress before any resolution or motion was acted on, noting, "Unanimity is the basis on which we mean to rise." It was not an easy task, but Dickinson possessed an iron determination. He succeeded in holding on to Duane of New York as an ally. Even at the risk of provoking the New Englanders to wrath, he followed his predetermined course. And his influence remained enormous.

Samuel Ward of Rhode Island on May 26 introduced four resolutions. Dickinson had guided the committees' hand in each of these. The first resolution noted that the colonies were "reduced to a dangerous and critical situation" and the British ministry by force of arms was attempting to carry into execution "several unconstitutional and offensive acts of the British Parliament." A second resolve, recognizing the outbreak of hostilities in Massachusetts Bay and the severe and cruel treatment of the inhabitants, proposed that the colonies be "immediately put into a State of De-

[11] "Instructions to Delegates," Gratz Collection, 3/14, HSP.

[12] Notes, Gratz Collections, 3/14, HSP. Other notes in L/HSP.

fense."[13] A third proposition, moved by John Jay and seconded by Dickinson, was unanimously agreed to only after ten days of "warm debate." This was the sending once again of "an humble and dutiful petition" to the king. The Congress recorded its belief that there was an ardent wish for "a restoration of the harmony formerly existing between our Mother country and these Colonies, the interruption of which must, at all events, be exceedingly injurious to both countries."[14] A fourth resolution, that measures be undertaken to open negotiations toward settling the dispute and be made part of the petition, was passed but without unanimous sanction. Dickinson had so far established a posture for action which John Adams described as having a sword in one hand and an olive branch in the other. The Massachusetts delegate approved preparations for a "vigorous defensive war," but the slow, lumbering progress toward practical resolution made him understandably impatient and even at times irrational.[15]

Should opponents object to Dickinson's calls for passive measures, he could point to his personal involvement in Pennsylvania defense activities. During the May session of the Assembly he had supported all such measures, serving on the committee designated to provide stores "necessary for the service of the Province."[16] Militia groups were being formed into companies of associators and when battalions were organized in Philadelphia, Dickinson, on May 23, 1775, was commissioned "Colonel of the First Battalion of Associators in the City and Liberties of Philadelphia."[17] His friend Thomas Mifflin was about to leave the Pennsylvania delegation to become General Washington's aide in Cambridge; Thomas McKean, a Delaware delegate, had also been commissioned a battalion colonel. These three friends each saw reason

[13] These two resolutions in Dickinson's hand are in the Gratz Collection, 3/14, HSP. They are printed in *JCC*, 2:64–65, without word change.

[14] *JCC*, 2:64–65; Frank Monaghan, *John Jay* (New York, 1935), p. 70.

[15] Adams to Moses Gill, June 10, 1775, Charles Francis Adams, ed., *Works of John Adams* (Boston, 1850), 9:356.

[16] *Votes*, 8:7234.

[17] Commission, Loudoun Papers, HSP.

dominating their actions. Declared a traitor in April,[18] Dickinson continued fearless in his quest for justice.

On June 3 a congressional committee with Dickinson as chairman was appointed to prepare a second petition to the king. Perhaps no other matter met with so much dissension as did this "Olive Branch" proposal. It was simple enough to understand why New Englanders, and most notably their spokesman John Adams, viewed a second effort dimly. The rest of the colonists by May were well aware of the crown's studied attitude in turning aside the petition of the First Congress. Yet Dickinson carried the delegates in support of a second petition. Pennsylvania was indeed the keystone or fulcrum. If Adams found allies in Virginia's delegation, Dickinson had strong supporters in South Carolina and New York. The debate was acrimonious. The Farmer, conscious of New England's belligerent attitude from the beginning, did not trust the motives of certain of these delegates. He sensed a willingness on their part, even some planning, to achieve separation. His own position stood in stark contrast.

John Adams was called out of the session. Seeing him leave, Dickinson immediately followed and met Adams in the State House yard. Dickinson often could rise to passionate anger. He accosted Adams furiously and demanded why New Englanders opposed any conciliation, threatening, "If you don't concur with us in our pacific system, I and a number of us will break off from you in New England, and we will carry on the opposition by ourselves in our own way." Adams reported that he responded judiciously to the effect that whichever way the Congress finally decided, any argument would demand support from both of them.[19] The burden was on Dickinson. Apart from a few loyal supporters, enthusiasm for the petition was weak. Dickinson's reputation, so early and deservedly won, coupled with the great sincerity and earnestness of his presentation, would greatly contribute to acquiescence by the delegates. Yet Dickinson could be stubborn and unyielding when he believed himself correct. In consequence, admiration, once so wholeheartedly given him, gradually began to dim.

[18] *Pennsylvania Packet*, April 17, 1775.

[19] Burnett, 1:108–9 n. 2; Adams, *Diary*, 3:318.

Dickinson was too often prone to cite the integrity of his opinion. In this case he noted: "A man's virtue may cost him his reputation and even his life. By virtue [I] mean an inflexible and undaunted adherence in public affairs to his sentiments concerning the interests of his country."[20] This observation Dickinson followed to the letter. He was blind to all contrary views.

A committee consisting of Dickinson, Thomas Johnson, John Rutledge, John Jay, and Benjamin Franklin was appointed to write the petition to the king. Dickinson, first named to the committee appointment, became its final author. Both Jay and Dickinson prepared preliminary drafts. Jay's, as we know it, was less cautious and in its conclusion even threatened independence. Dickinson, in the final petition, eliminated all wording or suggestions that might cause royal irritation. Its very prudence permitted passage by an already divided and argumentative Congress.[21] A "humble petition" in every way, it did not enumerate the causes of colonial dissension. Blame was placed on the king's ministers. It warned that the "violent resentments and incurable animosities [of] civil discords are apt to exasperate and inflame the contending parties" and prayed the king to put end to "the further effusion of blood, and for averting the impending calamities that threaten the British Empire." Without setting forth specific means of finding solutions, the petition concluded: "For by such arrangements as your Majesty's wisdom can form for collecting the united sense of your American people, we are convinced your Majesty would receive such satisfactory proofs of the disposition of the colonists towards their sovereign and parent state, that the wished for opportunity would soon be restored to them, of evincing the sincerity of their professions, by every testimony of devotion becoming the most dutiful subjects, and the most affectionate colonists."[22] The draft, presented to the Congress on July 5, was approved. Little debate followed. There had been little original enthusiasm for it and no criticism on the floor of significance. Two

[20] Scrap of notes, Gratz Collection, 3/14, HSP.

[21] Richard B. Morris, ed., *John Jay:The Making of a Revolutionary* (New York, 1975), pp. 147–54.

[22] *JCC*, 2:158–61.

days later the petition was engrossed and signed by every delegate.

Dickinson was the chief instigator of the Petition to the King. He gained no friends in his determination to foster it; the finished document was basically limited to an entreaty urging the king to act. The day after its unanimous approval, Dickinson attempted to explain his position to Arthur Lee.

> Our rights have been already stated, our claims made; war is actually begun, and we are carrying it on vigorously. This conduct, and our other publications, will show that our spirits are not lowered. If Administration be desirous to stopping the effusion of *British* blood, the opportunity is now offered to them by an unexceptionable Petition, praying for an accommodation. If they reject this application with contempt, the more humble it is the more such treatment will confirm the minds of our countrymen to endure all the misfortunes that may attend the contest.[23]

Dickinson's critics overlooked the Pennsylvania delegate's activity in defense measures. At home, as well, fuel was added to the political flames kindled by Philadelphia radicals, who were impatient for assertive action by their congressional delegates. Dickinson's slow, measured, legalistic pace in the Congress annoyed them. They ignored his support for defense in the Assembly and his commission as colonel in the Philadelphia militia. The Congress itself a month later established a committee "to put Militia on a proper state of defense of America," and Dickinson was a member of it. Curiously, no other member of Congress served so actively in colonial defense. Moreover, Dickinson was the only commissioned militia officer in the Pennsylvania delegation. Other factors, his rigid personal stance, inflexibility, and failure to compromise, blinded many.

The Congress appointed George Washington commander in chief in June 1775 and wrote rules and regulations for the armed forces. Meanwhile, a committee of five was named to draw up a declaration for Washington to read to his troops on his arrival at Cambridge. The next day a document for that purpose, purportedly written by John Rutledge, was reported out to the Congress.

---

[23] Peter Force, *American Archives*, 4th Ser. (Washington, D. C., 1839), 2:1604.

After considerable debate the declaration was recommitted. Dickinson and Thomas Jefferson were added to the committee. Dickinson had criticized the document as harsh and William Livingston, a committee member, thought there was too "much faultfinding and declamation, with little sense or dignity."[24] Jefferson wrote a new declaration and turned it over to Dickinson for suggestions. As he proceeded to edit it, Dickinson's words, phrases, and paragraphs came to dominate the whole. The final Declaration on the Causes and Necessity of Taking up Arms was first read to the thunderous acclaim of assembled troops. Afterwards reread as an inspiring document, modern historians have finally reached a consensus over its authorship.[25]

In addition to stylistic changes, Dickinson made changes in the content itself. These included noting the previous efforts toward conciliation, which Jefferson had omitted out of hand, and eliminating a suggestive denial of all parliamentary authority. In the end the Congress accepted what was indeed Dickinson's draft without further revision. Dickinson did not hesitate to insert cutting descriptions: "The pernicious project," "insidious maneuver," and "Ministerial Rapacity." Jefferson's general thought, however, was not obscured. As James Parton, a Jefferson biographer, later observed, where the Virginian had written "we mean not to dissolve that union . . . necessity has not *yet*," Dickinson held back his corrective pen.[26] That emphatic point suited Dickinson's sense of balance. And his own ringing paragraph gave the lie to any charge of timidity:

> Our cause is just. Our union is perfect. Our internal re-
> sources are great, and if necessary, foreign assistance is un-
> doubtedly attainable. . . . With hearts fortified with these
> animating reflections, we most solemnly, before God and the
> World, declare, that, exerting the utmost energy of those

[24] *JCC*, 2:128 n.

[25] Ibid., 128–57; Julian P. Boyd, "The Disputed Authorship of the Declaration on the Causes and Necessity of Taking Up Arms, 1775," *PMHB* 74 (1950): 51–73.

[26] James Parton, *Life of Thomas Jefferson*, 7th ed. (Boston, 1883), pp. 170–171.

powers which our beneficent Creator hath graciously be-
stowed upon us, the arms we have been compelled by our
enemies to assume, we will in defiance of every hazard, with
unabating firmness and perseverence, employ for the preservation of our liberties being with one mind resolved to die
freemen rather than live slaves.

When the declaration was read to General Putnam's division after
they paraded on Prospect Hill, they "shouted in three huzzahs a
loud AMEN!"

The Pennsylvania Assembly reconvened on June 20. A member
of both the Congress and the Assembly, Dickinson found himself
busy with varied assigned duties. Happily, the House was in session only a week, during which time resolutions were passed providing for the future defense of the province and establishing a
twenty-five-man Committee of Safety. Dickinson was first to be
named to the committee, of which Benjamin Franklin became
chairman. In early July, Dickinson and his fellow battalion colonels Roberdeau, Cadwalader, and Ross, were appointed to inspect
military stores, to make necessary repairs, to suggest a person to
serve as an assistant commissary, and to provide a model for a spear
or pike. Defense measures were provided for possible land and sea
invasion, and, on September 14, one of the naval craft that had
been ordered was named the *Dickinson*. Dickinson's attendance at
the Committee of Safety was infrequent. After the first few meetings he failed to appear again until the end of August.[27]

John Dickinson could not possibly meet all his assigned responsibilities: Pennsylvania assemblyman, congressional delegate,
member of significant committees of each body, and colonel of the
First Battalion. No other delegate was so busy. The day the Pennsylvania Assembly reconvened in June, the three battalions of
Philadelphia and the Liberties marched to the Commons, where
they were reviewed by General Washington, their new commander in chief.[28]

[27] Minutes of the Council of Safety, *Minutes of the Provincial Council of
Pennsylvania* (Harrisburg, Pa., 1852), 10:279–82. Hereafter cited as *Colonial
Records*.

[28] Moore, 1:100, quoting *Rivington's Gazette*, June 29, 1775.

Sessions of the Congress dragged into a third month. The delegates, who met daily, were impatient, frequently irked at their associates, and eager to return home. Eliphalet Dyer of Connecticut, angry with Pennsylvania because of a festering dispute between the two colonies over the Wyoming Valley, suggested that Dickinson "has taken a part very different from what I believe was expected from the country in general or from his constituents."[29] John Adams found Dickinson intransigent, seemingly opposed to every measure Adams favored. News of Bunker Hill in June affected Adams acutely. The Pennsylvania leader had little conception of Massachusetts's problems; Dickinson's main concern was to balance the growing radical forces in his own colony with the ever conservative Quaker and merchant elements.[30] His opponents fretted as Dickinson continued to dominate his fellow delegates.

On July 21, after the Congress resolved itself into a committee of the whole, Franklin presented a plan for a perpetual union of the colonies. Although Franklin in one article suggested that the confederated union would hold only until the "Terms of Reconciliation proposed in the Petition of the last Congress to the King are agreed to" and until certain treaties and reparations were made, implied demands in other articles went beyond the more temperate views Dickinson favored. They seemed to him to cut all ties with England. (Each state also was to have voting strength in proportion to population, thus practically silencing Delaware, about which situation Dickinson, as a property owner, would be concerned.) The time was not ripe for such a proposal. After discussion in a subsequent session, Franklin's articles of confederation were put aside.[31]

Just as Dickinson had had a plan of action at the beginning of the Congress, John Adams had his, one that he acknowledged supporting "from first to last." Yet the only major concession he had obtained from the Congress was the early resolve that approved Massachusetts's setting up an independent government. He had

[29] Dyer to William Judd, July 23, 1775, Burnett, 1:173.

[30] Adams to James Warren, July 11, 1775, *Warren-Adams Letters, 1743–1814* (Boston, 1917–25), 1:73.

[31] *JCC*, 2:195–99.

demurred over the second Petition to the King but affirmed that it could not be avoided lest disunion follow. He hoped for more radical undertakings. As he wrote in a "secret and confidential" note to James Warren, "We ought immediately to dissolve all Ministerial Tyrannies, and Custom houses, set up governments of our own . . . confederate together . . . and open our ports to all nations immediately."[32]

The same day Franklin's articles were proposed, a committee appointed to devise ways to protect the trade of the colonies made its report. This was largely the work of Franklin and Richard Henry Lee. The resolutions proposed that within six months all customshouses of the "Confederate Colonies" be closed and that "all the Ports of the said Colonies are hereby declared to be henceforth open to the ships of every state in Europe that will admit our commerce and protect it."[33] This "Great Idea," as Adams saw it, was doomed to defeat.[34] Once more Dickinson led the opposition, with the support of New York and Maryland. Critics feared that it would add to further dissension and lead to acknowledged rebellion. It was this rejection, perhaps more than the second petition, that fired Adams's ire toward Dickinson.

The Congress adjourned on August 2. The confident notes of hope sounded at the conclusion of the First Congress were now absent. There were major differences in the concepts held by the delegates. The Second Congress assumed responsibilities of a central government; the Association was no longer considered adequate to the exigencies of the time. Tempers had frayed; new proposals had been offered but frequently tabled. Enmities increased. The sultry midsummer weather seemed to add to dissension. Dickinson had succeeded in holding the line against more aggressive measures. He failed only in his earlier hope to send a representative to Britain to present the king with colonial grievances.[35] The

[32] Adams to Warren, July 6, 1775, *Warren-Adams Letters*, 1:73.

[33] *JCC*, 2:200.

[34] Adams to Warren, July 11, 1775, *Warren-Adams Letters*, 1:80.

[35] There are several pages of paragraphs, all rough jottings, written some time during the Congress in which Dickinson proposed such an emissary. Gratz Collection, 3/14, HSP.

dynamics of revolution, however, were creating a new atmosphere.

On July 24 John Adams had written his friend Warren that the Congress a month before should have assumed "the whole legislative, executive and judicial [power] of the whole continent and have completely modeled a constitution," raised a navy and opened wide all ports, "arrested every friend to Government on the continent and held them as hostages for the poor victims in Boston." Only then should they open the door for peace and reconciliation; only after doing these things should they petition and negotiate. Frustrations seemed to him to stem from the determined opposition of John Dickinson. Adams pointed the finger of blame at him, declaring, "A certain great Fortune and piddling genius, whose fame has been trumpeted so loudly, has given a silly cast to our whole doings." The day before he wrote his wife, Abigail, complaining about Dickinson, "whose abilities and virtues formally [*sic*] trumpeted too much in America, have been found wanting." He sneered that, by taking arms, Dickinson "pretended to be very valiant." [36]

Adams's letters contained much confidential information that delegates had been pledged to keep secret. These personal communications were given to Benjamin Hichborn, an official courier, who was riding back to Boston. Crossing Rhode Island by ferry, Hichborn was seized by British officers and taken prisoner. The documents he carried, including the letters, were forwarded to General Gage in Boston. The Warren letter, which clearly revealed congressional dissension, was published in Draper's *Massachusetts Gazette* on August 17. Published and republished, copied from the column by many hands, the venomous description soon was repeated in Philadelphia. In public Dickinson disguised his own reaction, but on a copy of the intercepted letter he wrote, "Letter from John Adams of Massachusetts Bay in which he abuses me for opposing the violent measures of himself and others in Congress." [37]

[36] Adams to Warren, July 24, 1775, *Warren-Adams Letters*, 1:36; Adams to Abigail Adams, July 23, 1775, Charles Francis Adams, ed., *Familiar Letters of John Adams and His Wife Abigail during the Revolution* (Boston, 1875), p. 84.

[37] L/HSP. There are several copies of the Adams letter to Warren in the files of Dickinson.

Charles Lee, like many others critical of Dickinson's intransigence and failure to meet the demands of the time, was sorry the letter had been published.[38] But contemporaries, and, later, historians, would repeat the libel as apt characterization. Latent and often unexpressed criticism, even jealousy, of Dickinson found comfort in the cutting description.

After the reconvening of the Congress on September 16, as Adams walked to the State House, he suddenly found himself close enough to Dickinson "to touch elbows." Adams doffed his hat and bowed ceremoniously. Dickinson ignored the Massachusetts delegate, continuing on his way in haughty dignity as if he had not seen his fellow deputy. Adams began recording in his diary any rumor that would lessen Dickinson's public standing. One caller, Jonathan Dickinson Sergeant of New Jersey, professed embarrassment to Adams about his name. The young man reported that John Dickinson had once made a poor showing on a visit to New Jersey and that he had sunk low in public esteem. Three days later Benjamin Rush pointed out blunders Dickinson had made, declaring that he was "warped by the Quaker interest and the church interest, too, [so that] his reputation was past the meridian and that avarice is growing upon him." Finding a receptive audience in Adams, Rush went on to complain about the activities of the Committee of Safety on which Dickinson served and which Rush considered unrepresentative of the people, asserting that it made laws though many of its members were not even members of the Assembly.[39]

The Pennsylvania Assembly met briefly the last week in September. Three items cast shadows of future importance. The officers of the three battalions of the Military Association of the City and Liberties of Philadelphia in a memorial asked for financial support and also pointed out "that people *sincerely* and *religiously* scrupulous [against bearing Arms] are a few in comparison to those who . . . made *conscience* a *convenience*; that a very considerable share of the property of this Province is in the hand of people professing to be of tender conscience in military matters." A

[38] Lee to Benjamin Rush, September 19, 1775, *Goodspeed Catalog 496*, Item 372.

[39] Adams, *Diary*, 2:173 and 182.

memorial of the Committee of Safety noted that there was need for more pecuniary aid and for the construction of powder magazines. It, too, made a pointed observation: "The liberty of all is at stake, every man should assist in its support, and that where the cause is common, and the benefits derived from an opposition are universal, it is not consonant to justice or equality that the burdens should be partial."[40] Distressing in another way was a letter concerning the further encroachments by Connecticut settlers above Sunbury, Pennsylvania, a problem that would admit of no easy solution. The Assembly adjourned without satisfying any of the questions posed. The House awaited new elections on October 14.

Votes for Dickinson surpassed all those given other representatives elected by the county of Philadelphia.[41] The result confirmed the underlying respect for and approval of his course of action. When the Assembly met later in November, Dickinson was reappointed to the Committee of Safety, which had indeed, as Rush suggested, seemed to assume certain lawmaking powers, particularly in matters of defense. He continued on the colony's Committee of Correspondence as well. His presence on these committees, whose membership was increasingly radical, was acknowledgment not only of the popularity of Dickinson's position but of their need for a token moderate.

Once again a memorial regarding Connecticut invaders of Northumberland and Northampton counties was presented. The dispute also concerned the Congress, which considered a resolution proposed by Connecticut establishing a temporary line between settlements of the two colonies. Pennsylvanians opposed this plan but were willing to acquiesce in any peaceful solution provided that no new settlements were made by Connecticut.[42]

The Quakers forwarded a long address to the Assembly concerning protection of their civil and religious liberties. This opened the gates to a flood of protests, memorials, petitions, and remonstrances from groups of military associations, both officers and pri-

[40] *Votes*, September 27, 1775, 8:7259–60.

[41] Marshall, *Diary*, p. 45.

[42] *Votes*, 8:7330–33.

vates, and from the unofficial revolutionary Committee of the City and Liberties of Philadelphia of which George Clymer was chairman. Their ire against the orthodox attitude of Quaker pacifism was compounded by the fact that many of the wealthiest men were exempted from any cooperation whatsoever.[43] The Assembly responded by appointing a committee which had a twofold responsibility. Dickinson was named first, and hence it is assumed was chairman, to "prepare a Set of Rules and Regulations for the better government of the Military Association of this Province; and . . . [to] essay a draught, directing the manner of levying taxes on non-associates, determining their mode of appeal, and how the said taxes shall be collected and applied."[44] Dickinson, who had an understanding of Quaker views, brought moderation to the final result. The rules and regulations were not completed until April, when resolutions concerning means of levying taxes on non-associators were also passed.

All during the November session Dickinson took an active part in the Assembly's proceedings on the second floor of the State House, above the congressional deliberations. He wrote new instructions for the delegates to the Congress which differed little from those previously made, asserting, "Though the oppressive measures of the British Parliament and Administration have compelled us to resist the violence by force of arms, yet we strictly enjoin you, that you, in behalf of this Colony, dissent from, and utterly reject, any propositions, should such be made, that may cause or lead to a separation from our Mother Country, or a change of the form of this Government."[45] These firm words were not consonant with the atmosphere of mounting irritation. On October 31 the king's proclamation of August 23 had been received, declaring all the colonies to be in open rebellion. In effect, it forbade his subjects from all correspondence with them.[46] A week

[43] Ibid., 8:7334; Marshall, *Diary*, pp. 49–50.

[44] *Votes*, 8:7352, 7473–90.

[45] Ibid., 8:7352–53.

[46] Marshall, *Diary*, p. 50.

later a report arrived from Richard Penn and Arthur Lee, who had been charged with delivering the "Olive Branch Petition" to the king. The petition had not been received "on the throne," and thus no answer would be forthcoming.[47]

The news was discouraging, indeed deeply disturbing. Continued and increased resistance was the only possible answer, yet Dickinson by neither word nor deed changed his stance. It was for him a time for reflection. From October through December he failed to appear at any meeting of the Committee of Safety, which was charged with obtaining military stores, providing storage magazines, and building boats. He divided his time between the Assembly, where he continued to dominate action, and the Congress. The daily trips to and from Fairhill were tiring. He asked to be excused from the congressional committee for importing arms, which met in the evenings.[48]

He received and answered letters addressed to him as a member of the congressional committee of Secret Correspondence. There were also personal letters. General Charles Lee wrote Dickinson on December 11 critical of the Pennsylvania Assembly's instructions to its congressional delegates. He reported that sentiment in the camp where he served believed the instructions implied that there was sentiment for independence. This he considered impolitic; it offered Britain an idea of which hitherto there had been no proof.[49] Lee's presumption was a logical one that the Pennsylvania delegate had probably not considered.

Early in December the Congress received word that William Franklin, the loyalist governor of New Jersey, had recommended to the Jersey legislature that separate petitions by that and other colonies might be more fruitful than the second petition of the Congress had proved to be. The Congress at once resolved that "in the present situation of affairs it will be very dangerous to the lib-

[47] *Votes*, 8:7352; *Pennsylvania Packet*, November 10, 1775.

[48] *Votes*, 8: passim, Assembly business from July 1775 to July 1776; *JCC*, 3:335.

[49] Lee to JD, December 11, 1775. Gratz Collection, HSP. Lee repeated his assertion in a letter of January 19, 1776, ibid.

erties and welfare of America" should any colony do so. It then tactfully sent three members, John Jay, George Wythe, and John Dickinson, to "confer with the Assembly of New Jersey."[50]

Dickinson addressed the New Jersey body in a half-hour appeal expressing a smoldering hope that some indication of acceptance of the "Olive Branch Petition" might even yet be forthcoming. Reviewing the actions of Congress, he suggested that Britain at first had considered that the position of the colonies was "a rope of sand and [we] would not fight." His appeal was both to the moderates and the conservatives, pointing out that had the Congress "drawn the sword and thrown away the scabbard, all lovers of liberty, all honest and virtuous men would have applauded, [but they again] humbly petitioned the King." He set forth the military successes to that date and observed, "We have nothing to fear . . . a country so united [as America] cannot be conquered." While he complimented the House on the petition and "noble answer" to their governor, he now asked them to stand by a united America. Finally, Dickinson warned "that neither Mercy nor Justice was to be expected from Great Britain." He was followed by Jay, who spoke for about twelve minutes and stressed that petitions were no longer the means of redress; "vigor and unanimity" were the only path. George Wythe commented briefly to the same end.[51] The members, properly impressed, refrained from separate action.

December proved dull. Delegates from various colonies absented themselves, to the distress of congressional leaders. John Adams himself requested leave. The Pennsylvania Assembly had adjourned November 25, not to meet again until mid-February.

A shift in emphasis and an increase in pressures toward independence were apparent that winter. Thomas Paine's publication *Common Sense* in January 1776 became the keynote for the changing temper in the months that followed.[52] In every way compelling, it was a clarion call to those who had hesitated or otherwise become

---

[50] *JCC*, 3:404.

[51] "Notes of What Mr. Dickinson Said before the House of Assembly of New Jersey," W. A. Whitehead et al., eds., *Documents Relating to the Colonial History of the State of New Jersey* (Newark, N. J., 1880–86), 10:689–91.

[52] Thomas Paine, *Common Sense* (Philadelphia, 1776).

apathetic. What the *Farmer's Letters* were to the pre-Revolutionary period, *Common Sense* was now to 1776. Liberty from arbitrary parliamentary measures and repressive enforcement was now translated into liberty from British rule. The book created strong support for the proponents of independence who, now emboldened, no longer disguised their long-sought goal.

Yet Dickinson held on to his strong position and maintained his influence. His personal hopes for reconciliation gradually faded, dashed by the king's adamancy. Nevertheless, deeply aware of Pennsylvania's divided people, his public attitude remained firm. But he now hedged the options. Over and over he stated, "The first wish of my soul is for the Liberty of America. The next is for constitutional reconciliation with Great Britain. If we cannot obtain the first without the second, let us seek a new establishment."[53]

The Congress was a unifying body, a de facto government for all the colonies, yet the many shades of personal opinion and varied instructions held by the delegates brought little unity into that legislature. The divisions were clearly marked in January 1776. On the ninth, James Wilson, with the king's speech declaring the colonies in open rebellion in hand, suggested that the colonial attitude was not understood and that it was misrepresented in England. He recommended that an address be written explaining the American position and disclaiming an intention of independency. A motion in support was adopted. But delegations were split over the idea, even that of Massachusetts. Sam Adams, leader in the absence of his cousin John, was furious, and threatened a separate confederacy for New England. Thomas Cushing influenced Robert Treat Paine and John Hancock to support Wilson's move and was promptly dropped from the Massachusetts delegation, with Elbridge Gerry being named in his place.[54]

The Pennsylvania delegation was now similarly divided. Thomas McKean, a Delaware deputy but highly influential in Pennsyl-

[53] There are many variations of this sentiment in notes, both fragmentary and complete in the Dickinson Papers in the collections both of the HSP and LCP.

[54] Stillé, pp. 169–73.

vania, together with Franklin sided with the popular Presbyterian party. This faction was cultivated by New England proponents of independence, who exercised no subtlety in their campaign to change Pennsylvania's congressional position.[55]

Within a week of Wilson's quest for a new appeal to Britain, Sam Adams proposed that Franklin's articles of confederation submitted the previous July be put on the agenda. Dickinson at once took the floor protesting the idea of confederacy. His arguments were to the point. No authority had been given any delegates, restrained or not by their colony's instructions, to vote for such a binding "independent and separate" government. That decision, he asserted, was the proper power of the people. He viewed the role of the Congress purely as one of defense and, if possible, reconciliation with Britain. The articles were finally dropped from further consideration. On the thirteenth, Wilson, after consultation with four moderate-to-conservative committee members, submited his proposed address to the inhabitants of the United Colonies, which he had earlier turned over to his mentor, Dickinson, who had cut and reworded certain portions. But Wilson did not accept all Dickinson's editing,[56] and in the end it made little difference. The address was tabled. Dickinson, whose support might have been crucial to its adoption, was otherwise concerned.

Charles Lee wrote Dickinson on January 19, en route to take command of New York, complaining of the complacency of the Continental Congress toward the dangers confronting that city. On Monday, February 12, a letter to the Congress from General Lee noted the arrival of a British troop transport in New York harbor. Fearing a landing of additional forces, he asked reinforcements to obtain a more secure defense. His specific request was for a battalion of the Philadelphia militia to support him, and to be instructed in "village fortification, camp duty, etc." Congress immediately acted upon the request and recommended to the convention or Committee of Safety of New Jersey that that colony

[55] Ibid., pp. 173–74.

[56] *JCC*, 4:134–64. See also the "Wilson-Dickinson" manuscript with emendations, L/HSP.

send detachments of minutemen to New York. A similar request was forwarded to the Committee of Safety for Pennsylvania.[57]

All four colonels of the Philadelphia battalions applied to Congress for the command of the detachments. As colonel of the First Battalion, John Dickinson insisted that it was his right to lead the companies. He refused any waiver of obligation because he was a member both of the Congress and Pennsylvania's General Assembly, which that very day was scheduled to reconvene. Members of the Committee of Safety and of the Assembly pressed him to remain in Philadelphia and to attend to the business at hand. But Dickinson would not be dissuaded. John Adams found himself waxing complimentary in a letter to Abigail, saying that "Mr. Dickinson's alacrity and spirit upon this occasion which certainly becomes his character, and sets a fine example, is much talked of and applauded."[58] On February 13 the four battalions were drawn up, and two companies from each were chosen to form a new battalion under Colonel Dickinson's command.

Dickinson addressed the assembled troops and the many citizens who had come out to see them. He spoke with "great vehemence and pathos." Adams observed that to awaken a martial spirit "it may be proper and necessary for such popular orators as Henry and Dickinson to assume a military character." Joseph Hewes of North Carolina thought it "diverting enough to see both officers and men soliciting to be employed in the service." Joseph Reed, who had been acting as secretary to George Washington, was chosen lieutenant colonel. The eight companies selected to make up the 720 men of the new battalion were ready for the march northward the next day. But, before the battalion could set out, word was received that General Clinton had retired from New York.[59] On February 15, it was officially noted that the "Congress have a proper sense of the spirit and patriotism of the Associators of the city and liberties of Philadelphia, in cheerfully offering and pre-

[57] *JCC*, 4:127–28.

[58] *Familiar Letters of John Adams to His Wife Abigail*, pp. 133–34.

[59] *JCC*, 4:128, Joseph Hewes to Samuel Johnson, Burnett, 1:345; John Hancock to George Washington, ibid., 345–46; Stillé, pp. 380–81.

paring to march, in order to assist in the defense of New York; but as the danger which occasioned an application for their service is at present over, Resolved, that their march to New York be suspended."

Dickinson's insistent answer to the call to military service, which met with so much approbation from all quarters, was soon forgotten. His patriotic position soon became invisible to his opponents. They were unable to comprehend the direction and rationale of the straight course Dickinson pursued, as he fearlessly continued protest against every action of Britain that infringed on the liberties of the colonists and joined with military preparedness in case or armed struggle, yet remained loath to face the question of separation.

Mary Norris Dickinson with her infant daughter Sally, by
Charles Willson Peale (1773). In the background is the State
House, Philadelphia. This would have been the view from
Dickinson's Chestnut Street house had she consented to live
there. (Historical Society of Pennsylvania)

Dickinson's Chestnut Street House (c. 1810), between Sixth and Seventh streets in Philadelphia, was four years in the building and of great elegance. Never occupied by the Dickinsons, it was seized briefly for hospital use in 1777, was occupied by the French ambassador in the later Revolutionary period, and became the home of Philemon Dickinson and later, Judge William Tilghman. (Print and Picture Collection, The Free Library of Philadelphia)

THE PATRIOTIC AMERICAN FARMER.
J-N D-K-NS——N Esq.ʳ BARRISTER at LAW:
Who with Attic Eloquence and Roman Spirit hath Asserted,
The Liberties of the BRITISH Colonies in America.

'Tis nobly done, to Stem Taxations Rage,
And raise, the thoughts of a degen'rate Age,
For Happiness, and Joy, from Freedom Spring;
But Life in Bondage, is a worthless Thing.

Printed for & Sold by R. Bell Bookseller

This print, published by R. Bell in 1768 from an engraving attributed to James Smither, hailed Dickinson for his *Farmer's Letters* and reflects the ceremony tended by his friends at the Colony, a fishing club near the Falls of the Schuylkill. Paul Revere copied the portrait for *Nathaniel Ames' (Boston) Almanac* of 1772. (The Library Company of Philadelphia)

The Dickinson Mansion, which John called "Poplar Hall," near Dover in Kent County, Delaware, was built by Samuel Dickinson in the late 1730's. The two smaller additions to the left were added shortly before 1754. A disastrous fire in 1804 required a change from the original hip roof with a triangular pedimented front. (Division of Historical and Cultural Affairs, State of Delaware)

☆ 7 ☆

Dickinson as
a Conservative

THE TIDES OF REVOLUTION could not be stilled. The Pennsylvania Assembly which Dickinson and the moderates easily
controlled was buffeted by petitions and demands from the officers and the privates of military associations and from the radical
Philadelphia City Committee. Paine's *Common Sense* pointed to
the dangers inherent in a government comprised of small groups
of electors and representatives. The charge was difficult to refute.
Meanwhile, the whigs in the Assembly were seriously split. Dickinson with Thomas Willing and Robert Morris, both wealthy
merchants, continued to dominate; yet other forces with Benjamin
Franklin as their leader were increasingly strong in influence.
Joseph Reed, George Clymer, and Daniel Roberdeau represented
those pressing the Assembly for more radical solutions. Once so
closely associated with these radicals and unceasing in his demands
for liberty, Dickinson became intransigent. For all the historical
analogies he cited, he failed to understand the factors that were
determining the American future. Liberty was a constitutional
question. Concerned with maintaining a moderate position, Dickinson could neither foresee changes nor comprehend the fact that
minority strength of itself can create a revolution. Politics is dynamic in its very nature. By the spring of 1776 the time for passive
means of protest had ended.

Problems of county underrepresentation were exacerbated by

suffrage restrictions, which already were under attack. Craftsmen and mechanics dubbed "Leather Aprons," becoming prosperous and increasingly influential, demanded representation. Dickinson and others at first tried to prevent the call for a provincial convention in July which they knew would act on such demands. Understanding the dangers of revolution, the attendant violence and social dislocations, Dickinson proved too cautious as a politician, vainly hoping somehow to ride out the storm rather than find the center of energy and turn it to advantage.

Pressures mounted in the spring of 1776. February witnessed an avalanche of petitions critical of the mode of levying taxes on nonassociators, asking for a revision of militia rules, citing a need for better military compensation, and seeking immediate naturalization for Germans and other foreigners serving in the militia.[1] All of these demands were received from officers and privates of military associations or committees of inspection. At the end of the month, western counties separately petitioned for an increase in their number of representatives. Dickinson was first named, thus assuming the chairmanship, to committees to revise militia regulations, to draft instructions for recruiting, and to bring in a bill relative to increased representation.

On March 22 Mary Cadwalader Dickinson died at Belleville, near Trenton, the home of Philemon Dickinson and his wife. The Philadelphia Dickinsons went up at once, taking with them the black gloves and other mourning accessories Philemon had requested.

Mary Dickinson had found living with her younger son more congenial than living with John's family, whose Norris kin were of another cast. Both the families were Quakers but of different Meetings, interpreting life in different ways. The Norris family, beginning with Isaac, grandfather of John's wife, were proprietary leaders since William Penn's day. The Cadwaladers, more worldly, were less strict in their religious tenets and followed professional interests rather than careers in government. The Norris family were of English descent, the Cadwaladers Welsh, which also served to set apart the two families. Yet both families were mem-

[1] *Votes*, 8:7462–90.

bers of the early Quaker aristocracy. Polly Dickinson was quieter and more closely bound to the proprieties and rules of the Friends than her mother-in-law. Philemon had married his first cousin, his mother's niece, and sometime later, after her death, he married his wife's sister. It was Cadwalader tolerance that permitted the mother to understand the forceful positions toward English aggression which both sons took, first John in his pamphlets and letters, then each son as he took up arms. Philemon was first commissioned as a colonel of the Hunterdon County, New Jersey, Battalion in the fall of 1775 and soon became a brigadier general, outranking his older brother militarily. Her Cadwalader kin were also active whigs.

When John in early April returned to Fairhill and to the business both of the Assembly and Congress, he found himself beset by dissension and rumbling criticism. The Philadelphia City Committee by the end of February had already shown its determination to force the conservatives into the open and to call a new provincial convention.[2] The whig factions had polarized. Radicals, demanding more democratic innovations in the Assembly as well as separation from England, kept up their barrage in petitions, letters to the editors of Philadelphia newspapers, and meetings in Philadelphia. Moderate whigs moved to the right; some, like the once popular William Allen and his sons, soon assumed a tory role.

Two significant resolutions passed the Assembly in response to the pressures exerted upon it. On March 4 the House agreed to take up the question of increased representation for the several back counties. Ten days later a bill passed adding seventeen new seats to the Assembly. Four of these were designated for Philadelphia.[3] The measure was an unhappy compromise, a gesture rather than a satisfactory solution. Suffrage had not been increased, and many in the city who did not meet existing voting qualifications were angered. However, on May 1, when elections were held in Philadelphia, the radicals lost. Only one of their slate, George

[2] Marshall, *Diary*, p. 61.

[3] *Votes*, 8:7446.

Clymer, was elected. The moderate, anti-Independence party elected three representatives, including Andrew Allen, the leading conservative.[4] The election was bitter. The radicals had reason to complain. Tom Paine suggested many qualified voters were already under arms and on the battlefield while others by suffrage restriction had been prevented from casting any ballot. The moderates remained in control even after new Assembly members arrived from western counties. But the margin was narrow.

Dickinson, meanwhile, failed to foresee the prospect before him. Years later, he asserted that after the second Petition to the King had been rejected, not a word had been spoken in the Congress favoring reconciliation. Even so Dickinson vainly continued to seek time in the hope that somehow the British ministry would recover from their "mad" course or, failing that, that encouraging word would be received from Silas Deane, who had been sent to France to seek its support.[5]

The Continental Congress, prodded by John Adams, fostered support for the Philadelphia dissidents, who echoed the restless demands of the frontier counties. On May 6 the Massachusetts deputy sought a congressional resolution which would advise all colonies to refrain from instructing their delegates. This was a rebuff to Dickinson, who had written the Pennsylvania instructions specifically enjoining its representatives from voting for separation. The resolution failed. Undaunted, Adams on May 15 successfully obtained a congressional resolution of even greater significance. This recommended that colonies institute new constitutons if those under which they governed were not sufficient "to the exigencies of their affairs." Writing to James Warren that day, Adams called the resolution equivalent to a declaration of independence, although "a formal declaration was still opposed by Dickinson and his party."[6]

As soon as word of the resolution got abroad, petitions and addresses from the city and counties, from associations and committees once again deluged the Pennsylvania Assembly. Buoyed by

[4] Thayer, pp. 178–79; Lincoln, pp. 246–47.

[5] Stillé, pp. 192, 195–96.

[6] JCC, 4:342, 358; Burnett, 1:445–46 n. 2.

this support and impatient for action, the City Committee at the behest of certain excited radicals on May 20 called for a "general gathering" in the State House yard. Two days later, seven thousand citizens stood in a soaking rain in support of the call. Daniel Roberdeau was given the chair. The business at hand was taken up item by item with a crescendo of enthusiasm. The strict instructions that bound the Pennsylvania delegates were read to a silent audience. Then came the resolution of the Congress, which drew shouts and salvos of applause. Thomas McKean, now a militia colonel, took the rostrum and asserted that the people of Pennsylvania themselves must inaugurate a new government through a provincial constitutional convention. A resolution was also presented which characterized the instructions of the Pennsylvania delegates as inimical to the liberties of the people and called for an immediate change. This was followed by a declaration that the Assembly, owing allegiance to the king, must be superseded by a government instituted by the people. A call for a conference of representatives from the city and counties to arrange for such a change was then passed. This meeting, as William Bradford was to note, marked "a *coup de grace* to the King's authority" in Pennsylvania.[7]

Dickinson as usual had gone down to his Delaware plantation in mid-May. James Wilson, the delegate who had once been his law student, had stayed close to Dickinson in all arguments opposing separation. When John Adams proposed his successful motion advising the formation of new governments by the people, both Wilson and Dickinson were absent from the Congress. Dickinson, however, was not disturbed by the resolution since he maintained Pennsylvania's government would withstand any such test. A week later, a startling preamble was introduced declaring that any oath or support of the crown should be suppressed by the new government. Wilson, back in his seat, saw it as a prelude to independence. He requested a delay in its passage, asserting that the Pennsylvania Assembly should be given time to act since the newly elected representatives were not yet present. New instructions for delegates were sought. Nevertheless, the Congress passed the preamble. The

[7] Lincoln, pp. 254–55; *Pennsylvania Gazette*, May 22, 1776; William Bradford, Jr., Memorandum Book and Register, May and June, 1976, HSP.

radicals now turned their ire toward Wilson, Dickinson being out
of town. In Carlisle, where his wife and children still resided, the
people bitterly accused him of deserting their interests. Now in
Philadelphia calumny toward Wilson mounted so high that twenty-two delegates to Congress signed a Defense in his support. This
temporarily lessened the attacks against him.[8]

In the Pennsylvania Assembly the moderates, by two votes, managed to hold onto their dwindling control. They undertook a
limited number of requested reforms. Committees were appointed,
and Dickinson was a member of each. But stemming the criticisms
launched against them was difficult.

On May 28 the Assembly received a remarkable petition from
the freemen and inhabitants of Cumberland County. Primarily
it asked for removal of the instructions to the Pennsylvania delegates. This address and news that Virginia was about to establish
a new government and lift their delegates' instructions resulted a
week later in a motion to appoint a committee to bring in new
instructions for delegates. But the radicals were foiled. Once again
Dickinson was appointed chairman.[9]

On June 6, the day following, a draft of new instructions was
submitted to the House. Other business was set aside, and both
morning and afternoon sessions were devoted to its consideration.
It took three days before the new instructions were ordered transcribed and signed by the Speaker. The Assembly grudgingly acknowledged that the situation of public affairs had altered. Many
justifications for the change were found, including the contempt
Britain accorded the last petition of the Congress, Parliament's
declaration of the colonies' being in rebellion, in the engagement
of mercenaries, and in the unyielding answer of the king toward
the petition of the Lord Mayor and other officials of the City of
London. For all these reasons the candle of hope for reconciliation
was flickering. Delegates were empowered to take any steps they
deemed necessary "for promoting the Liberty, Safety and Interests

[8] Charles Coleman Sellers, *Dickinson College, a History* (Middletown, Conn.,
1973), pp. 39, 422; Charles Page Smith, *James Wilson* (Chapel Hill, N. C., 1956),
p. 83.

[9] *Votes*, 8:7520–24, 7535.

of America; reserving to the people of this Colony the sole and exclusive right of regulating the internal government and police of the same."[10] It was a document that balanced opinions and yet echoed the voice of Dickinson. On the one hand, it lifted the limitations on delegate action; on the other, it strove to head off the motion of Congress that gave impetus for a change in the governmental structure. But in the latter regard it failed.

The *Pennsylvania Gazette* on June 26 ran a long editorial "To the People" castigating the actions and inaction of the Assembly. Pointing out that while the Proprietary party had "ruinous decisions of reconciliation in view," the Popular party supported separation and suspicions. But, it noted, "in between these two, a certain gentleman, the framer of the first instructions to the Delegates steered an indefinite course, sometimes agreeing with one side, sometimes with the other, sometimes with neither; seeming upon the whole to have no fixed object in view than HIMSELF." In sum, the editor described the preamble of the instructions as "vague, general and unsatisactory" and accused the assemblymen of deserting "the public trust in a time of the greatest danger and difficulty. . . . The revolution is now begun."

The question for the moderates now was how to prevent the total ebb of their political power and avoid both anarchy and civil war. After Richard Henry Lee's motion in Congress on June 7 that the United Colonies "of right ought to be free and independent States," few failed to foresee its eventual passage. Any moderate stand taken in the Pennsylvania Assembly was doomed to defeat. Two efforts were frustrated: an attempt to hold a constitutional convention under the aegis of the Assembly itself and a move to have the proposed two brigadier general appointments made by the House.[11] The radicals negated each by nonattendance, making it impossible to obtain a quorum for either discussion or vote. Positive actions for defense and the abolition of oaths of allegiance were ignored by the revolutionaries in their zeal to prevent other actions. The Assembly could not function, and on June 14 it adjourned. The *Pennsylvania Packet* observed that by "deser-

[10] Ibid., 8:7543.

[11] Thayer, pp. 182–83.

tion and cowardice" the Assembly had turned over the government to the second Provincial Conference to be convened four days later in Carpenter's Hall.[12]

The conference delegates were led by its Philadelphia proponents, including Franklin, Bayard, Christopher Marshall, Rush, and McKean. The last was chairman. The delegates were an impressive cross section of the state. Henceforth, new voices would lead Pennsylvania policies. The main business was a call for a constitutional convention. The conference also removed former suffrage restrictions. All associators, even though not meeting previous voting requirements, were given the vote provided they were twenty-one, had lived in Pennsylvania one year, and had paid either provincial or county taxes. Only those renouncing allegiance to Great Britain were to be eligible to vote in the July 8 election.[13] The result of this liberalization meant a new constituency and hence a new power base.

Thomas Rodney on May 12 wrote his brother Caesar about a rumor that Dickinson had become an Independent, adding "I trust that this subject will not be disputed much longer. . . . Independence is the only guardian of freedom in America." On May 19 Dickinson met Thomas Rodney on the street in Dover. Unabashed, Rodney asked his opinion of the new congressional resolution recommending changes in colonial governments. Agreeing that there would be certain advantages to it, Dickinson observed "that it would not prevent but perhaps promote a more speedy reconciliation because the longer they let Government exist before they offer terms the more firm that government would be, and therefore the more difficult to effect a reconciliation." The answer puzzled Rodney. Dickinson, Rodney believed, still had some "glimmering hopes" for reconciliation without independence.[14]

Thomas McKean, his close friend since his youth, had long since parted political company with Dickinson. Charles Thomson, so closely allied in the early years of protest and now bound in kinship through marriage, was distressed. Deploring the cuts and

[12] *Pennsylvania Packet*, June 24, 1776.

[13] Thayer, pp. 184–85.

[14] Thomas Rodney to Caesar Rodney, May 12, May 19, 1776, RSR/HSD.

criticisms leveled at his friend, Thomson laid them in part to jealousy of Dickinson's talents by the Lees of Virginia and others. He was aware of his friend's fear that America would be too weak in arms to win. But he also remembered Dickinson's saying that he would consider the contest "as a family quarrel, which may be made up at any time, and harmony be again restored, but [that] the moment she employs foreign mercenaries to cut our throats, I will join you in preparing for a declaration of independence." By mid-June the colonies knew that Hessian troops were engaged. Thomson reminded Dickinson of his pledge to come to the side of independence. Acknowledging that he had indeed so promised, Dickinson nevertheless could not bring himself to that decision.[15]

Dickinson's correspondents seemed unanimous in their support of independence, and they did not hesitate to explain their positions. Thomson Mason of Virginia a year before had suggested that had all colonies firmly united like New England and taken up a position of defense, Britain would have renounced its claim. But now he wrote: "The sword of discord is now drawn and nothing can regain the scabbard. . . . If we seem too desirous of peace . . . a long and bloody civil war will be the inevitable consequence."[16] Dickinson himself, so close to the established ruling elite of Philadelphia and fearful of civil strife, continued to hope for a consensus in that city and in Pennsylvania on the issue. But any unanimity among Pennsylvania delegates was clearly impossible. Thomas Willing was firmly against any separation, and Robert Morris too stood staunchly by Dickinson's side. James Wilson was beginning to waver.

Dickinson, his constituents, and his allies watched the inevitable sweep of events beginning in June. McKean's plan for polling the battalions on June 10 in support of independence, the seizing of an unfortunate Philadelphia Jew accused of disloyalty, the pillaging of the house of another suspect, as well as increased vigilante activity, were unhappy harbingers of further trouble.[17]

[15] "Charles Thomson's opinion of the Declaration of Independence," Deborah Logan Diary, L/HSP, X, 9.

[16] Thomson Mason to JD, June 17, 1775, MDL/HSP.

[17] Thayer, pp. 180–83.

Dickinson had two arenas in which he could express himself in an attempt to sway others to his viewpoint, his positions as colonel of the First Battalion of Associators and as a Pennsylvania delegate to Congress.

To the officers of the associators, political questions were of growing importance. On Thursday, June 6, a meeting of all battalion officers was held to protest the suggestion that the Assembly appoint the brigadier generals, which they considered a scheme of the conservative elements to maintain unreasonable control. One officer, pointing out why Assembly action could not be trusted, cited the voting instructions by which Pennsylvania delegates to Congress had been bound. Colonel Dickinson was present; yet the speaker minced no words. He asserted that "the author and abettor of these instructions would find they had lost the confidence and affections of the people." Dickinson replied with what was described as a "masterly defense." William Bradford, Jr., reported the occasion:

> "We are blamed," said he [Dickinson], "for appointing men who had not the confidence of the people and we are also blamed because we gave not those suspected unlimited powers: you say the assembly has no right to alter the Constitution without the consent of the people, and you condemn the Assembly because they gave not their delegates power to alter it." He shone in a spirited and beautiful manner when he took notice of the words leveled at him. He own[ed] himself the author of the instructions and appeal[ed] to his maker for his integrity. "The loss of life," said he, "or of what is dearer than life itself, the affection of my countrymen shall not deter me from acting as an honest man. These threats then that we just now heard might have been spared. I defy them—I regard them not—I stand as unmoved by them, as the rock among the waves that dash against it—I can defy the world, Sir, but—I defy not heaven: nor will I ever barter my conscience for the esteem of mankind. So let my country treat me as she pleases still I will act as my conscience directs." These were his words and appeared to be the unpremeditated effusions of the heart. His graceful actions, the emotions of his countenance and a plaintive yet manly voice strongly impressed

upon my judgment. He was clearly wrong yet I believed him right.[18]

The eloquent address failed to sway the officers; but, in spite of themselves, they were impressed by the depth of Dickinson's sincerity, a quality that was his most impressive and most winning characteristic.

Four days later the forces backing independence actively sought support from the associators of Philadelphia and the Liberties. The First, Second, Fourth, and Fifth battalions consisted of about two thousand officers and men. The votes of each battalion showed the influence of their commanding officers. In Dickinson's First Battalion four officers and twenty-three privates voted against separation from Britain; in the Second only two privates voted negatively, while the Fourth and Fifth Battalions were unanimous in support of independence. A lieutenant of the Third Battalion refused to put the question before the men. The *Evening Post* reported: " 'How our delegates in Congress may act' says a Pennsylvanian, 'we know not, though we have a right to know, and intend to promote an inquiry into that purpose.' Take heed, Tories: you are at your last gasp! You have had many warnings and many kind invitations."[19]

While Dickinson tried to sidetrack every radical issue in the Assembly, giving way only of necessity, the Congress hastened the inevitable decision on separation. Dickinson's position was abundantly clear. More than most men he recognized other factors—the seriousness of intercolonial disputes and the lack of governmental machinery to settle them.

As a member of the Congress, Dickinson saw the gulfs that separated sectional interests, the suspicion and mistrust between the colonial delegates themselves. As Pennsylvania assemblyman he was aware of the problems his own colony endured in its relations with Connecticut in its northern stretch and with Virginia in the southwest. Neither colony had felt limited in its designs on Pennsylvania soil by the greater struggle in which they were all in-

[18] Bradford, Memorandum Book and Register, HSP.

[19] *Pennsylvania Evening Post*, June 11, 1776; Moore, *Diary of the Revolution*, 1:250.

volved. In 1774, 1775, and now in June 1776, the disputes continued. Nor was the question one that dealt with unoccupied Pennsylvania land. Much was already surveyed, was owned by Pennsylvania speculators, and included strategic centers such as Pittsburgh.[20] With good reason Dickinson pointed out the need for greater union.

As a member of the congressional Committee of Secret Correspondence, which was involved with foreign affairs, more than most other delegates he knew British and European attitudes toward the American struggle. Silas Deane in March had sailed on a secret mission to France. Word had not yet been received from him or from Madrid where assistance was also being sought. Deane's instructions had been written March 3 by Dickinson and edited by Franklin, Robert Morris, and Benjamin Harrison. All committee members signed them, noting, "If we should, as there is great appearance we shall, come to a total separation from Great Britain," France would consequently be looked upon as a power whose friendship would be hoped for.[21]

The threefold resolution Richard Henry Lee had brought in on June 7 had been duly moved and seconded:

> That these United Colonies are and of right, ought to be, free and independent states, that they are absolved from all allegiance to the British Crown, and that all political connection between them and the State of Great Britain, is and ought to be, totally dissolved.
> —That it is expedient forthwith to take the most effectual measures for forming foreign alliances.
> —That a plan of confederation be prepared and transmitted to the respective Colonies for their consideration and approbation.[22]

[20] Bernhard Knollenberg, "John Dickinson vs. John Adams, 1774–1776," *Proceedings of the American Philosophical Society* 107 (1963):142–43; *Votes*; Thomas Perkins Abernethy, *Western Lands and the American Revolution* (New York, 1937).

[21] J. H. Powell, *George Washington and the Jack Ass* (South Brunswick, N. J., 1969), pp. 165, 318–23.

[22] *JCC*, 5:425–26.

Consideration of Lee's motion began the next day, Saturday, and resumed the following Monday. The ensuing debate was warm; Dickinson, Wilson, Robert Livingston, and Edward Rutledge all were against "the power of all N. England, Virginia and Georgia." Agreement postponed consideration of the first resolution until July 1, but in order to lose no time in case Congress then agreed to the motion, a committee was appointed to prepare a declaration regarding it. Two other resolutions followed: "That a Committee be appointed to prepare and digest the form of a confederation to be entered into between these colonies," and "that a Committee be appointed to prepare a plan of treaties to be proposed to foreign powers." [23]

On June 12 Dickinson was appointed a member of the last two committees. That charged with preparation of articles of confederation included one representative from each colony; the one to prepare a plan of treaties had five members: Dickinson, Franklin, John Adams, Benjamin Harrison, and Robert Morris.

The twelve-man committee appointed to write articles of confederation included all colonial viewpoints and embraced many rivalries. Dickinson was chairman of the committee. Sectional concerns, such as fisheries and slavery, western lands and ocean trade, local measures and national needs, split the delegates. Within the week Josiah Bartlett of New Hampshire noted that "some difficulties have arisen, I fear it will take some time before it will be finally settled." Voting, whether by colony, as was then the case, or in proportion to population, was a first hurdle to surmount. Edward Rutledge of South Carolina, so much in sympathy with Dickinson's views regarding separation, was distressed at some of the proposals. He wrote John Jay asking him to come down from New York for the important business of July 1 when the declaration and reports of the other two committees would be taken up. Dickinson had prepared a draft of a confederation plan; in Rutledge's view, it had "the vice of all his productions to a considerable degree; I mean the vice of refining too much. Unless it's greatly curtailed it can never pass. . . . If the plan now proposed should be adopted, nothing less than ruin [would come] to some Colonies." He feared

[23] Powell, *George Washington*, p. 138; *JCC*, 5:431, 433.

[159]

"making everything bend to what they call the good of the whole."[24]

Dickinson did not resolve all the divergent views. Time, for one thing, was too short. The chairman had studied the previous plans for confederation—those proposed at Albany, Galloway's plan laid before the First Continental Congress, and, less than a year before, the articles that Franklin had submitted to the Congress. He found strengths and weaknesses in the earlier proposals and concluded that only one solution was possible to achieve permanency: a strong union, in a sense "one and indivisible."

Not until July 12, a week after the Declaration of Independence was passed and Dickinson no longer present was the draft of the articles of confederation submitted to the Congress. Dickinson had avoided as many disputatious matters as he could. Uppermost in his mind was the need to submerge state jealousies by a strong national emphasis. Parochial viewpoints of the delegates were at once aroused by its unhesitating demands: "No Colony or Colonies, without the consent of the United States. . . . Every Colony shall abide by the Determinations of the United States. . . . The United States shall have authority for. . . . The United States shall have the sole and exclusive Right and Power. . . . No Colony without the consent of the United States. . . ." The negative brakes upon the colonies, for whom the very word *independence* had come to be so significant, were not eased by the article that declared "Each colony shall retain and enjoy as much of its present laws, rights and customs, as it may think fit, and reserves to itself the sole and exclusive regulation and government of its internal police." Even so these privileges were limited. Such rights were allowed only as long as they did not interfere with the articles of this confederation.[25] For example, although several colonies had various religious restrictions, the articles provided that religious toleration was to be enjoyed by every sect.

Committee members frequently differed with the chairman on many points; yet the whole clearly reflected Dickinson's philoso-

[24] Bartlett to John Langdon, June 17, 1776, Rutledge to Jay, June 29, 1776, Burnett, 1:476–77, 517.

[25] Powell, *George Washington*, p. 143; *JCC*, 2:546–54.

phy of government and his intention to provide strength to the central government. Above all else disunion must be avoided. Restrictions and amendments as well as further "refinements" were made by the Congress before final passage. Not until March 1, 1781, were the considerably revised Articles of Confederation put into effect. Dickinson's draft was remarkable, a considerable advance over similar plans for confederation in world history.[26] There was also good reason to regard him as "a master of legal subtleties."[27] And, significantly, the draft emphasized the "national government" of strength that he felt the parlous times required.

Monday, July 1, was the day set for the consideration of the proposed declaration of independence. The three preceding weeks had brought changes in the instructions given the delegates of various colonies. Every delegate seemed to have his own count as they took their seats.[28] Each colony was to vote as a unit, but many delegations were split.

After letters from general officers of the army to the Congress were read, routine business was acted upon. A resolution of the Maryland Convention removing restrictions was read, but a letter from the Provincial Congress in New York still restrained their delegates from voting affirmatively for separation, though some devoutly hoped for an imminent change. Nine colonies were needed to carry any such declaration. The New Jersey, Delaware, and Pennsylvania delegation votes were unknown factors. South Carolina under Edward Rutledge's influence was cool to the proposed measure. After Maryland's assent, approval of one other colony was necessary.[29]

The session then sat as a committee of the whole, and Benjamin Harrison took the chair. Lee's motion to adopt a declaration was

[26] Andrew C. McLaughlin, *The Confederation and the Constitution* (New York, 1905), p. 49.

[27] Merrill Jensen, *The New Nation* (New York, 1950), p. 25. See also Jack N. Rakove, *The Beginning of National Politics* (New York, 1979), pp. 151–58.

[28] *JCC*, 5:503.

[29] Ibid., 5:504–5 n.; Burnett, 1:408, 503–4, 514.

again laid before the House; a proposed declaration was likewise submitted. The adoption of the first motion became the issue of the day.

Dickinson knew exactly what the session foreordained. He also knew how the votes were likely to tally, more positively after the new Maryland instructions were read. That weekend he had sat down to write out his opposing views, a summary of all he had thought and expressed on so many occasions both public and private. What remains of this effort are a few introductory pages, notes, and a written-out conclusion.[30] Dickinson realized his fight was undoubtedly final. If any characteristic marked him, it was his fearless honesty. He never flinched at standing up to be counted. Dickinson was captain of the opposition, and regardless of the consequences, he did not intend to desert those who believed as he did and who had followed his leadership. He had risked his life, fortune, and security in the years past by unceasing opposition to British measures, but as their representative he did not willingly wish to risk the lives and security of his constituents.[31] Thus, when Dickinson rose to speak his final words of caution and regret, he observed: "I tremble under the oppressive Honor of sharing in its Determination. I feel Myself unequal to the Burthen assigned Me. I believe, I had almost said, I rejoice, that the Time is approaching, when I shall be relieved of its Weight. . . . My Conduct, this Day, I expect will give the finishing Blow to my once too great . . . [now] too diminished Popularity." To him the danger of setting forth on the uncharted course of independence was like braving "the storm in a skiff made of paper."

The appeal leaned upon history past and present, notably concerned with the timing which Dickinson felt made any declaration of independence inadmissible. He enlarged upon possible conflicts between Spain and Portugal, the alliance of Spain to France, the need for closer understanding between the American colonies themselves. The belief that such a declaration would animate the

[30] J. H. Powell put together Dickinson's speech opposing the Declaration from manuscript notes in the MDL Collection, HSP, and printed it in "Notes and Documents," *PMHB* 65 (1940):468–81.

[31] *Vindication*, in Stillé, p. 368.

people and in turn encourage foreign powers to send aid, Dickinson thought specious. Successful campaigns would win the colonies' support, not words. France, moreover, should be consulted in any such move. "We wait only for her determination to declare our Independence. We must not talk generally of foreign Powers but only of those we expect to favor us. Let us assure Spain that we never will give any Assistance to her Colonies. Let France become guarantee for us in [an] arrangement of this kind."

Not only should the colonies establish governments, but they together should take the form of a state. Though separation might be inevitable, it was in America's interest to keep Britain in the opinion that "we mean reconciliation as long as possible." It might even be that, having endured unsuccessful campaigns, Great Britain would redress all the grievances recited in the first Petition to the King.

Each advantage that had been set forth favoring the declaration Dickinson took up in turn and answered:

> The animating of our Troops? I answer, it is unnecessary. Union of the Colonies? I answer, this is also unnecessary. It may weaken that Union, when the people find themselves engaged in a cause rendered more cruel by such a Declaration without Prospect of an end to their calamities, by a continuation of the war.
>
> People are changeable. In bitterness of soul they may complain against our rashness & ask why we did not apply first to foreign powers, Why we did not settle differences among ourselves, . . . Why we did not wait till we were better prepar'd, or till we had made an experiment of our strength?
>
> A third advantage to be expected from a Declaration is said to be the proof it would furnish of our strength of spirit. But this is possibly only the first campaign of the war. France & Spain may be alarm'd & provoked with each other; Masserano was an insult to France. There is not the least evidence of her granting us favorable terms. Her probable condition the glory of recovering Canada will be enough for her. She will get that & then dictate terms to us.

Dickinson continued,

A partition of these Colonies will take place if Great Britain can't conquer us. To escape from the protection we have in British rule by declaring independence would be like destroying a house before we have got another in winter, with a small family; then asking a neighbour to take us in and finding he is unprepared.

It is claimed that the spirit of the Colonies calls for such a Declaration. I answer, that the spirit of the Colonies is not to be relied on. Not only Treaties with foreign powers but among ourselves should precede this Declaration. We should know on what grounds we are to stand with regard to one another. We ought to settle the issues raised by the Declaration of Virginia about colonists in their [western] limits. And, too, the Committee on Confederation dispute almost every Article—Some of us totally despair of any reasonable terms of Confederation.

Dickinson concluded unhappily, "When our Enemies are pressing us so vigorously, when we are in so wretched a state of preparation, when sentiment and designs of our expected friends are so unknown to us, I am alarm'd at this Declaration being so vehemently presented." Dickinson saw a "Doomsday Book of America" and wondered if in twenty or thirty years the commonwealth of colonies would not be too unwieldy and separate into two at the Hudson River.

Dickinson's address was recognized by his fellow delegates as a recapitulation of all the objections that had been said and written during the preceding months. John Adams, recounting the proceedings of that day, wrote that Dickinson "conducted the debate not only with great ingenuity and eloquence, but with equal politeness and candor."[32]

No member rose to answer Dickinson. It was a time for reflection. Finally Adams, recognized as the "author of all the mischief," felt compelled to give reply. After he concluded, the debate came to an end. The New Jersey delegation entered the hall late. They asked that the arguments pro and con be repeated. Adams summarized the various positions regarding the motion. The New Jersey delegates found the arguments "demonstrated not only the

[32] Adams, *Diary*, 3:396.

justice but the expediency of the measure."[33] The Committee of the whole proceeded to a vote.

The die was cast. New York abstained, Delaware was divided, South Carolina voted no. Pennsylvania's vote was three affirmative votes to four negatives cast by Dickinson, Robert Morris, Charles Humphreys, and Willing; James Wilson, influenced by the many pressures against his previous stand, deserted his mentor's camp. But the newly granted freedom of Maryland delegates to vote as they saw fit and now the New Jersey delegation brought the affirmative votes to nine.

Nine hours had exhausted the colonial delegates. When John Hancock resumed his chair and Harrison reported that Congress had agreed to the resolution for independence, Rutledge rose and asked that the official vote of Congress be deferred until the next day. It was so ordered. Congress adjourned with the expectation that South Carolina would certainly change its vote and just as surely that the Declaration of Independence would be adopted. John Adams, for all his vehement urging of that decision, now paused to speculate soberly on the results as if for the first time: "A bloody conflict we are destined to endure. . . . I don't expect that our new Government will be so quiet, as I could wish, nor that happy Harmony, Confidence, and affection between the Colonies, that every good American ought to study, labor and pray for, a long time."[34]

The oppressive heat of Monday was broken by heavy rain and thunderclaps on Tuesday. The question of independence was resumed. The outcome was already known.

Thomas McKean, when he found his vote and hence Delaware's affirmative stand checked by George Read's negative vote, sent a dispatch posthaste to Caesar Rodney, the third delegate, then in Dover. After an all-night journey, beset by many difficulties, Rodney arrived the next morning.[35] His vote placed Delaware in support of the declaration. South Carolina's men had met and, as ex-

[33] John Adams to Mercy Warren, August 17, 1807, Burnett, 2:523n.

[34] Adams to Samuel Chase, July 1, 1776, letter book, MaHS.

[35] John M. Coleman, *Thomas McKean: Forgotten Leader of the Revolution* (Rockaway, N. J., 1975), pp. 173–74.

pected, chose to side with independence. With New York asking to be excused from the count, Pennsylvania was the colony which could make the Congress's action united. Pennsylvania delegates made their individual decisions. John Dickinson and Robert Morris withdrew "behind the bar," and thus by their abstention Pennsylvania cast an affirmative vote. Congress could truthfully report that the Declaration of Independence had passed "without a single dissenting" vote of the colonies.[36]

Dickinson's position in those momentous days demanded moral courage. He did not shrink from the leadership that had been given him. Dickinson's constituents believed in him and would continue to show their esteem. Dickinson could not in good conscience refrain from a final summary of the conservative opinion on July 1. Then, on July 2, he faced the facts. To vote affirmatively would have been as emotionally impossible as it would have been insincere. Recognizing the need for Congress to speak with a single voice, he joined Morris in abstention and thereby assured Pennsylvania's support of the declaration. History is fickle. Continuing wrath clouded Dickinson's reputation from that moment; Morris escaped that fate.

Dickinson's great popularity and fame as a defender of liberty was tarnished more by the words of his foes than by his own words or deeds. He did lose "immortality" by not subscribing to the great document on independence. Ezra Stiles solemnly noted, "He now goes into oblivion or a dishonorable reminiscence with posterity."[37]

On July 3 the weather turned clear and cool, matching the settled tempers of the Congress. Rumors that British transports had arrived in New York harbor were rife. A letter from New Jersey asked for military assistance, and Congress immediately ordered the Committee of Safety of Pennsylvania to send as many troops as possible to Monmouth County. It also asked Pennsylvania counties to raise troops by battalions or companies quickly and march them to Philadelphia. Those assembled in Bucks, Berks, and

[36] Stillé, pp. 196–97.

[37] Franklin B. Dexter, ed., *The Literary Diary of Ezra Stiles* (New York, 1901), 2:182.

Northampton counties were to set out at once for New Brunswick.[38] The Philadelphia battalions of associators were mobilized and prepared to march northward to face the British in New York and to hold English sympathizers in check in Amboy.[39] On July 4 the arrival of 113 British transports at Sandy Hook was confirmed. Congress urgently requested a "Conference of the Committee of Safety, the Committee of Inspection of this City, the Delegates of New York, New Jersey and Pennsylvania, and The Commanding Officers of the Association, to devise the most expeditious mode of raising and marching the Militia of this Province to the assistance of the neighboring Colonies."[40] Britain had now shown its hand.

Dickinson, as colonel of the First Philadelphia Battalion of Associators, answered the call to defense with alacrity. Debate was over; military decisions were now of prime importance. Dickinson and his men were the first to leave for northern New Jersey. The strain of that week had left him exhausted and ill. After riding as far as Trenton, he was forced to rest there a day and continue the trip to camp by carriage. On July 10 he arrived at Elizabeth, surrounded by exhausted and sullen men upset by their sudden uprooting from their Philadelphia homes and confused by their own inexperience as military men.

[38] *JCC*, 5:508.

[39] Scharf and Westcott, *History of Philadelphia*, 1:329.

[40] *Minutes of the Provincial Council of Pennsylvania*, 10:631.

☆ 8 ☆

Outrageous
Fortune

A FORTNIGHT AFTER THE Declaration of Independence, Dickinson and the First Battalion of Philadelphia Associators were facing the British in northern New Jersey.

When the *Pennsylvania Gazette* of July 10 was published, Dickinson was already en route to Elizabethtown. But before he left, he learned the result of the meeting of the officers and privates of the fifty-three battalions of Pennsylvania associators in Lancaster. The Philadelphia companies had succeeded in preventing the Pennsylvania Assembly from nominating two brigadier generals of the militia. At the meeting the protest made by the officers of the five battalions of the City and Liberties was read and an election held which elevated Daniel Roberdeau and James Ewing to the rank of brigadier general. There were no legal grounds for their appointment, but the decision was accepted by the Committee of Safety and later agreed to by the Provincial Convention. Dickinson, who in February had successfully demanded his right as ranking colonel of the First Battalion to lead the march to New York, was now both ignored and outranked, although in the field with his troops. General Roberdeau, contrariwise, assigned to Philadelphia, thus stayed close to revolutionary political action.

Hugh Mercer was the general commanding North Jersey, with headquarters at Perth Amboy. Not until late in July did the Philadelphia militia finally take up its assigned positions. Mercer experienced difficulties almost daily. Even before the arrival of reinforcements, many of the Jersey militia expressed anxiety to return to their fields for harvest. There was trouble, too, from some loyalists who had taken up arms against the patriotic defenders.[1] Dickinson's first headquarters was at Elizabethtown. He was faced with both inadequate military supplies and, much worse, grumbling companies of militia. Problems of military supplies were most easily solved. Mercer at once ordered up ammunition and two pieces of cannon for the First Battalion's use. Steps were taken to build twenty "proper boats" to transport troops across the sound from Perth Amboy to Staten Island. A map of that island was prepared at Dickinson's request by Captain Mercereau.[2] A bridge was constructed across the Hackensack River and an armed vessel lay by to prevent attacks. Dickinson's force moved back from Brown's Ferry to the Rahway River, and a report of activity was then sent to the commanding general.[3]

But the most distressing problems Dickinson encountered were the threats of desertion by his men and the actual return of many to Pennsylvania. These fair-weather associators had not foreseen military action. Some had joined the battalion earlier in defense of their reputations or in a popular wave of enthusiasm. The sudden call to leave home and job was unexpected; sacrifice had not been envisaged. General Mercer asked Dickinson to use his "utmost address to induce the militia to perform their duty." One officer commented, "If Col. Dickinson will give his sentiments to the battalion this afternoon, I am convinced it will be effectual in quieting the present disturbance."

Dickinson made an earnest appeal. He pointed out that the soldiers had come at the request of Congress and any recall must be by Congress. The political leaders in Congress were the best judges

[1] Peter Force, *American Archives*, 5th ser., (Washington, D. C., 1853), 1:140; Leonard Lundon, *Cockpit of the Revolution: The War for Independence in New Jersey* (Princeton, 1940), pp. 115–20.

[2] Force, 1:620, 674.

[3] Hugh Mercer to JD, August 1, 1776, Item 14, L-D/LCP.

of military demands; "it is an act of disobedience to them to go back when they think we ought to stay. . . . Are they not wise and just? Have we not put everything into their hands and shall we set an example for undermining their authority? If others irritate us there is an end of the contest." He noted that measures had been taken to form what was called the Flying Camp for their relief and that he had spoken to General Livingston about their concerns as well as written to Philadelphia.[4]

Dickinson's reasoned words had no effect. On August 10 General Mercer informed Washington: "Colonel Dickinson writes me that thirty of his men have gone off with their arms this morning. I have written to the Congress to take measures to stop this infamous desertion, and the Convention of New Jersey to raise their militia to take up the [places of the] deserters."[5]

The First Battalion had just settled into camp when Dickinson received a letter from Daniel Roberdeau. The newly elected brigadier general was now active in the affairs of the radical Provincial Convention that had opened in Philadelphia on July 15. He requested the return of John Morris, Jr., and Jacob Garrigues, who had been appointed secretary and assistant secretary of that body. The tone of the announcement was cordial, Roberdeau noting, "I hope to have the happiness of seeing you soon."[6]

Dickinson had both feared and tried to head off the convention, which came to write the most radical constitution framed by any new state. Morris, Dickinson's cousin, kept him in touch with every action. In two weeks he wrote, "I wish most heartily that you could have been with them on this important subject," and he enclosed a tentative bill of rights which had been printed for the consideration of the members.[7] A few days later Morris reported: "It gives me the greatest pleasure to find, by all who come from camp, that you are regaining that influence which your su-

[4] Fragment of Notes of Dickinson's Appeal, n.d., Item 391, L-D/LCP.

[5] Force, 1:885.

[6] Roberdeau to JD, July 16, 1776, Item 24, L-D/LCP.

[7] Morris to JD, July 30, 1776, Item 24, L-D/LCP. The original printed Declaration of Rights in the LCP collection has significant changes and additions made by Dickinson.

perior wisdom and abilities must soon or later give you. For the sake of everyone who loves you, as well as for the sake of your country in general, cultivate it with the closest attention—for more than a thousand reasons,—it is absolutely necessary—I wish to God, you were here."[8]

Morris continued to forward news of the convention, although that body summarily dismissed Dickinson as delegate to Congress. He was also aware of the colonel's problems in the field. Samuel Morris, his son, was a member of the First Battalion, and he therefore knew the restlessness of the men in the ranks. Writing Dickinson, he promised:

> You may depend that the Convention is most sincerely in earnest to do everything in their power, consistent with the general safety, for the relief of the brave militia. . . . But to make this relief and the general safety to [come] hand in hand, is, you will know, the great Desideration. . . . Your letter to me last Sunday as also yours to the president of the 6th instant had a good effect in accelerating the measures taken. . . .
>
> Pray endeavor to impress upon the battalion and others the idea that the convention have not any object more at heart than the speedy relief and happiness of their brave and virtuous fellow-citizens.[9]

Mary Dickinson was faithful in her correspondence as well. She had had no letters, she wrote, from her husband since he had been in Trenton, but periodical reports from Jemmy Ewing, Tommy Franklin, and B. Lloyd had been welcomed. She was glad that he was apparently well accommodated. Plunket Fleeson, the upholsterer and cabinetmaker, was making a camp bed for him and would soon have it finished. As she wrote by the bed on which their baby lay asleep, Mary Dickinson could not help adding, "Ten thousand fears continually rack my tortured mind," thinking of the dangers he confronted.[10]

[8] Morris to JD, n.d., Item 24, L-D/LCP.

[9] Ibid., Sunday, August 11, 1776.

[10] Mary Dickinson to JD, undated letters and July 29, 1776, L/HSP, VIII, 74–75.

"Employed by a thousand various and new cares and attentions" to military matters, Dickinson wrote Charles Thomson: "Let me observe that no youthful lover ever stript off his clothes to step in Bed to his blooming beautiful bride with more delight than I have cast off my popularity. You may recollect circumstances, that are convincing, that my resignation was voluntary, I might have said ardent. Whether I shall ever put on the cumbersome robes [again] I know not and care not." Actually, Dickinson was still deeply concerned with affairs of state. He kept up with his correspondence. He wrote John Hancock requesting him to forward a letter addressed to him from England, and in his letter to Thomson he enclosed two others, one he had written General Lee, another to John Rutledge. He asked Thomson to "jog" Hancock and Robert Morris to answer his letters.[11]

A week later Dickinson wrote Thomson that "the enemy are moving and an attack on New York is quickly expected." He contemplated actual battles with equanimity.

> As for myself, I can form no idea of a more noble fate, than after being the constant advocate for and promoter of every measure that could possibly lead to peace or prevent her return from being barr'd up—after cheerfully and deliberately sacrificing my popularity, and all the emoluments I might so certainly have derived from it to principles—after suffering all the indignities that my countrymen now bearing rule are inclined if they could so plentifully to shower down on my innocent head, willingly to resign my life, if Divine Providence shall please so to dispose of me, even for the defense and happiness of those unkind countrymen, whom I cannot forbear to esteem as fellow citizens, amidst their fury against me. However, I covet not the glory of such an exit from the stage of life—where duty and honor require my presence, there I shall be—But much, much rather would I choose that these severe masters would give me up to my dear connections, my books and my fields, an intercourse and employment for which my constitution [is] better form'd, than to relish all the united glories, could I

[11] JD to Thomson, August 6, 1776, Thomson Papers, I, DLC.

attain them, of every heroic death from the Roman Curtius to the British Wolfe.[12]

Two incidents conspired to disturb Dickinson's peace of mind. Removed as a delegate to the Congress, he was even more depressed over a frank and revealing conversation he had had in his quarters on August 1 with an unnamed former political ally. The next day Dickinson drafted a tortured defense.[13] "Inexpressible was my astonishment at the detail of falsehoods you mentioned to be circulated against me concerning my expressions of sentiments relating to Presbyterians and their clergy—such as 'my having now discovered and abhorring the designs of that society in general and ridiculing the manners and pretenses of their ministers.'" These were indeed false rumors. He had innocently thought the coolness he had occasionally observed was due to his necessarily closer relationship by marriage to the Society of Friends and to certain jealousy. This

> jealousy of some gentlemen of merit, especially among the Presbyterians, desirous of drawing to themselves all the weight that could be derived from that body and a very convenient step to the attainment of this distinguished station was to destroy that confidence with which I had been so long, so uncommonly & so affectionately honored by them. I mean more especially Col. Reed and Doctor Rush. . . . Those two gentlemen, at a time when my breast contained as sincere and unsuspicious a friendship for them as they could wish . . . while on every occasion I religiously performed a friend's duty in vindicating their character from every reflection that came to my hearing—totally estranged themselves for me and did not act kindly with respect to my reputation.

He then defended his position regarding the Declaration of Independence. Dickinson remained firm in his belief that *"at this time,"*

---

[12] Ibid., August 10, 1776.

[13] Draft of a letter by Dickinson on which he noted, "A letter from me at Elizabethtown, August 25, 1776," box 6-D-90, box 1, Robert R. Logan Collection, HSP. Afterwards cited as RRL/HSP.

as he wrote General Charles Lee on July 25, separation would not promote happiness, asserting,

> I have tried, I have toil'd to thrust the belief of the proposition into my mind. I have represented myself, that you and several other good & sensible men think it as clear as any axiom in Euclid—that my reputation, at least by popularity, must inevitably be sacrificed by my obstinate heresy— yet, I have so much of the spirit of martyrdom in me, that I have been consciously compelled to endure in my political capacity the fires & faggots of persecution, rather than resign my impious persuasion.[14]

Dickinson did possess a "spirit of martyrdom." There was unhappy truth to the blunt reply to Thomson, who chastized him for his comments about his old allies. As only a "sincere and affectionate" friend may do, Thomson set forth just criticisms of Dickinson's attitude.

> I know the rectitude of your heart & the honesty & uprightness of your intentions; but still I cannot help regretting, that by a perseverance which you were fully convinced was fruitless, you have thrown the affairs of this state into the hands of men totally unequal to them. I fondly hope & trust however that divine providence, which has hitherto so signally appeared in favour of our cause, will preserve you from danger and restore you not to "your books & fields," but to your country, to correct the errors, which I fear those "now bearing rule" will through ignorance—not intention—commit, in settling the form of government.
> There are some expressions in your letter, which I am sorry for; because they seem to flow from a wounded spirit. Consider I beseech you and do justice to your "unkind countrymen." They did not desert you. You left them. Possibly they were wrong, in quickening their march and advancing to the goal with such rapid speed. They thought they were right, and the only fury they show'd against you was to chuse other leaders to conduct them. I wish they had chosen better; & that you could have headed them, or they waited a little for you. But sure I am when their fervour is

[14] JD to Lee, July 25, 1776, transcribed copy, HSP.

abated they will do justice to your merit. And I hope soon to see you restored to the confidence & honours of your country.[15]

Thomson's sound advice did little to comfort him. Dickinson sadly commented, "I desire nothing more from my countrymen than they should acknowledge the rectitude of my mind; and if they err on that point, I will strive to console myself by remembering that there is a Judge who cannot mistake. However, I trust they cannot err on that point."[16]

In mid-August, Dickinson wrote his aunt, Mrs. Mary Norris, that he was "remarkably hearty in body, and blessed be God, quiet and resigned in mind receiving every event that happens, not only with content[ment], but even with cheerfulness." News of an imminent attack on New York had arrived; "the State of America will be decided in a few weeks or days. Gen'l Washington has invited our militia to reinforce them. The duty is so evident, the occasion so vast, that I spoke to my battalion, and offered to lead them to New York, in defense of our Country, our wives, children and friends. I have not received their answer—whatever it may be, I feel a conscious satisfaction in having done what I *ought* to have done, *and no more*."[17]

George Ross and Thomas Matlack, both colonels, hoped a company might be formed from men belonging to the original battalions, and if that were possible, those "Brave and Worthy Associators" who had been in service for six weeks could return to their homes.[18] Finally, by September 1, Colonel Dickinson and his battalion returned to Philadelphia.

When in camp, although Dickinson had vigorously disapproved of the Provincial Convention being held in Philadelphia that July and August, in spite of himself he found the documents sent to

[15] Thomson to JD, August 16, 1776, L/HSP, VIII, 78.

[16] Draft of letter by Dickinson to ———, August 25, 1776, L/HSP.

[17] JD to Mrs. Mary Norris, August 14, 1776, MDL/HSP.

[18] Ross and Matlack to "Col. John Dickinson," August 29, 1776, Item 24, L-D/LCP.

him by Morris of great interest. He went over the first printing of the declaration of rights carefully. Parts of some articles he crossed out; to others he made additions.[19]

Among his suggestions was an emendation that government existed for the common benefit and that the people had the right to alter it. In the margin Dickinson explained: "Whenever the ends of government are perverted and public liberty is manifestly endangered by any magistrate or a treacherous combination of several, or whenever a government shall be found inadequate to the purposes for which it was framed, the people have a right and ought to establish a new [one] or reform the old government in such a manner as shall by the community be judged most conducive to the public level." Elsewhere he added that any man accused of crime should "be informed of the accusations against him and in due time to prepare for his defense," be confronted by his accusers and witnesses, be able to compel their attendance, and have the right to examine them. He believed "that the Freedom of the Press is one of the great bulwarks of liberty" and so noted. He likewise concurred in limiting the terms of elected officials, so that they "may be restrained from oppression." Dickinson at this point withheld much public comment, not because of his satisfaction with the document, but rather because there was too much to which he objected.

When, early in September, Dickinson returned to Philadelphia, the convention was still in session. He ignored it and stayed out of the city as much as possible, either remaining at Fairhill or visiting his Delaware plantation. He made no bones about the fact that his "honor had been repeatedly wounded" by many slights. Fellow officers kept him from precipitously resigning his colonelcy, as he had planned to do. Then on September 28 the convention confirmed the earlier choice of Roberdeau and Ewing as brigadier generals. Two days later Dickinson resigned his commission. He later explained that "I resolved, in the first place never to be accountable to such men [who led Pennsylvania] for any military command—secondly, to seek my fortune and a kinder usage in an-

[19] See the printed copy of the preamble to the constitution of Pennsylvania with Dickinson's marginal notes in LCP.

other state—and thirdly, to serve as a volunteer in the next call of the militia of the city and neighborhood, if it should happen before my departure."[20]

The regularly established government of the state was without power to act. The Pennsylvania Assembly had adjourned in June in embarrassment. When an attempt was made to reconvene in August, a quorum could not be obtained. A call in late September met a similar fate. Dickinson knew there was no use to pretend the Assembly elected in October 1775 still possessed authority. He did not bother to take his seat. Its responsibilities had been taken over by the convention.

The new constitution for Pennsylvania was distributed as a twelve-page folio and also printed in two Philadelphia newspapers. The Provincial Convention proclaimed loudly that their work had the approval of the people. The representatives, however, merely assumed all their actions were the popular will and that the citizens sanctioned the document they produced. Any unity in support of that document was soon lost in a cacophony of protesting voices. Complaints were aimed not only at the extralegal assumption of power by the convention but increasingly at specific details of the constitution itself.

Many former friends and sponsors of the convention joined the protests. Benjamin Rush, Christopher Marshall, George Clymer, and Thomas McKean for one reason or another found it unacceptable.[21] Termed ultraradical, it was certainly more democratic than those written in most other states, although the new constitutions of Georgia and Vermon bore certain similarities.

Supporters who had once hoped it might be a permanent document now sought to make the result temporary. Some criticism was aimed at the fact that a new class of people was now being brought into power through an extended suffrage. The arrogant manner in which the convention had acted, not only creating a

---

[20] *Vindication*, in Stillé, p. 392. This "Vindication," here and subsequently referred to, was Dickinson's own defense of his actions relative to accusations made against him in the Pennsylvania political campaign of 1782.

[21] David Hawke, *In the Midst of a Revolution* (Philadelphia, 1961), pp. 191–93.

frame of government but putting it into effect without submitting it to the people for a vote, was additional cause for antagonism. The bill of rights and the structure of government found specific complaints. Religion, the unicameral legislature, the dependence of the judiciary on a single House, the right of the new Assembly to impeach every executive or judicial officer before six members of the Executive Council, who themselves were dependent on the Assembly, and the lack of a court of appeals were all strongly criticized. Not least, the oaths to be taken by both the voters and the elected were loudly denounced. Every man before his vote could be cast, together with every elected officer of the government, had either to swear or affirm he would not "directly or indirectly do any act or thing prejudicial or injurious to the constitution, or government thereof, as established by the convention."[22]

Philadelphia opponents closed ranks. Dickinson once again was in league with McKean, who thought a formal objection to the new government so important that he came up from Delaware, where he was running for the Assembly.[23] The critics carefully planned a protest meeting. Printed tickets were distributed for a meeting in Philosophical Hall on October 17. That afternoon, Christopher Marshall reported, "a large number of respectable citizens [met] in order to set aside sundry and improper unconstitutional rules laid down by the late convention."[24] Of the assembled group another anticonstitution man observed that "all the rich great men and the wise men, the lawyers and the doctors" were on their side.[25]

The organizers hoped to forestall the proposed November election for the Assembly and to prevent the constitution from being put into effect. Colonel Bayard, once a proponent of the convention, was chairman of the meeting. Both sides were democratically

[22] J. Paul Selsam, *The Pennsylvania Constitution of 1776* (Philadelphia, 1936), pp. 224, 21.

[23] Coleman, p. 203.

[24] Marshall, *Diary*, entry for October 17, 1776.

[25] *Pennsylvania Gazette*, November 13, 1776.

heard. Dickinson and McKean spoke against the Constitution. James Cannon, Timothy Matlack, Dr. Thomas Young, and Colonel James Smith of York spoke in support of it. When darkness settled in, the meeting was adjourned until the following morning. Arguments of the day before were reviewed, and after mature consideration, resolutions were passed by "a large majority." In sum, the constitution was declared "confused, inconsistent, and dangerous." It was agreed that "no Counsellors ought to be chosen at the election to be held on the fifth day of November next."

Resolutions were only one part of the campaign. Explanatory letters, newspaper accounts, and the resolves were sent to friends in counties throughout the state. The Philadelphia objections came as a shock to delegates from the back country who had returned home pleased with the convention's work.[26] Philadelphia protests continued, however, and the constitutionalists were kept busy denying the allegations made against the new government. Broadsides were issued. After another meeting of citizens in Philosophical Hall on November 2, a flyer stating that there were more evils to the new frame of government than were "pointed out by the pen or tongue of any man" was circulated.[27] But the proponents still dominated the masses; it was apparent that the old government was dead. Undaunted, the opponents worked out a strategy they hoped would be successful: refuse to vote for any supporters of the new constitution, seek to dissuade all voters from taking the required oaths, and, finally, rather than vote for the Supreme Executive Council, vote whether any such councillors should be elected. Each side nominated its own slate of candidates to run for office.

In the election in Philadelphia City and County the anticonstitutionalist tickets won decisively. Dickinson once more was elected to the Assembly.[28] Many voters refused to take the prescribed oaths. However, the conservative Philadelphia representatives failed to win control in the Assembly. Western counties elected supporters of the new constitution, many of whom had been dele-

[26] Hawke, p. 92.

[27] *Pennsylvania Gazette*, November 13, 1776.

[28] *Vindication*, in Stillé, p. 391n.

gates either to the Provincial Conference or to the subsequent convention.

The minority, however, possessed a negative power in the Assembly. These members could prevent a quorum for legislative business by absenting themselves. The Assembly met on November 27, and only when Dickinson, Robert Morris, and Clymer threatened to leave was business begun. Having stated their opposition to the new constitution under which the Assembly was meeting, Dickinson, as spokesman for the dissenters, set forth their predetermined proposals for revisions.[29]

These were rejected by the majority. Dickinson thereupon left the Assembly. Looking back on that decision, he recounted that "the behavior of some persons on that day, and the disagreeable circumstance of entering into contests scarcely to be avoided with gentlemen I had for a long time esteemed, added to what had passed before" had caused him to retire.[30] The Delaware Assembly in November asked him to be their delegate to Congress, but he refused, citing bad health. He needed time for reflection.

The Assembly was paralyzed into inaction. A more pressing question of the moment, however, was the course of General Howe's army, which had invaded New Jersey and was heading south toward the Quaker City. Congress threatened to assume the responsibility of governing Pennsylvania if its Assembly could not do so. It forwarded requirements for military supplies and defense to the Council of Safety, which was acting as an executve body for the city and state. For these needs it granted large sums of money to the state.

By December 1776 Philadelphia was in a state of turmoil and confusion. On the second, the Council of Safety ordered shops and schools shut, and all energies were turned to the defense of the city. The Assembly now acted out of dire necessity. That body, however, lost members in the calls to join their regiments. Congress finally intervened and placed Philadelphia under martial law on December 10.[31] Families who were able to do so moved out

[29] Ibid.

[30] Ibid.

[31] *JCC*, 5:1017.

of the city to safety. On the twelfth Congress began a move to Baltimore where a temporary capital was to be established.

Dickinson made his own plans. First, sensible to the chance of harmful treatment toward his family by a conquering enemy in reprisal for his prominent political activities, he prepared for their removal from any possible scene of action. Second, he determined that he would stay behind and, enrolled as a private in the militia, help in the American defense.

Without consulting his wife, he arranged for a relative in Philadelphia to accompany Mary Dickinson and their little daughter Sally to Kent County, sixty miles south, to the Dickinson estate. The kinsman arrived and the carriage stood at the door. The resultant scene, Dickinson later wrote, was indescribable. Mrs. Dickinson refused to leave without her husband. Neither words nor promises would in any way appease her unhappy and agitated state. Dickinson had no alternative but to accompany his family to Delaware.[32]

The Dickinsons left Fairhill on the afternoon of December 12. Instead of taking the most direct route and the ferry to Chester, the family detoured, crossing the Schuylkill about a mile above the falls, to avoid the main highway crowded with refugees. The next day they lodged at the same inn as the John Hancocks, who were carrying their two-week-old baby toward Baltimore. On the fourteenth, the Dickinsons arrived at New Castle. At each stop they heard frightening tales of the Jersey occupation and the British advance.

The next morning Dickinson wrote his brother, then at camp where he faced the enemy advance. Philemon's family had already fled their New Jersey home and had found refuge in Maryland. Their estate, Belleville, was occupied by the British. The note was hurried and simple: "Receive no more continental money on your bonds and mortgages—the British troops have conquered the Jerseys, and your being in camp, are sufficient reasons—Be sure you remember this—It will end better for you." He did not sign the message, but sealed it, addressed it to "Brigadier General Phile-

---

[32] An account is found in the *Vindication*, in Stillé. A much-worked-over manuscript entitled "To The Public" adds to the published version, as do many unarranged pages of other drafts in L/HSP.

mon Dickinson, at the American camp," and sent it to Philadelphia. There the letter was given to Dickinson's black servant, who was told that passes issued by the Council of Safety were necessary to travel to the camp. When the servant was asked why he wanted the pass, the council learned about the letter.

The council had no reason to investigate a letter addressed to a general who was not only on active duty but was also commanding officer of the New Jersey militia. The spur to its action lay only in its suspicion and dislike of his brother John. The letter was seized and judged to be compromising; the unfortunate black was thrown in jail. The council then wrote General Washington explaining the background, enclosing a copy of the letter, and saying that although General Dickinson had requested it, the council was holding the original. It had already advised General Dickinson to contact his commanding officer, who would decide if it were proper to turn the message over to him.[33]

When the Dickinsons arrived in Kent, they had to crowd into only two rooms in their mansion house because it had been rented. Within a week, Dickinson learned of the seizure of the letter and the council's actions. The council had also seized Dickinson's yet-unoccupied elegant Chestnut Street house for use as a military hospital. Then came ill-natured rumors suggesting Dickinson had advised his brother to refuse all Continental money, to resign his commission, and to join the enemy, as well as statements that John had refused Continental money and was attempting to go over to the British.[34] Unhappily pressed by the conditions under which his family had to live, Dickinson was deeply tormented. He had only one recourse, that of facing his critics in Philadelphia. Ever mindful of his "reputation," he left his family and rode back to Philadelphia.

On Sunday, January 12, Dickinson arrived in the city. The successes of the American army at Princeton and Trenton had temporarily halted the expected British invasion and mitigated earlier

[33] Council of Safety to Washington, December 17, 1776, Force, *American Archives*, 5th ser., 3:1254–55.

[34] *Vindication*, in Stillé, p. 406.

fears in the Quaker City. Martial law still prevailed, however, and the Council of Safety ran the government.[35] Dickinson went directly to the lodge where the council sat. Only three members were present. They told him to return the next day. This he did. Dickinson complained about the council's confiscation of the letter and of the way they had gone on to represent his conduct in such a manner as to prejudice his reputation. He asserted that he appeared before them not as a criminal but to seek justice for the injuries done to him. To Dickinson's "very great astonishment" the answer was to the effect that

> they were induced to open the letter by a *complaint* made to one of the members, of my having refused to receive Continental money in payment of a debt, which *complaint* they *soon afterwards found to be false*; That their design in opening the letter was to *discover where I was*; that the servant was somehow or other sent to jail *by accident*; that my House was appropriated to the use of sick soldiers because of its *conveniency*, and would have been taken for this purpose, if I had been at home; that as a Council of Safety they had done no act to represent my conduct to the prejudice of my reputation and were not accountable for anything done by individuals of the Board.[36]

This was no figment of Dickinson's sometimes exaggerated sense of persecution. The radicals now in power were happy to humble him. He had opposed them not only on declaring independence but also on implementing the new constitution of the state. Indeed, he still hoped to overthrow it.

Dickinson demanded an inquiry, a public hearing, and a copy of the note he had written as well as the letter the council had sent General Washington. The council turned deaf ears to all Dickinson's entreaties. Not only did he regard their actions as cruel, but he charged that they had unfairly inferred that his writing of the letter was "unfriendly to *America*." To that David Rittenhouse, the council spokesman, replied that "he never regarded the letter

[35] Selsam, pp. 238, 240.

[36] Manuscript, "To The Public," L/HSP.

as any evidence of such intentions, but as a letter written by a person who dispair'd of the American cause, and he did not believe his brethren considered it in any other light."

Dickinson failed to receive satisfaction. Subsequently each day he returned to seek some favorable resolution of the matter. He threatened a direct appeal to the public if the council did not make amends. Over and over he explained what he had intended in the note to Philemon; that being paid by Jersey debtors in Continental currency at that time would embarrass Philemon since, being in the field, he had no chance to hold it securely; that he himself, contrary to rumor, had accepted such currency, actions he could substantiate. No apologies were offered. Then on Friday, Dickinson received word that there had been an accident on his estate and that his family sorely needed him. Heavy-hearted, he rode back to Delaware.

Dickinson could not rest. When he arrived in Kent he immediately sat down and wrote the Council of Safety setting forth all the arguments he had laid before them in person.[37] His goal was a formal apology. But the council considered the matter closed. Suspicion lingered in the public's mind, and five years later these charges were again raised to Dickinson detriment. The unfortunate incident rankled. Dickinson then would write an open letter to the public. But it was an exercise undertaken in vain.

The fear of British invasion across the Delaware River into Pennsylvania had been stemmed by Washington's victory at Trenton. Mrs. Dickinson and Sally returned to Fairhill as soon as possible. Dickinson saw them settled, but he did not linger long at their side. Although the Congress did not come back from its Baltimore seat until March, he resolved to stay in Kent County, far away from the critical atmosphere of Philadelphia. His anxieties over the conflict remained. The mounting military struggle caused him to write George Read and express a continuing hope for some accommodation with Britain; to him it appeared that "the winter is the only time that [is] allowed to think of peace before we suffer

[37] This was, according to the *Vindication*, written (finally) on January 21 (Stillé, pp. 405-7).

indescribable calamities!"[38] But the winter and spring passed without any such resolution of the war.

Early in 1777 General Howe determined on a new advance to Philadelphia. In July troops embarked in 160 vessels and sailed south along the Jersey and Delaware coasts. Moving up Chesapeake Bay, on August 25 they disembarked at Head of the Elk in Maryland, from whence the British troops moved eastward toward Newark. American forces were ordered to Wilmington the very day Howe's troops landed on the Eastern Shore. Eleven thousand regular troops, 1,800 Pennsylvania militia, a regiment of horse, and one artillery company went forward. In a brilliant and unexpected maneuver, Howe at Newark turned his men northward into Pennsylvania rather than continue to Wilmington. The British and American forces were finally engaged at Brandywine.[39]

General Caesar Rodney of Delaware with troops largely raised in Kent had been ordered by Washington to press forward to Head of the Elk and obtain American stores of ammunition housed there. The order came too late; the cache was already in the hands of the enemy.[40]

Dickinson took the action he had previously declared he would. Joining as a private in the local company raised by Captain Stephen Lewis which advanced to the Brandywine, Dickinson noted that he had served "with a musket upon my shoulder, during the whole tour of duty." On one mission Dickinson rode through the familiar countryside collecting much-needed ammunition and similar supplies. He was fearless in assignments, determined to prove his patriotism. On one occasion he boldly asked for fifty men to lead a sortie to the Christiana Bridge. Because the enemy surrounded that area and the mission would be a difficult one to undertake, General Rodney refused his consent.[41]

[38] Read, p. 2, letter quoting Dickinson, January 22, 1777.

[39] Benson J. Lossing, *Field Book of the Revolution* (New York, 1851–52), 2:168–178.

[40] Stillé, p. 394; Lossing, pp. 170–75.

[41] Stillé, pp. 214–15; *Vindication*, in Stillé, p. 394. Rumors of Dickinson's military activity were both frequent and often incorrect. Hannah Moore,

Washington failed to stop Howe at Brandywine Creek on September 11. The next day a British contingent advanced on Wilmington and seized the governor of Delaware. Thomas McKean, Speaker of the Lower House of Assembly, arrived in Delaware on September 20 and took over as chief executive. On September 24, recognizing Dickinson's value and experience, McKean appointed him a brigadier general. Dickinson refused the commission.[42]

General Howe continued his advance. On October 4 at Germantown the Americans were defeated again.[43] The intervening battle of Brandywine had prevented Mary Dickinson from returning to Delaware. Alarmed at the advance of the British, she sought refuge for herself and Sally with her Aunt Mary Norris in Philadelphia. Dickinson wrote her on October 30, knowing with some certainty of the British occupation and the impossibility of her continuing to live at Fairhill or in Philadelphia.

> My Dear Wife—Mr. Mifflin has been so kind as to undertake to come from Philadelphia with you and our dear child. I heartily rejoice in such an opportunity. Come immediately. . . . The carriage is at Bringhurst's; the harness James has. Mr. Mifflin engages to provide some way of getting you out of town. I wish you to lodge the first night at the Humphreys's; the next you may get to some friend's at Wilmington. I entreat that you will not cross the Ferry of Christeen. I also earnestly desire that you will not pass any ferry or bridge in the carriage; I beg earnestly that you and our precious one may get out at such places. . . . I dread your coming in a two-wheeled carriage. If any of your friends supply you with horses they shall be well taken care of.[44]

The arrangements worked, and the Dickinsons were reunited in Delaware. Less than a month later, on November 22, Fairhill

---

writing Milcah Martha Moore (Mrs. Charles Moore) on the "4th Day," 1777, wrote, "John Dickinson is aid-de-camp to Gen'l Rodney and was seen well since the Battle." (Thomas Stewardson Letters, I, HSP).

[42] Commission, September 26, 1777, and resignation, December 19, 1777, RSR/HSD.

[43] Lossing, pp. 111–13.

[44] JD to his wife, October 30, 1777, L/HSP, VIII, 8.

was put to the torch. In the belief that many of the large deserted county residences to the north of Philadelphia were used as hideouts by Americans, the British had begun to burn them. Seventeen houses in all were destroyed. Colonel Twistelton is said to have sent word to General Howe that he had burned "that damned rebel Dickinson's house."[45] It was reported that Galloway was present on the occasion and protested that the property was entailed to a minor. It was also rumored that it was through Galloway's efforts that further destruction by fire was stopped.

As soon as the British evacuated Philadelphia in June 1778, Mrs. Dickinson and Sally returned to Mrs. Norris's. In August she gave birth to a son who was named for his father; a month later the baby died.[46] The main building at Fairhill had been almost entirely destroyed, but the dependencies, including the library, had been saved. In December "John Dickinson of Kent County on Delaware, Esquire, and Mary his wife" conveyed the plantation called Fairhill, containing about 498 acres to Mary Norris, effective in July 1790, subject to the leases then held by tenants.[47] The intention of Mary Dickinson's father was thus resolved by the transfer to the male line of the Norris family.

Dickinson remained in Kent. In 1778 he contracted with Joshua Underwood to build a four-horse stable, such as he had erected elsewhere for Dickinson, and a shed with corncribs and mangers next to it, a hen house, a bathhouse fifteen feet square, a distillery —all of hewn logs—and a frame pigeon house. A new roof was to be put on the mansion, and all the buildings were to be completed before Christmas 1780, the priority of each to be decided by Dickinson.[48] There was no doubt that he had made up his mind to continue living in Delaware.

That fall he visited his family in Philadelphia and had opportunity to gauge the political mood of Pennsylvania. On November

[45] Stillé, p. 315.

[46] Family Bible, L/HSP.

[47] Conveyance of Property, December 14, 1778, witnessed by John Mifflin, Jr., and Isaac Norris, L/HSP.

[48] Business papers, L/HSP, XXXV, 79.

28, 1778, the Pennsylvania Assembly resolved to give the people a chance to vote on the constitution in April. But after receiving disapproving petitions, the Assembly rescinded the referendum.

The state of the new nation was even less encouraging. The Declaration of Independence had not engendered the enthusiasm that had been predicted. Confidence had almost given way to despair. Washington and his army were at White Plains watching Clinton in New York City, while the British launched their southern campaign. Currency problems were acute. Paper money was issued without backing. States did not fill the military quotas as requested by the Congress. General Washington seemed correct when he stated that "America was on the brink of destruction."[49]

On February 1, 1779, Delaware again asked Dickinson to become its delegate to the Congress.[50] Dickinson this time accepted the appointment. Caesar Rodney, McKean, and others in power in Delaware were considered radicals. George Read, a moderate, doubtless had urged McKean to appoint Dickinson as a delegate. Dickinson did not take his seat until April 23.[51]

With his formal commission, Dickinson brought Delaware's ratification of the Articles of Confederation, a document considerably amended since he had drafted it. He found old friends among congressional delegates, but many other earlier leaders whom he admired were no longer present. The Congress welcomed him back, as did John Jay, who congratulated him on the appointment to "a place which you formerly filled with advantage to your country and reputation to yourself."[52]

Caesar Rodney had become president of Delaware State, and an official correspondence now began between these two Kent County neighbors. Late in April, Rodney wrote about "a matter which gives me and, I think, must give every real friend to American

[49] Stillé, p. 219, quoting Washington. Also see Washington to John Augustine Washington, May 12, 1779, John C. Fitzpatrick, ed., *The Writings of George Washington* (Washington, D. C., 1936), 15:57–62.

[50] Order of the (Delaware) Council ratifying the Articles of Confederation, Ryden, pp. 293–94, 300n.

[51] *JCC*, 14:501.

[52] Stillé, p. 217, quoting Jay to JD, March 22, 1779.

Independence great concern—I mean the management in the Quarter-Masters and Commissaries departments." The enormous costs of forage, provisions, and transportation he feared would ruin "one of the most glorious causes a people ever engaged in." Dickinson agreed about these problems, and, in late May, the Congress took up the need for retrenchment and reform in these departments. A committee was appointed for this study, and Rodney was pleased to find the Delaware delegate's name was "at the head" of it.[53]

Dickinson informed Rodney that

> we have most momentory business to transact. It may happen in managing the affairs of so extensive a Confederacy, that particular states may be more interested in certain points than other states or than the confederacy in general.
>
> My opinion is clear, that the interest of each state being objects comprehended within the Confederation, are to be regarded as the interests of the whole, & as such to be contended for and defended. [On] interests of this kind, difficulties, I apprehend, will not arise, but on interests beyond these limits they may. On these, my opinion is also clear, that as a delegate I am bound to prefer the general interests of the confederacy to the partial interests of constituent Members, how manysoever they be, & however respectable and meritorious; and further, that if ever such a competition should arise, it is my duty to prefer the particular interests of the State that honours me with her confidence & invests me with a share of her power, to the particular interests of any other state on this continent.[54]

Financial problems of the new country were paramount. On May 11 a congressional committee of three consisting of Dickinson, William Henry Drayton, and James Duane was appointed to "prepare an address to the several states on the present situation of affairs, and particularly on the necessity of paying their respective quotas." On May 25 the document was presented to Congress. In its final form it was the work of Dickinson. The address, pointing

[53] Rodney to JD, April 29, 1779, L-D/LCP; *JCC*, 14:754, 622; Rodney to JD, June 13, 1779, Loudoun Papers, HSP.

[54] JD to Rodney, May 10, 1779, Ryden, pp. 300–301.

out the increasing depreciation of the Continental currency, emphasized the need for immediate efforts to stem the "mischief."
Its conclusion was a stirring appeal:

> Fill up your battalions—be prepared in every part to repel
> the incursions of your enemies—place your several quotas in
> the continental treasury—lend money for public uses—sink
> the emissions of your respective states—provide effectually
> for expediting the conveyance of supplies for your armies
> and fleets, and for your allies—prevent the produce of the
> country from being monopolized—effectually superintend
> the behavior of public officers—diligently promote piety—
> virtue, brotherly love, learning, frugality and moderation;
> and may you be approved before Almighty God worthy of
> those blessings we devoutly wish you to enjoy.[55]

Indeed, as Dickinson told Thomas Rodney, Caesar's brother, in
July, the currency difficulties were "prodigious," and with the
daily and hourly rising cost of purchases, loans and taxes seemed
almost purposeless.[56] His own hope was to prevent further remis-
sions of paper money, a very unlikely possibility.

During the summer of 1779 the future control of North Atlantic
fisheries revealed sectional concerns and personality conflicts in
the Congress. Arthur Lee and Silas Deane, who with Benjamin
Franklin beginning in 1777 had been American commissioners to
France, had feuded over details, and charges of mismanagement
arose. Both were eventually relieved of their responsibilities.
Deane was a friend of Charles Thomson; Lee was supported by
John Adams. The Lee-Deane conflict entered the halls of Congress.
New Englanders and allies, the so-called Lee-Adams interest, were
opposed by Dickinson, Robert Morris, and Secretary Thomson.[57]

Dickinson's position on the fishing rights was not only opposed
to that of his northern colleagues but, unhappily, also contrary to
that of his Delaware colleagues, McKean and Nicholas Vandyke.
Dickinson did not want either fishing rights or commercial rights

[55] *JCC*, 14:569, 649–57.

[56] JD to Rodney, July 22, 1779, Gratz Collection, HSP.

[57] Business papers, L/HSP, XXXV, 79.

to interfere with other projected peace efforts. He decided to write out his views to President Henry Laurens, explaining his position and deploring the growing animosity toward him for his stand. It was once again an almost paranoiac complaint. At the same time he stated proposals that he hoped would lead to peace with Britain. Dickinson eschewed negative criticisms yet he determinedly voiced his opinion on these matters, certain that they would stand the test of time. He declared that he was not inflexible:

> Two Rules I have laid down for myself throughout this contest, to which I have constantly adhered, and still design by the Divine favor to adhere—first—on all occasions where I am call'd upon as a trustee for my countrymen to deliberate on questions important to their happiness, disdaining all personal advantages to be deriv'd from a suppression of my real sentiments, and defying all dangers to be risqued by a declaration of them openly to avow them; and Secondly—after discharging this duty, whenever the public Resolutions are taken, to regard them the opposite to my opinion as sacred because they lead to public measures in which the Commonweal must be interested, and to join in supporting them as earnestly as if my voice had been given for them.[58]

On July 29 differences within the Delaware delegation were resolved. It was finally decided that if, after a treaty of peace had been concluded, Great Britain molested any American citizen or inhabitant while he was taking fish on the banks in the North Atlantic or elsewhere in the area, such an action would be considered a common cause of the states should Congress declare it a breach of the peace. Later Dickinson submitted a resolution that would require assent to these rights by both France and Spain as well as guarantees for free commerce and navigation of the Mississippi.[59]

Dickinson prayed that the year would crown all the labor to that end "with peace, Liberty—Safety." In June he wrote President Rodney and, after noting military successes in South Carolina,

[58] JD to Henry Laurens, July 22, 1779, Laurens Papers, South Carolina Historical Society.

[59] *JCC*, 14:896–97.

declared: "Let us all at this important crisis intensely recollect our duties to heaven & our country—cooperate in our several stations with the efforts of our gallant brethren in the field, and after vanquishing lions in fair fight, not suffer ourselves to be ruined in our internal & domestic affairs by the most contemptible vermin that ever crept upon the earth."[60]

In his letter to Laurens, Dickinson also regretted that congressional movement toward peace was so slow. He enclosed a "Draft of Instructions for the Negotiation of Peace" proposing several resolutions to be conveyed by a minister plenipotentiary appointed to treat with Great Britain on the subject. A treaty of peace, he thought, ought to be concluded before a treaty of commerce should be made. If Britain should refuse a treaty of "perpetual peace" and propose a truce in its stead, Dickinson would have regarded that favorably. But in all instances the Alliance of 1778 demanded that France and Spain be consulted.

Dickinson had already been criticized for his position in the fishing rights dispute. He now feared that other "reproaches" would be incurred as a result of the peaceful stand he proposed. Nevertheless, he vowed to Laurens that he would act in the way he himself deemed honorable, saying, "If the present day is too warm for me to be calmly judg'd, I ever credit my country for justice some years hence."

Dickinson's fears were not justified. President Laurens appointed Dickinson to two committees, one to draft the commission for a minister plenipotentiary to Great Britain and the other to state the terms for the negotiation of a treaty of amity and commerce with Great Britain. Each of these proposals passed. In addition, the French minister, about to return to the Court of Versailles, had raised questions about a treaty with Britain. Dickinson was called upon to answer Minister Gerard's parting statements to the Congress and prepare a message for him to carry to the French king.[61]

The conflict over Deane, who had by now returned to America, and Arthur Lee, who had remained in Paris, continued. In June,

[60] JD to Rodney, June 10, 1779, RSR/HSD.

[61] JCC, 14:744, 922, 1018.

Lee was recalled. Dickinson had a warm and affectionate esteem for Lee, and his vote against his old friend was a painful one to cast. In the debate over the question, Dickinson failed to speak in Lee's favor. His final decision was made because of Lee's coolness toward his fellow commissioner at the Court of Versailles and his serious differences with Dr. Franklin. To comfort his brother on the recall, William Lee suspiciously suggested that "the conduct of D-k-n may be accounted for, as he was always violently against *Independence*. He acted, spoke and voted against it! Therefore, he may have designs of oversetting Independence."[62]

His climb once again to patriotic recognition and political power had been slow, but his months in the Congress in 1779 served as catharsis for John Dickinson. The eager earlier radicals, such as Rush and McKean and President Rodney, found themselves in accord with him. Political success was next achieved at the polls, and Dickinson was again to win it first in Delaware.

[62] JD to Arthur Lee, March 30, 1780, letter draft, Item 19, L-D/LCP; William Lee to Arthur Lee, September 28, 1779, Worthington C. Ford, ed., *Letters of William Lee* (Brooklyn, N. Y., 1891), 3:753.

Reentering
the Arena

Dickinson had done yeoman's service in Congress in 1779. He did not return in 1780 but sought time for reflection. No subject was so dear to him as prospect of peace. He had exerted every energy to that cause.

The climate of the country had changed. The years 1779–80 were years of defeat and despair. Examples of selfishness and of refusals to cooperate under law were everywhere apparent. Yet in Philadelphia, Dickinson noted a belligerent determination to support the war. He knew well enough that an active and radical minority counted more than a divided or apathetic majority. There had even been violent assaults on persons and property. On October 5, 1779, a mob of armed citizens and dissatisfied militiamen, angered by internal war profiteering, moved up Walnut Street to the beat of drums toward the house of James Wilson. There conservatives and moderates, patriots all, helped in the defense of "Fort Wilson." Only the arrival of President Reed, backed by city militia, dispersed the crowd at a critical point in the confrontation.[1] Delaware also was bitterly divided politically and often at the mercy of loyalist disruptions and tory raids inland from the bay.

On his trips to his estates in Kent, Dickinson found relief from

[1] Frederick D. Stone, "Philadelphia Society One Hundred Years Ago," *PMHB* 3 (1879):390–93; also *PMHB* 5 (1881):475–76.

the radical violence of Philadelphia and the political dissensions of Delaware. Mary Dickinson, however, was always unhappy there. To avoid miasmic summers in Jones Neck with the usual plague of mosquitoes and other insects, she spent those months in the Quaker City. Her husband's acceptance of the commission as a Delaware delegate to the Congress in 1779 temporarily eased their domestic problem. At the close of that year the three Dickinsons dutifully returned to Kent. There were times, of course, when Dickinson had found it necessary to leave Mary and Sally at the Delaware plantation. Concerned about his wife's reticence, he urged her to go out and visit their friends in his absence and to enjoy other activity.[2] Mary, trying to make the best of her residency there, had transferred her letter to the Duck Creek Friends' Meeting.

Now on his arrival at Jones Neck in the fall of 1780 he wrote Mary:

> Our place affords a luxuriant Prospect of Plenty—the clover lawn as green as a favorable Season can make it—About twenty head of cattle grazing and gamboling over the verdure—The trees bending down to the grass with red and reddening apples—peaches & damascenes without number. Two mills promising by their flow sounds like fine cider & spirits, prodigious fields of corn—a beautiful sheet of buckwheat flowering—the winter grain is all peeping out of the ground—& around the house as many turkeys & chickens of various broods as you or our precious one would wish to see—What blessings—What gratitude should they excite— With such sentiments & with your company—partaking how would they delight![3]

Yet neither bucolic life nor plantation responsibilities deadened Dickinson's mind to the pressing problems of the day. Efforts toward peace with Britain in 1779 had not succeeded. He believed that the time once again was ripe to urge Great Britain to acknowledge American independence. Not military success but the per-

[2] Susannah Wright to Hannah Thomson, February 7, 1779, L/HSP; Letter, May 19, 1781, L/HSP, VIII, 88.

[3] JD to his wife, September 30, 1780, L/HSP, VIII, 86.

sistent determination of the people to win should be considered. There were four persuasive reasons for Britain to come to terms. America had no intention of giving up.

> 1st—The *Unanimity* of America in support of independence. All information to the contrary is utterly false—the only people discontent with that declaration are those who will not bear arms & the creatures of the late government....
>
> 2nd—The zeal of America in support of independence. ... If G[reat] B[ritain] could conquer the sea coast—a vast multitude would retire over the mountains and carry on a War aggrivated [*sic*] by every consideration [?] which must end in G[reat] B[ritain]'s being driven from the continent— all language is too faint to represent the ardor of America on this head.
>
> 3rdly—Her strength—such an army as we never had before. Our people growing up yearly & more than repairing the waste of war—arms & military exercises as the amusements of our youth—They grow up soldiers as they do tradesmen & husbandmen.
>
> 4th—Our resources—we have endured *all we can* by stopping foreign imports—our distress was great because the methods for supporting ourselves internally were strange & new—We have endured the first shock—How our inventions & supplies, go hand in hand with our wants.[4]

Immediate peace would result in good terms for Britain; delayed efforts on its part would bring worse conditions. To whom his reasoned appeal as a private citizen was addressed we do not know. His sense of duty was strong. He certainly had no desire to see military conflicts continue and he saw a chance to influence the course of events propitiously.

In Delaware the lack of political unity was disastrous. George Read in 1780–81 held conservative power in New Castle County, while Caesar Rodney had won earlier support from the more radical forces in Kent and Sussex. New Castle reflected mercantile views; the two lower counties, agrarian opinion. At best, the three counties of the state were reluctantly revolutionary, divided not

4 Undated manuscript, L/HSP.

only by economic interest but also by religious persuasion.[5]

Early in December 1780, through Read's efforts, Dickinson was chosen by a vote of 179 to 12 to fill a vacated New Castle seat in the Delaware House of Assembly. In reasoned detail, seasoned with flattery, Read urged Dickinson to accept. He cleverly pointed out that, apart from the desire of the electorate, Dickinson's private interests were involved. Read believed that after a few more years of careless and ignorant mismanagement such as Delaware was experiencing little property would be left to be cared for. If whigs and tories worked together for better government, a beneficial calm should result.[6]

Dickinson, looking to Pennsylvania for political advancement, refused the seat. He bided his time, making frequent trips to see his wife and daughter. In mid-August 1781, shortly after arriving in Philadelphia, he received a letter from William Molleston in Dover. The news was shocking.

> Yesterday morning a party of refugees consisting of 15 men and boys were so hardy as to come as far as the house, confin'd every person that came in their way as they did the servants till they plundered the house and kitchen of all provisions and liquors except a small keg of cherry rum, they apply'd themselves to the furniture of which they took blankets, sheets, all the curtains—leaving the parlour and book room or study untouched for want of time and a team to carry them off. They left no piece of plate they could find—no acc't of their being in [St. Jones] Neck came to Dover till after the[y] had left your house. . . . We went with about 60 men but too late to effect anything, they having taken the nearest way to the beach . . . at the same time asking the Negroes if any of them would go with them. They all refused except a Negro man of the name Isaac.

That same day letters arrived from Sheriff McComb and Charles Ridgely, a neighbor, who further assessed the damage. The marauders reportedly had told the Negroes that "they would rather

[5] J. H. Powell, "John Dickinson, President of the Delaware State, 1781–1782," *Delaware History* 1 (1946):16–17.

[6] Read to JD, December 2, 1780, Item 14, L-D/LCP.

have their Master than all they had taken."[7] Dickinson left at once. His losses were estimated at more than £1,500.

Raids along the coast of Delaware Bay by British marauders and by loyalists had been frequent. This unhappy incident continued to show that many still saw Dickinson only as the early agitator and opponent. Contrariwise, in Pennsylvania his political enemies continued to call his patriotism into question.

In the Pennsylvania election of October 9, 1781, Dickinson's name was listed as candidate for the Assembly from the Northern Liberties. Delaware politicians at the same time continued to solicit his participation in their state campaign. Read was certain to win power over Caesar Rodney, who was about to leave the presidency of Delaware after three years in that office. Dickinson, however, had no natural constituency in Delaware though he owned property in both Kent and New Castle. He continued to assert that he had no wish to pursue a political career in the state. Nevertheless, on October 1 he was elected to the Executive Council of Delaware from New Castle County.[8] Dickinson declared his disinterest, but news from Philadelphia the following week changed his mind. He had been viciously attacked in the Pennsylvania campaign. Those who made up what could be called the Militia party, which supported the new Constitution, once again had used Dickinson's stand against independence to his detriment.

Dickinson understood the problems facing the small state of Delaware torn between patriots and loyalists. McKean had written him about the use of Continental money as legal tender, the need to put Delaware regiments on a "respectable footing," and the neglect of the civil government, particularly in the administration of justice. If the latter was not corrected, McKean asserted, "the country will be governed by a parcel of ignorant and extortionate men." McKean had declined to serve any longer as a Delaware delegate to the Congress, not having received "a farthing" for two years; Nicholas Van Dyke found it necessary to take the same step.

[7] Molleston to JD, August 11, 1781, L-D/LCP; McComb to JD, August 11, 1781; Ridgely to JD, August 10, 1781, L-D/HSP.

[8] *Pennsylvania Packet*, October 9, 1781.

Caesar Rodney, also, as president, alert to the deficiencies of Delaware, had not hesitated to seek advice from Dickinson.[9] George Read, Rodney's political opponent, also renewed his efforts to win Dickinson's involvement.

Mary Dickinson, although unwilling to move to Delaware, wrote endearing letters to her husband after his return there to assess the damage to his mansion. She expressed a wish that he would not remain as long at the plantation as he usually did. "Love me, I deserve it," she wrote, "if for no other reason for loving thee with an affection founded on virtue." More and more she had become dependent upon her husband and desperately lonely during his prolonged absences. Gentle in all her ways, Mary Dickinson at the same time, and indeed early in their marriage, demanded his attention. Her own family had been close-knit and the distaff side found little interest outside Meeting and kin, of whom there were many. In part this accounted for her not accompanying John to Dover. Dickinson wrote her often. She responded unhappily, "I never suffered so much in my life as I do now." In addition she worried about her husband's spiritual welfare, writing him,

> I endeavor to leave ev'rything belonging to me to that Gracious Being who has led me to this day of trial—Let me entreat thee my dearest frd by all the tyes of a love that reaches beyond the grave—not to give up that anchor which has been there. Thee has been led thro' scenes of great difficulty—think not all is vain—but be assured we may possess eternal substance, that will endure when ev'ry fleeting vision shall be no more—remember me the weakest of mortals—and be an assistant in virtues rugged path.[10]

As Dickinson continued to supervise his plantation, he faced the need to avoid financial loss in a time of easy paper-money payment. He accepted some rents in grain and for others made contracts that were sometimes severe. He kept his records in meticulous

[9] McKean to JD, December 25, 1780, draft letter, L/HSP; Rodney to JD and George Read, June 6, 1781, MDL/HSP, III.

[10] Mary Dickinson to JD, n.d., and September 24, 1781, MDL/HSP.

order, noting sales and payments, the hides tanned, the yarn purchased, and spinning production.[11]

Dickinson still had a half dozen slaves living on the Delaware plantation. Without his wife to care for them as his mother had once done, they were a burden. Increasingly, too, their services were not needed since most of his land was leased to others. These factors, perhaps combined with Mary's aversion to the institution of slavery, led to Dickinson's decision to manumit his slaves in Kent in 1781. On September 29 Dickinson executed a deed of manumission for six of his remaining slaves: Joseph Martin, 40; Violet, 30; William, 20; Pompey, 14; and two girls, Nancy and Rose. According to the law, which required security for any slaves manumitted, four of these were indentured for different terms, while Violet chose to remain in the Dickinson service, and another black was similarly retained. Two other slaves were unaccounted for, and Isaac, who had run away with the tory refugees, was ignored.[12]

The Delaware Assembly was set to meet on October 20 to choose a new president. Though Dickinson protested his election to the Council, he did not refuse service. The day before, on October 19, Thomas Rodney in Wilmington wrote his brother Caesar in Dover suggesting it would be difficult to find a presidential candidate who would meet with "general approbation." He predicted that Dickinson would be appointed Speaker of the Council and Caesar Speaker of the Assembly. In that case Rodney believed that Dickinson would not stay in the state, and the government would thus once again devolve on Caesar Rodney in lieu of an officially elected president.[13]

The Assembly did not obtain a quorum until the twenty-fifth. When the oaths were administered, Dickinson assumed a Quaker stance and chose to affirm his allegiance to the state and then de-

[11] The R. R. Logan Collection, HSP, contains bundles of receipts, contracts, and similar documents, formal and informal. Notebook for 1781, Item 28, L-D/LCD.

[12] Powell, "Dickinson, President of Delaware," p. 11.

[13] Thomas Rodney to Caesar Rodney, October 19, 1781, Ridgely Papers, HSD.

clare his faith rather than taking an oath as he had always done before.[14] This action subtly marked a change in his religious attitude, as did the freeing of his slaves the month before. One senses the influence of his absent wife, whose letters so often implored Dickinson toward new religious commitments.

With new vigor the Assembly and Council got down to work, aroused to increased energy by news of the American victory at Yorktown.[15] The Assembly found strength in the association of Read in the House and Dickinson in the Council of which Thomas Collins was named speaker. Two important measures of immediate concern were those dealing with reorganization of the militia and with piracy of Delaware Bay. At once, drawing on his extensive knowledge in this field, Dickinson prepared a bill covering militia organization, training, and administration. The second problem involved the raids up the small streams that flowed into the Delaware Bay such as the one from which Dickinson had suffered. He drafted a bill for "punishing and discouraging offenses committed in taking vessels out of the Harbours of this State" and removing trials of those captured from the admiralty courts to local courts, which were more likely to judge offenders severely.[16] Of the many bills passed during the three weeks the Assembly met, he wrote six of the most important ones and prepared notes in support of another five. This session laid a firmer foundation for Delaware's future than had any since independence was declared.[17]

On November 6, before adjournment, both houses of the Assembly met to ballot for the new president. Seven councillors and nineteen members of the House were present. John Dickinson received twenty-five of the twenty-six votes cast for the office. His own ballot was the lone dissent. Dickinson's greatest worry now lay in reporting the decision to his wife. He wrote her the next day: "Yesterday I was elected unanimously by both Houses of the Legis-

[14] Delaware Miscellany, Minutes of the Council of Delaware State (hereafter cited as MCDS).

[15] Powell, "Dickinson, President of Delaware," pp. 26–30, 31, 32.

[16] Both the proposed bills in Dickinson's hand are found in the 1781 Legislative Papers, Public Archives, Delaware State, Dover.

[17] Powell, "Dickinson, President of Delaware," p. 32.

lature President of this State, notwithstanding the most positive and solemn declarations by me, that I could not accept the office. In short, it is absolutely forced upon me with one voice not only of the legislature, but of the people. How to avoid [it] I know not." Indeed, the day before the election, he had sent off the servants and household goods to Christiana Bridge where they were to be loaded on shallops for Philadelphia. He asked Mary to speak to Dr. Rush, who had been among his most active political sponsors in Philadelphia, and to inform him of the unexpected turn of events which he had been unable to prevent.[18] Pennsylvania's rejection of Dickinson at the polls was at the same time softened by the confidence Delaware showed him.

On November 13, 1781, Dickinson celebrated his forty-ninth birthday by being inaugurated president of Delaware State. In his acceptance speech, he questioned his ability to discharge the office as well as his supporters expected, but, health permitting, he declared that his integrity, the common cause, and his love of country might make up for any other deficiency. Dickinson challenged the Assembly to determine what laws should be altered, repealed, or made anew. He ended with an appeal that reflected the best spirit within him.

> May a happy harmony, in sentiment and measures, so beneficial to society, always prevail among us, or, if there must be division, let it only be between those who generously contend for the freedom, independence and prosperity of their country, and such as weakly wish for a dangerous and dishonorable submission to enemies. . . .
>
> Let us more and more promote a spirit of benevolence, equity and liberality, and heartily join together in discouraging every kind of vice and immorality, being assured that "Righteousness exalteth a nation, but Sin is a reproach to any people."[19]

War breeds profiteering and other evils as part of the violence and the moral laxity attending it. Delaware suffered from fluc-

[18] JD to his wife, November 7, 1781, L/HSP, VIII, 8.

[19] MCDS, pp. 677–99. The original of this address is in the R. R. Logan Collection, HSP.

tuating prices, inordinate costs of goods, and cheating within the Commissary Department. The virtue envisaged by early patriots had been overwhelmed by greed and selfish interest. Dickinson, six days after his inauguration, issued a Proclamation against Vice and Immorality. In the largest sense this was a clarion call to unite a people. It posed a philosophy of government in which Dickinson saw the state as the creative force determining a prosperous and happy citizenry. It assailed the evils of "Drunkenness, blasphemy, profane swearing, profanation of the Lord's Day" as well as evils of "Gaming Houses, and other lewd and disorderly houses." All judges and magistrates were charged to enforce, with dispatch, the laws against such violators. The state was seen as the responsible agent for maintaining an orderly and healthy atmosphere.[20]

The public and private reactions to President Dickinson's proclamation were immediate. He had struck a popular note which set forth a path for government to follow and which marked a new leadership for Delaware.

Dickinson had expected to rejoin his family in Philadelphia by November 18. He delayed nearly a month and then advised his wife that it would be necessary to live in Wilmington. He received attractive offers for a residence there, such as Thomas Rodney's own house. But Mary Dickinson hesitated to pull up stakes, just as her husband had hesitated to cut the political lines that bound him to Pennsylvania. Finally, in the summer of 1782, a decision was made, and a house was prepared for them. But they were never to occupy it.[21]

In the meanwhile, the enthusiasm that Dickinson's actions engendered in Delaware was reported in the Philadelphia newspapers with steady frequency. Much remained to be cleared up from Rodney's term as governor, and new legislation to stabilize the state was put into operation. Military matters were in particular disarray. Since the British had marched across the state four years before, Delaware had not raised its quota of troops to serve the

[20] The proclamation was published as a broadside in Wilmington in a run twice the number of broadsides usually being printed.

[21] Thomas Rodney to JD, May 22, 1782, Gratz Collection, HSP; *Colonial and Revolutionary Documents of Delaware*, 2:760–61.

Confederation. Dickinson promised General Nathanael Green, then with Delaware regiments in South Carolina, to institute vigorous measures to fill the ranks at once.[22] A similar problem was the lack of funds to pay both officers and men. Some officers even advanced sums from their own pockets to support the families of indigent privates. Among Dickinson's early official actions was his promise, made to a Captain McKennan, that he would "on all occasions receive a singular pleasure in forwarding every measure of relief or benefit to such of my fellow citizens as are encountering difficulties and dangers in defense of their country."[23]

The Assembly met in Dover on January 9. In his message on the nineteenth, President Dickinson reviewed the steps that had been taken by the Continental Congress to assure "political happiness."[24] The prognosis was good: victory had been achieved by the army at Yorktown in October, French aid continued, the vexing currency problems were in the process of reformation, and trade was increasing. But relaxation on the part of the state and its citizenry, he believed, was the greatest danger to be faced. A major worry lay in America's movement away from France. Britain had sought to separate the two countries, and now, although the war was not yet over, America was becoming careless about maintaining ties to its ally.

Relations between Delaware and the Confederation required deliberate and immediate compliance. Foremost was the need to forward the funds Congress required. There were other measures to be provided as well. General Washington in December had written that a temporary hospital was to be established at Wilmington to care for wounded soldiers brought from southern fields of action. The state was requested to find and furnish a suitable building for the purpose and to obtain carriages to bring forward the incapacitated soldiers from Head of the Elk. Delaware could provide only the building. The treasury was empty and unable to

[22] JD to Greene, October 24, 1781, Item 60, L-D/LCP.

[23] Finney to JD, January 15, 1782, JD to Captain McKennan, November 14, 1781, draft letter, Items 60, 23, L-D/LCP.

[24] *Colonial and Revolutionary Documents of Delaware*, 1:123–27.

pay for the purchase of wagons, firewood, straw, and other supplies. Dickinson lent funds of his own for all these desperately sought items.[25] In his message to the Assembly he ignored his own generosity but underscored the need for hospital resources and medical officers.

Many other responsibilities had to be assumed: a cooperative undertaking with Pennsylvania and New Jersey in clearing the bay and river of marauders, an increase in the recruitment of militia, codification of laws regarding such service, establishing provision for clothing Delaware regiments, and seeking better regulation and collection of taxes.

The Assembly rose to the challenges the president set before them. Acts were passed in all instances; and, underscoring the state's place in the Confederation, four new delegates to Congress were appointed. The choices were strange yet in large measure determined by two factors: the need for the state to have two men always present on the floor and the lack of money to pay the delegates sufficiently for their service in Philadelphia. James Madison had suggested a financial saving by appointing out-of-state delegates.[26] The representatives designated were Caesar Rodney, then in Philadelphia; Thomas McKean, once from Delaware but now chief justice of Pennsylvania; Samuel Wharton, a Pennsylvanian who had only two years before returned from England but now was a resident of Philadelphia; and General Philemon Dickinson, the governor's brother, whose home was in New Jersey. The latter two held more moderate points of view than the others. Only Rodney was a "proper" Delawarean, although McKean and Philemon Dickinson owned property in the state. With the exception of Rodney, opponents termed the men "foreigners." It was Wharton who, although friend of both George Read and the governor, had most criticism leveled against him.[27] Dickinson himself wrote

[25] Washington to JD, December 3, 1781, Fitzpatrick, *Writings of Washington*, 23:368–69.

[26] Read, pp. 279–80, quoting Madison.

[27] Column by "A Watchman of Delaware," *Pennsylvania Journal*, April 6, 1782; Thomas Rodney to Caesar Rodney, February 9, 1782, Ryden, pp. 432–33.

the instructions for the delegates, specifying in great detail their duties and the measures Delaware expected them to sponsor or support. In case of uncertainty in the question of decisions to be made, the delegates were to communicate with the president of the state, who in turn would consult with the legislature should it be necessary to obtain their advice.[28]

Spring arrived and once again ships in the bay were preyed upon. In early April, after boldly seizing a loaded shallop at a wharf at New Castle, British and Loyalist raiders attacked a schooner at anchor. Although the enemy had been driven away by townspeople, raiders at some distance fired "four pounders" into the town.[29]

Financial matters were a concern of all the states, yet even more serious were monetary deficiencies of the Confederation. Robert Morris, superintendent of finance, reported to Congress the dire financial straits in which the country found itself. In November 1781 eight million dollars had been requisitioned from the states. All failed to levy taxes to supply the amount. Congress, almost at bay, appointed two committees to visit the states and to confer secretly about this serious financial state of affairs. Dickinson was in Pennsylvania visiting his family in May, and George Clymer and John Rutledge met with him there. Their account was shocking. For one thing, states used all their tax collections for their own needs. It seemed imperative that each state have separate levies, one for themselves and another for Continental use. Delaware's financial debt owed to the Confederation was clear. Moreover, while the state was obligated to have had a complement of 679 men in its regiment, only 190 men were in the field. France, now without financial resources and itself forced to borrow, could no longer lend financial support to America.[30]

Speedy action for corrective measures was imperative. Despite a smallpox epidemic in Dover, Dickinson called for the Assembly to convene as quickly as possible. On June 14, he appeared personally before a joint session, and the next day he sent a formal

28 MCDS, pp. 715–17.

29 *Pennsylvania Packet*, April 4, 1782.

30 Powell, "Dickinson, President of Delaware," pp. 115–16.

message to the Assembly recommending that the state send congratulations to the French ambassador on the birth of the dauphin and include a resolve that no peace negotiations would be contemplated except with France. No action should be permitted that would separate America from France. Although Britain's ministry had changed, its purpose had not; instead it bent "the force against our friends, and at last [would] return to the accomplishment of the original object—our destruction."[31] On the domestic side, he emphasized the need to eradicate the public debt.

In response the Assembly unanimously resolved that the French alliance would be strictly maintained and no treaty with England made without France's concurrence; it agreed that Delaware should take every measure to strengthen Congress in an effort to obtain "peace consistent with our federal Union and national faith." It passed an act that separated tax accounts into two parts and another that made it possible to levy realistic congressional taxes on land despite the fluctuating monetary values. It also made appropriations for the Delaware regiment and appointed a committee for codification and publication of state laws. Brief though it was, the Assembly session provided strong measures.[32]

Resolutions on the birth of the dauphin were followed by a celebration of rejoicing in Dover on June 22. Dickinson viewed it as a diplomatic affair. An elaborate triumphal arch with appropriate inscriptions was erected, and at twelve o'clock militia and officers ranged themselves on a line with assembled artillery and fired a "few de joye." An account Dickinson carefully sent to the Philadelphia newspapers reported that "the highest satisfaction was expressed by every person present on the auspicious event that contributes so much to the happiness of our august ally and the French Nation." Afterward the president, the legislators, and army officers dined together. Thirteen toasts were drunk; the last pledged: "May the independence of America add to the happiness of Mankind in every part of the World." A month later, in Philadelphia, President Dickinson attended an elaborate reception cele-

[31] MCDS, pp. 728–31.

[32] Powell, "Dickinson, President of Delaware," pp. 119–20.

brating the dauphin's birth in the house and gardens of his Chestnut Street mansion, now rented to the French ambassador.[33]

Raids from the bay continued, and tax income remained inadequate for state requirements. Dickinson, on his personal bond, again borrowed money for Delaware's most pressing needs. The militia, both in recruiting and in organization, presented difficulties. Throughout the summer the president sought remedies for improvement. He proposed a military review in October of all the companies and alerted General Thomas Collins in Kent, John Dagworthy in Sussex, and Samuel Patterson in New Castle to that end.[34] Militia laws were sent to the leaders, and 450 abstracts of Baron Steuben's treatises were forwarded for distribution. Dickinson, the state's commander in chief, came down from Philadelphia for the purpose, first stopping to review the New Castle regiments under General Patterson. He progressed leisurely down the state road and after a three-day ride arrived at Lewes where he spent four days reviewing the regiments under Colonels Hall and Polk. Dickinson then turned back toward his mansion at Jones Neck and reviewed the Kent County troops under General Collins. He devoted ten days in all to this task and was pleased at the improvement obtained within that year.[35]

The Assembly met again on November 1. In his message Dickinson informed the legislators of the progress of the peace negotiations and other developments of the Confederation. But other matters had intervened to win his attention. Pennsylvania, like a siren, lured him from the now more peaceful waters of Delaware to the rougher seas of that state's politics.

When, in October 1781, Dickinson was proposed as a candidate for the Pennsylvania Assembly, it had been fully expected that he would be elected. A counterrevolution was in the making, but it had not succeeded in reaching full strength. The controlling radi-

---

[33] "Rejoicings on the Birth of the Dauphin," Item 4, L-D/LCP; "The French Fete in Philadelphia in Honor of the Dauphin's Birthday, 1762" (letter by Benjamin Rush), *PMHB* 21 (1896):260.

[34] Letters of these commanding officers are in the MDL and RRL collections, HSP.

[35] Powell, "Dickinson, President of Delaware," p. 129.

cal party owed a measure of its continuing success in the elections to illegal pressures, gaining votes from the militia.[36] Nor were the conservative anti-Constitutionalists united on their own candidates. Dickinson's defeat was part of this struggle.

While Dickinson was serving in Delaware, Pennsylvania politics continued to boil. On the one hand were those radicals, at times violent, who supported the constitution and continued to control the loyalty of the militia. Opposed to them were the Republicans, conservatives who founded the Republican Society and still sought to overturn the new constitution. They largely represented mercantile and commercial interests rather than the "mechanics," who supported the older Presbyterian party. William Moore, a moderate Constitutionalist, had been elected president of the state in 1781, but James Potter, a hard-line radical, was vice-president. The Assembly chose Frederick A. Muhlenberg, a Republican, as Speaker, and that majority faction held an upper hand throughout the year, particularly in financial undertakings. The Republican forces now sought to gain support on current issues rather than simply to assail the state's constitution.[37]

On October 10, 1782, Dickinson, president of Delaware, was elected to the Supreme Executive Council of Pennsylvania. Benjamin Rush sat down that morning to write him and to predict an auspicious outcome: "The day is at last come that will give freedom and happiness to Pennsylvania. . . . The wishes, the hopes, the affections of every good man in *our* State now centre in you." The president of Pennsylvania, by law, was chosen from among the councillors by the Assembly. Dickinson doubted that the Republicans would be able to control the vote, telling Rush, "[Our] opponents are indefatigable, and stimulated by their private interests." However, Charles Pettit of Philadelphia, in a letter to a Maryland friend, General Otho H. Williams of Baltimore, had predicted that "Mr. Dickinson, the present Governor of Delaware State, will be transplanted in the Chair of Pennsylvania. . . . There is no other member of Council that can with decency be raised up

[36] R. L. Brunhouse, *The Counter-Revolution in Pennsylvania, 1776–1790* (Harrisburg, 1942), pp. 105–7.

[37] Ibid., p. 120.

as a competitor. He is a man of education and of polished manners, but I should think him better adapted to a time of peace than of war."[38]

Upon his election, Dickinson went up to Philadelphia. In their marriage of thirteen years four children had been born to Mary and John. The first child, called Sally, had lived, and was now twelve years old. Three other children had been born to them, a daughter and two sons. The first two died shortly after birth; the second son was stillborn in 1779. On November 6, Mary Dickinson, aged forty-three, gave birth to a fifth child, called Maria, who was to live and bring them increased joy. Dickinson, who would be fifty-one within a week, did not attend the Council meeting that day. The next morning, however, he was in the chair, and later with other members joined the House in the Assembly Room of the State House. By a vote of 41 to 32, he was then elected president of Pennsylvania over James Potter, a Radical. James Ewing became vice-president.

As soon as the Pennsylvania Assembly finished counting the presidential votes on November 7, Dickinson was officially proclaimed "Captain General and Commander-in-Chief in and over the Commonwealth of Pennsylvania." A procession was then formed beginning with "Constables and their staves, Sub-Sheriffs with the wands, [the] High Sheriff with his wand, Coroner with his wand, Judges of the Supreme Court" and all other officials, as well as the "Provost and Faculty of the University, General and field officers of the militia, [and] Citizens." They marched in rank to the Court House at the foot of Market Street. There the proclamation was publicly read, and Dickinson and Ewing took the oath of office required by the constitution.[39]

In his acceptance of the office, Dickinson issued a challenge: "Let every individual constantly remember, that he is a citizen as well as a man—Let him love his country, that is his fellow citizens

---

[38] Rush to JD, October 10, 1782, Rush Papers, HSP; JD to Rush, Dover, October 28, 1782, Winterthur Museum Library Manscript Collection (60x6, 1–7); Pettit to Williams, October 15, 1782, O. H. Williams Papers, II, 165, Maryland Historical Society.

[39] *Colonial Records*, 12:414–16.

and be as anxious for their combined glory and happiness as for his own. . . . May Pennsylvanian faith become the common expression to signify consumate honesty in public affairs."[40]

Dickinson immediately wrote to John Cook, the Speaker of the Delaware Legislative Council, directing him to assume administrative duties of that state, but for two months Dickinson was president of both Pennsylvania and Delaware. Then, on January 11, he sent a message to the Delaware Assembly explaining as best he could his reason for accepting Pennsylvania's call and pointing out his earlier protest at Delaware's action of the previous year in honoring him.[41] His formal resignation came on January 14. The Delaware Assembly took his desertion with little grace, believing it not only contrary to the spirit of the constitution but "inconsistent with the dignity, freedom and interest" of their state.

Response to Dickinson's election was immediate. John Jay, in Paris, wrote John Vaughan in Philadelphia that "Mr. Dickinson has talents and good intentions: and I think it will not be his fault if Pennsylvania does not derive advantage from his administration —Parties must be expected in Republics and provided the people are well informed, their errors are seldom of very long duration. Newspapers will sometimes be licentious but they had better be so than in the contrary extremes." Testimonials to President Dickinson's sagacity and honor arrived to cheer him: from the inhabitants and freemen of Germantown Township, from the officers of the troops in the Continental Army, and from many others.[42]

But the congratulations failed to offset bitter, virulent, personal attacks being made on him in the newspapers by one who signed himself "Valerius." The attacks had begun on October 30 in the *Freeman's Journal* before his elevation to the presidency and continued throughout November. The Constitutionalists, realizing they were almost certain to lose control of the Assembly, had also been conducting a vendetta in the press. As Dickinson later stated,

[40] Undated notes of Dickinson in his inaugural address, Item 56, L-D/LCP.

[41] *Colonial and Revolutionary Documents of Delaware*, 2:760–61.

[42] Jay to Vaughan, Paris, February 15, 1783, Madeira-Vaughan Collection (B, V462), APS; Asamead Scrap Book, p. 38, HSP; Address of . . . German Lutheran Churches, Item 53, L-D/LCP.

"I stood still—cast away all defense—and bared my breast to receive every blow, either openly or covertly aimed at me."[43] Indeed, he went so far as to write the English-language newspaper publishers in the city, noting the attacks against his character and stating that he was willing to have all pieces published against him, but that he would prefer they print "nothing in his defense or Favor."[44] After his election as president, the personal assaults grew more violent. Dickinson bided his time and promised his associates that in due course he would give answer to the charges against him.[45] On December 24 Dickinson's first letter in his own defense, addressed "To my Opponents in the late Elections of Councillor . . . and of President," appeared in the *Pennsylvania Gazette*. Others followed in the next four weeks, all giving evidence of his anguish. They were republished by the three other Philadelphia papers.

Dickinson had specifically been charged with four actions that were considered disloyal: he had opposed the Declaration of Independence, disapproved of the new state constitution, deserted his battalion when it became a part of the Continental Army, and weakened public confidence in Continental currency by advising his brother to refuse acceptance of it. Dickinson attempted to answer each in turn.

Dickinson could not refute the charge that he had opposed the Declaration of Independence. He had led the opposition right down to the first day of July. He now explained that he had believed the action inevitable but that he considered its timing unpropitious, that allies should have been obtained before such action occurred, and that articles of confederation were first necessary to bind the states together.

The record was also clear on Dickinson's opposition to the new state constitution. He avoided any defense of his actions on this point, although he did not reject his previous position and his advocacy of an orderly revision.

[43] *Vindication*, in Stillé, p. 365.

[44] Notes, L/HSP, VIII, 90.

[45] Benjamin Rush to John Montgomery, November 26, 1782, Rush Papers, HSP.

The charge that he deserted his battalion was patently false. Nevertheless, Dickinson carefully outlined his military service for those who may not have known about it. He pointed out that after resigning his colonelcy of the First Battalion and retiring to Delaware, he had served with the militia as a private when the state was invaded by the British and, that still later, he had refused a commission as brigadier general.

Of the four accusations, the one that dealt with the unsigned note to his brother advising Philemon to refuse Continental currency was the most difficult to explain. When the Council of Safety refused to forward it and in other ways took punitive measures, Dickinson had sought to offer suitable explanations. He repeated these now, but they still sounded specious.

Had Dickinson either refused to answer or at most replied in one brief column in the newspaper instead of five long ones, the effect might have been more successful.[46] All the Republicans had felt stung by the charges against him; they did not want their success turned into ashes. Moreover, after the barbs directed at the president were concluded, "Valerius," in subsequent columns, had attacked other Republican favorites such as John Montgomery, James Wilson, and Speaker Muhlenberg.[47]

Dickinson's replies were everywhere discussed. To some they may have seemed adequate. James Otis, of Massachusetts, asked Dickinson for another copy of this "vindication," writing his one-time associate, "Within a few weeks indeed have fallen into my hands part of your publication since your elevation to the chief seat in the power of a grateful country . . . [news] from the pen is at all times devoured with the greatest avidity by me and others, [and] form but an imperfect idea of the whole."[48]

The identity of "Valerius" has never been discovered. Contemporaries thought it might be Joseph Reed, but Reed himself wrote Dickinson to correct an error in the "Vindication," a statement that he had opposed the constitution, and Dickinson apologized.

[46] Powell, "John Dickinson as President of Pennsylvania," *Pennsylvania History* 28 (1961):254–63.

[47] *Freeman's Journal*, January 15, 1783.

[48] Otis to JD, February 10, 1783, L/HSP, VIII, 94.

Certain members of the Dickinson family laid the blame on John Armstrong, Jr., who in March became secretary of the Supreme Executive Council. Yet this accusation is unlikely unless Armstrong was wholly dishonest in a letter written to his father, an old friend of Dickinson, describing "Valerius" as "an angry turbulent fellow." He further suggested, "It is cruel to disturb his [Dickinson's] term of sufferings and toil till October next—especially when we consider the bed of thorns he has sat upon 6 long years."[49]

The state had set aside the handsome house of Mrs. Grace Galloway as the presidential residence. Located on the southeast corner of Sixth and Market streets, the property had been confiscated following the defection of Joseph Galloway to England. On his removal from the mansion, Joseph Reed, as outgoing president, sent a note to his successor, and Dickinson at once set about making repairs to the house for which £150 had been appropriated.[50] The house was little over a block from the State House. As the new president walked to the Council Chambers there, he passed the garden of the mansion he had so hopefully and indeed lovingly built, but in which he had never lived. Throughout the Revolutionary War years it was the residence of the French ambassador and subsequently the home of his brother Philemon and his family.

Moving into the President's House entailed many considerations, not the least of them being furnishings. Probably little had been saved in the destruction of Fairhill, but library armchairs at least had been among the salvaged items, similar to ones that had been made for the Logans of Stenton. Once again Dickinson could plan for a stylish house in Philadelphia and order new furniture. The chairs and sofas were in high style. The chairs bore great similarity to those ordered by Charles Thomson, and one of the sofas is attributed to Thomas Tufft. The ensemble was both handsome and elegant, a measure of Dickinson's taste and position.[51]

[49] Brunhouse, pp. 124–25; Reed to JD, January 4, 1783, L/HSP, VIII; Armstrong, Jr., to Armstrong, February 26, 1783, *PMHB* 5 (1881):108.

[50] Reed to JD, n.d., L/HSP, XXXVI, 6.

[51] William McPherson Horner, *Blue Book of Philadelphia Furniture* (Philadelphia, 1935): Joseph Downs, *Philadelphia Furniture: The Queen Anne and*

Now with the whole family settled in Philadelphia, Mary formally rejoined the Philadelphia Monthly Meeting.

Dickinson's Proclamation against Vice and Immorality had achieved such a warm and healthy response in Delaware that the new president decided to issue a similar proclamation in Pennsylvania. This he did on November 20. Enthusiasm for such a moral, corrective position proved limited. The French ambassador reported that although the Presbyterians were happy with the proclamation, Dickinson had displeased the Episcopalians, many other sects, and atheists.[52]

Morality had little to do with Dickinson's most vexatious problem as chief executive—border disputes. Pennsylvania and Connecticut settlers still struggled over claims in the Wyoming Valley, and the southwestern boundary of Pennsylvania was likewise disputed between that state and Virginia.

No permanent boundary line separated Pennsylvania and Virginia in the southwest, and settlers' protests thwarted attempts to run even a temporary line there. The whole question was further complicated when Congress sought to have the states cede their western lands to that body. Not until 1783 did Virginia and Pennsylvania, in order to establish a boundary between themselves, name a commission with four members representing each side.[53] The determination was a happy event in President Dickinson's first year. When the commissioners were finally appointed, Dickinson outlined instructions for them, including five-mile markings in the extension of the Mason and Dixon Line with physical observations recorded for future mapping of the area.[54]

Chippendale Periods (New York, 1972), vol. 3, items 273, 137. One of the armchairs is in the Dickinsoniana Collection, Dickinson College; another is at the Dickinson Mansion in Dover. A pair of Dickinson's sidechairs are in the Historical Society of Pennsylvania; sofas are at the Winterthur Museum.

[52] *Colonial Records*, 13:433–35; La Luzerne, Correspondance Politique, Etats-unis, XXII, Ministière Affaires Etrangères.

[53] Brunhouse, pp. 113–14; John E. Potter, "The Pennsylvania and Virginia Boundary Controversy," *PMHB* 38 (1911):418. Dickinson's "Proclamation Fixing the Boundaries" was made March 20, 1783.

[54] Penn Papers, Pennsylvania Miscellaneous, Penn and Baltimore, 1768–1834 (March 28, 1794), p. 107, HSP.

The Wyoming Valley conflict and the violence among settlers there, which Dickinson had considered almost fatally divisive before the Declaration of Independence, were brought to what was hoped to be a final conclusion by a special court established by Congress. In 1778 the Congress had sent troops to this disputed area lying along the northern branch of the Susquehanna. Peace was possible only as long as the soldiers were stationed there.[55] A trial before the Court in Trenton brought James Wilson and Joseph Reed into temporary harmony in their defense of Pennsylvania's claims. The "Trenton decree" of December 30, 1782, declared that Pennsylvania had jurisdiction in the disputed area. Much of the land was owned by Pennsylvania Republican land speculators, a fact that helped taint the political resolutions of the question.

In his first presidential message to the General Assembly in 1783, Dickinson noted the judicial resolution of the conflict, considering this a "peaceful and conclusive settlement" of the dispute. But the disputes in the Wyoming Valley persisted. Problems lay not so much between the two states as between the settlers' claims. Dickinson believed the settlement of claims by magistrates should be adequate to preserve the peace. Connecticut settlers in the area petitioned Connecticut delegates in Congress for help in assisting them. Edward Hand, as a Pennsylvania delegate, urged Dickinson to have the Assembly explain what the state had already done so that "we may be able to show the humane and generous intentions of that Honorable Body towards those people."[56] But the legislature was irked at the continuing dissension. Dickinson resisted the assembly's wish to send in more troops than the two companies previously detailed there. He also opposed the appointment of John Armstrong, Jr., the Council's secretary, as adjutant general because Armstrong was anathema to the Connecticut settlers. Nevertheless, Armstrong was sent to the Wyoming section.

In a proclamation of October 5, 1783, President Dickinson re-

[55] *JCC*, 11:636, June 23, 1778; *Pennsylvania Archives*, 1st ser., 6:371, 9:510–11, 674–724; 11:431–59; *Colonial Records*, 13:10–11, 426, 475–77, 486–90.

[56] Hand to JD, January 17, 1784, Dreer Collection, HSP; see also Hand to JD, April 2, 1784, Gratz Collection, HSP.

viewed the action of the state in appointing commissioners the previous February and expressed hope for a friendly compromise with the settlers, putting an end to the violent confrontations that had occurred in May, July, August, and September. Pennsylvania would continue to seek remedy for those whose cases merited "considerations of equity or humanity."[57]

The Connecticut delegates continued to raise the question in the Congress. Yet neither Pennsylvania nor Congress took any immediate action. The Wyoming Valley remained a festering problem until 1786 when, after the Radicals had assumed political control of the commonwealth and Dickinson was out of office, adequate moves were made toward the settlement of land titles.

Peace rumors had been circulating since the surrender of Cornwallis at Yorktown in 1781. Dickinson had long hoped for that happy resolution to the war, but now he was suspicious of Britain's intentions. On New Year's Day, 1783, he wrote General Anthony Wayne, "The best informed here think we shall have peace next spring. I cannot believe it. . . . It would not be surprising if the *apparent zeal* of Great Britain in negotiating should prove an artifice to draw from the belligerent powers demands, afterward to be laid before Parliament as 'incompatible with the dignity of the crown and the essential interests of the Kingdom'—for the purpose of inflaming the nations to a continuance of the war." But peace did come. Preliminary articles were signed and after ratification by the American ministers plenipotentiary and their allies, France and Spain, the United States in Congress announced the declaration on April 11, 1783. Dickinson issued a proclamation announcing peace on April 16 to be read throughout the state.[58]

Dickinson was concerned with the lack of financial support for the officers a.:d soldiers who had fought the war. In 1781 there had been a near disaster in a mutiny of the Pennsylvania Line. Demands had been for immediate relief in pay and in physical needs; a march on Philadelphia had been repulsed only in the nick of time. When, in the beginning of 1783, the end to the war seemed certain, the weaknesses of the Confederation, so loosely held to-

---

[57] *Colonial Records*, 14:219, 224.

[58] JD to Wayne, January 1, 1783, Wayne Papers, XIV, HSP.

gether by the conflict itself, became more apparent. Robert Morris, superintendent of finance, continued to set forth the exigencies to be dealt with, but his urgent messages fell on deaf ears. The army, officers and men, faced a bleak future with all the promises of bounties, grants, and pay ignored. Reaction was inevitable.

On March 11, at Newburgh, New York, an anonymous address, written by John Armstrong, Jr., confirmed the problems of demobilization. The officers asserted their intention to remain under arms until all financial debts had been satisfied by the Congress. Taking a strong position, Washington succeeded in quieting the revolt. Then, as commander in chief, he advised the Congress that it should not disband the army until all accounts had been settled.[59] The Congress, on its part, had hoped to furlough the men before final settlements were made. A compromise was effected which gave the men the choice of either accepting immediate furlough or remaining under arms until all accounts were satisfied. This Washington announced as an order on June 6.

The Newburgh address was only one event of that highly volatile spring. Congress was still divided into factions: some members favored even greater decentralization, others opting for more centralization. With peace, the trend lay toward diminishing any strength for the Confederation, which, in turn, increased the role of the individual states.

Philadelphia had become a seedbed of rumors. Some soldiers who had been a part of the mutiny of 1781 were in the barracks there. Ships bringing restless Pennsylvania veterans from southern theaters and Maryland troops, who had agreed to furloughs, arrived on June 12. All rumors sooner or later dealt with that most telling item of all—the possibility of furlough without a settlement of the accounts due the men.

Early in June, Sergeant James Bennett of the Pennsylvania Line was stopped by two officers on Second Street in Philadelphia. These men, Lieutenant John Sullivan of the Dragoons and Captain Henry Carbery, a Marylander and veteran of the 1781 mutiny, no longer on duty, told him that the Congress had resolved to demobilize the army without pay or bounty provisions. They sug-

---

[59] Fitzpatrick, *Writings of Washington*, 26:342; *JCC*, 24:364.

gested that only by taking up arms in protest would the justice due them be achieved. They also promised to provide leadership for such a movement.[60] Returning to the barracks, Bennett told his fellow soldiers of the alledged plan to disperse the men without settlement. Infuriated, a group of sergeants at once sent a statement to the Congress demanding settlements and asserting that they would not accept furloughs. Congress passed it on to military leaders for resolution.

Then, on Thursday, June 19, Dickinson received letters warning him of the "march, temper, and intentions" of a group of mutinous troops advancing on Philadelphia from Lancaster.[61] He immediately discussed the soldiers' advance with Robert Morris, with whom he shared a common concern for financial stability in government. Each, too, was a firm supporter of measures which would strengthen the Confederation. The information from Lancaster was that the march on the capital was instigated from Philadelphia and that the soldiers planned to rob the Bank of North America as a source of the pay due them. Morris unequivocally advised Dickinson to call up the local militia and to keep the advancing soldiers out of the city. The president, however, held a more reasoned opinion. He remembered the irresponsible attack by the Philadelphia militia on James Wilson's house in 1779 and understood the soldiers' grievances.

The Congress and the Supreme Executive Council both met in the State House. The Council sent the Lancaster letters downstairs to the session of the Congress. A committee consisting of Alexander Hamilton, New York; Oliver Ellsworth, Connecticut; and Richard Peters of Pennsylvania was appointed to recommend action. Its suggestions, similar to those of Morris, were two: either reduce the party by force or prevent the soldiers from crossing the Schuylkill. The committee believed the mutiny would spread if the men's advance was not stopped.

[60] Kenneth R. Bowling, "The Philadelphia Mutiny of 1783: Federal-State Confrontation at the Close of the War for Independence," *PMHB* 101 (1977): 419–50; James Thomas Flexner, *The Young Hamilton: A Biography* (Boston, 1978), pp. 417–25.

[61] *The Diplomatic Correspondence of the United States of America, 1783–1789* (Washington, D. C., 1833–34), 1:11–14.

Dickinson, in concert with his Council, felt otherwise. They thought it unlikely that the militia would take up arms against soldiers whose selfless patriotism was now met with apparent indifference. If that were the unhappy result, the state would be severely crippled in its power. Moreover, violence had not been openly threatened. Consequently, the Council resolved that "from the good order observed in the March, the tranquil temper of the troops already here, and the measures pursued by government to make them easy and contented, the language of invitation, and good humor became more advisable than any immediate exertion of authority."[62] The tactic was one of restraint and moderation. It was also in direct opposition to Hamilton's advice. Taking authority into its own hands, the congressional committee ordered the assistant secretary of war, William Jackson, to meet the troops and keep them from entering the city. Nevertheless, the Lancaster troops, on Friday, the twentieth, marched to the Philadelphia barracks, where provisions had been made for them to stay among the already restive troops there.

The situation was further exacerbated by a decision made by some highly placed official of the federal government; payroll certificates, in lieu of cash, would no longer be given soldiers unless they accepted the Congress's furlough, a furlough without payment of accounts. Hamilton, Assistant Secretary of War Jackson, and Gouverneur Morris, the assistant secretary of finance, likewise agitated the men during an evening visit. They urged the troops to accept the furlough without settlement and proposed a one month's pay in cash if the men would go home. The men refused.

The next day Dickinson again visited Robert Morris. Once more Morris urged the president to call out the militia;[63] he reiterated his concern about the threats to the authority and dignity of the Confederation. Dickinson continued to refuse the advice. Then, between 12:30 and 1.00 P.M., almost three hundred soldiers set off from the barracks and marched to the State House to demand satisfaction. It was Saturday, and the Congress was not sched-

[62] Ibid., pp. 16, 18, 19, 25.

[63] Bowling, p. 420.

uled to meet. The Supreme Executive Council, however, was in regular session. The Pennsylvania troops now turned to their own state for recompense.

The soldiers delivered a note to the Council seeking redress of grievances and demanding that the troops be given authority to appoint new officers. The Council was given twenty minutes to comply.[64] The arrogance of the demands brought a unanimous rejection.

The Congress then unexpectedly convened[65] in an emergency session requested by Hamilton on the basis of a fear that the bank might be robbed that evening. Fortunately, the mutinous troops made no attempt to confront the representatives as they entered the building. Although a quorum was not obtained, Dickinson carried the Council's rejection of the soldiers' demands down to the congressmen and explained that the Council opposed a call-up of the militia until some "outrage" or violence occurred. Meanwhile, General Arthur St. Clair conferred with the boisterous, drinking soldiers outside in the street and arranged a compromise. The Council agreed to hear the soldiers' claims provided they were "decently expressed and constitutionally presented."[66] The soldiers withdrew.

The delegates of Congress left the State House, and President Boudinot returned to his quarters. He immediately sat down and wrote General Washington asking him to send a dependable regiment to Philadelphia to restore order. A special session of the Congress at six that evening authorized his request, and Hamilton and his committee were commissioned to obtain effective measures at once from the Pennsylvania Council in support of governmental authority. Should adequate measures not be undertaken immediately to that end, the Congress resolved to move to New Jersey. Congress, in Boudinot's words, considered the lack of Coun-

[64] *Colonial Records*, 13:605.

[65] E. Boudinot to the Ministers Plenipotentiary in Paris, July 15, 1783, Burnett, 7:193, 222.

[66] *Colonial Records*, 13:605.

cil support a "wound to the dignity of the Federal Government."
The cause of the mutiny itself was ignored.[67]

On Sunday, the twenty-second, the Executive Council met at
the president's home. The night before, Robert Morris had called
on Dickinson, once again urging him to call out the militia. Now
for the first time the Council had in hand resolves of the Congress,
not just those of the committee, asking that "effectual measures"
be taken because the authority of the United States had been
"grossly insulted by the disorderly and menacing appearance of a
body of armed soldiers."

The Council acknowledged the need for secrecy, but it also
agreed that before any determination was made regarding the request, "measures to ascertain the temper of the city" should be
taken. If the results should prove that an action such as calling
out the militia was inadvisable, then none would be taken. A conference was held with Colonel Hamilton. Council noted that many
preparations would have to be made and pointed out that the
state's munitions magazine had been seized and consequently ammunition could not be procured. Hamilton assured the Council
that any quantity of arms could be commanded in fifteen minutes.
Before adjournment, the Council resolved: "In consequence, that
the sense of the city upon this subject be collected with all possible
secrecy and dispatch; that the members of the Council individual-
ly exert themselves in this business, and that the field officers of
the militia be immediately consulted."[68] The Council, however,
was not informed about Boudinot's letter to Washington, nor until
the next morning, when the Council again met, were the Saurday
evening resolutions of the Congress given that body.

The inquiry of militia officers included all but one of the commanding officers. All the while Dickinson refused to be intimidated either by the soldiers or by the Congress. Neither he nor
any member of the Council was aware that Boudinot, annoyed as
much as Hamilton had been by the moderate tone of the Penn-

[67] *JCC*, 24:419; William T. Hutchinson and William M. E. Rachal, eds.,
Papers of James Madison (Chicago, 1962–79), 7:177–180; Burnett, 7:194.

[68] *Colonial Records*, 13:606–7.

sylvania leaders, was intent on moving to New Jersey as soon as possible. Dickinson's stolid position infuriated them.

On Tuesday morning Dickinson brought the field officers of the militia into the sessions of the Council. All the resolutions of the Congress, explanations of them as presented by the committee, and the message the soldiers had sent the Council on Saturday were set forth. With this background the officers now gave their sentiments upon the practicality of assembling the militia in such force and manner as to accomplish the purposes of the congressional resolution. A senior field officer, after deliberating with his fellow officers, presented their united opinion that "it would be imprudent to call upon the militia now, as we are convinced it would be ineffective. If the negotiation for settling the disturbances does not succeed, and the soldiers should insist on unjust and unreasonable things, or should commit any outrage, we are willing to make all the exertion in our power for preserving the peace, and supporting the public authority." The militia officers thus confirmed the views of Dickinson and the Executive Council. Shortly after this session, President Dickinson received a note from the president of the Congress. The Congress had adjourned to New Jersey.[69]

When, on Wednesday, the Council met in regular session, Captains Christie and Symonds, representing the soldiers' committee, appeared with three papers, which included an apology, signed by James Bennett, the sergeant who had spread the initial rumors leading to the mutiny. The Council refused to receive the papers unless certain conditions were met: the troops must put themselves under the command of their officers and "make a full and satisfactory submission to Congress." The captains then suggested that the soldiers were likely to react by rioting. At this point, the Council acted fearlessly and with dispatch. The lieutenant of the city militia was immediately directed to call up a guard of five hundred privates and as many officers as needed "as a measure indispensably and immediately necessary to secure government from

---

[69] Manuscript draft by Dickinson of consultation with field officers, June 24, 1783, L-D/LCP; Dickinson account of the meeting, *Colonial Records*, 13:654–66.

insult, the state from disturbance and the city from injury."[70]

Benjamin Rush, who seems to have been at the center of every Philadelphia event, went by the barracks where he got into conversation with some of the dissident soldiers. After listening to his arguments, the men inquired whether they would receive pardon if they submitted to the government. Dr. Rush replied that he thought the government would agree to that, and he then went at once to call on Dickinson, who received the suggestion "with avidity." The doctor carried the president's opinion back to the men. In the meantime, the officers who had originally inspired the mutiny had fled town. The men decided to submit. That evening all but the Lancaster troops marched to the president's house in Market Street where they formally once more put themselves under the command of their officers. Dickinson came out, climbed on a table, and with a servant holding a candle at his side, addressed the men, chastising them for their "unprecedented and heinous fault." He promised to request Congress to pardon them but asked that they prove their regret for their mutinous actions by joining the militia to quell the Lancaster renegades if those troops did not return home the next day.[71] By Thursday evening Nagle, the leader of the Lancaster troops, and his men were on the homeward march, and Dickinson could report to Boudinot that Philadelphia had returned to normal.

The mutiny had a significance far beyond the revolt itself. It became the "first major confrontation between a state and the United States government" and raised the question of the extent to which police power should be used by a republican government. Not only did it resolve the question of the Congress's long-discussed removal from Philadelphia, but it also ended the constitutional crisis of 1783 by crippling those who sought a more centralized federal government.[72]

No delegate was more angered by the unyielding position of Dickinson than Alexander Hamilton. He wrote George Clinton,

[70] Bowling, p. 442.

[71] Benjamin Rush to [John Adams], April, 1812, copy Rush Papers, LCP.

[72] Bowling, p. 449.

governor of New York, that the "Executive of this state [Pennsylvania] was to the last degree weak and disgusting. In short, they pretended it was out of their power to bring out the militia, without making the experiment." The majority of the delegates supported Hamilton in his willingness to experiment with possible tragic violence. Oliver Ellsworth, reporting the events to the governor of Connecticut, could not understand the Council's failure to follow the Congress's request. He wondered whether "they had not the spirit or power enough to do it, or did not think it necessary."[73] Congressional communication lacked clarity.

Dickinson's conduct met divided reactions. Pennsylvanians seemed to approve. Benjamin Rush assured Congressman John Montgomery: "You have nothing to fear for the character of Mr. Dickinson. His conduct is highly approved of by all classes and parties. I think the Constitutionalists give him most credit for his behavior." Richard Peters, another Pennsylvania delegate, thought the removal of Congress would be temporary and believed the question of which side—the United States or Pennsylvania—was justified would "always remain a matter of opinion upon which each may decide from possibly opposite motives." Timothy Pickering more than a quarter of a century later expressed his opinion that if Dickinson had called up the militia on that occasion, the capital of the United States would not only have remained in Philadelphia and obviated the wasteful move to establish one on the Potomac but would also have saved the country from what he regarded as the disasters of Jefferson's and Madison's administrations.[74]

For Dickinson the two weeks left lasting but undeserved scars on his record as president of the state. The removal of Congress was a major blow, overshadowing his courageous stance in successfully quelling the revolt. The Republicans were concerned

[73] Hamilton to Clinton, June 29, 1783, Hamilton to Edmund Randolph, June 30, 1783, Ellsworth to Joseph Read, July 1, 1783, John Montgomery to Benjamin Rush, July 8, 1783, Ellsworth to Trumbull, July 10, 1783, Burnett, 7:203, 207–8, 209–10, 215, 220.

[74] Rush to Montgomery, July 7, 1783, Dickinson College, Rush Papers, LCP; Motion of Richard Peters, Oct. 10, 1783, Burnett, 7:329–31; Letter, Timothy Pickering Papers, LI, 236, MaHS.

with maintaining their political power. Efforts were immediately made to get the Congress to return to Philadelphia. Robert Morris joined city residents in late July in signing a citizens' address to the Congress written by Thomas Paine. The address attempted to assure the Congress of the city's promise to uphold the national honor if that body once again took up residence in Philadelphia. Dickinson disapproved of the plan, and Charles Thomson failed to convince him that it would be best if the petition were forwarded in the name of the Council.[75] The city and state could not have been more solicitous of the Congress. In July the citizens' address was forwarded; in August the Council decided to extend an appeal; and in September the General Assembly offered its olive branch. The efforts came to naught. Congress had no intention of coming back to Pennsylvania.

The autumn elections of 1783 were successful for the Republicans who won despite strident accusations against them by the Constitutionalists. The radicals charged the Republicans would be soft on the tory exiles who were about to return following the peace treaty. When the votes were all in, the Republicans continued to hold control of the Assembly by a slim margin. On November 6 Dickinson and Ewing once again were elected president and vice-president of the Supreme Executive Council.[76]

The most significant election that fall, however, was for the Council of Censors. The constitution of 1776 provided for a council made up of two representatives from each county and two from Philadelphia City, elected every seven years, to review the working of the constitution and evidences of its defects. Republicans saw a legal opportunity to achieve a new constitutional convention, and they exercised every means to win adherents to their cause by the election of sympathetic candidates. Radical leaders countered the Republican appeals with letters and broadsides, warning their followers, "The time is near at hand, when all that is dear to the Friends of Liberty, and the Constitution, will be determined. The next election will decide our fate."[77] When the

[75] Thomson to JD, July 11, 1783, L-D/LCP.

[76] *Colonial Records*, 8:736–38.

[77] Broadsides, II, 264, HSP.

votes were in, the Republicans had thirteen members, the Constitutionalists twelve in the Council of Censors. The edge was slight, and the ultimate goal of calling a convention was frustrated since that required a two-thirds vote.

The Council of Censors was a unique feature of the Pennsylvania constitution. The only ultimate check on the legislative and executive branches, it was also the sole agent for any constitutional change. Three tasks were to be investigated: first, had the constitution been properly adhered to; second, had taxes been justly levied and collected throughout the state; and, third, was the constitution in any part defective and in need of amendment. The organizing session was held November 13, 1783. By January a report was issued which embodied all the changes the Republicans had been urging since the constitution had been put into effect. Recommendations included proposals for a governor with veto power as a single executive; a bicameral legislature; the ability of either house to originate bills (except money bills); an increase in the residence requirement for voting to two years; enfranchisement of foreigners who had taken up land and subscribed to an oath; judicial tenure for good behavior rather than specified terms; and the establishment of a militia. The minority of censors officially declared their dissent, giving their reasons for every objection. On June 21, the first session concluded.[78]

A second session convened on August 5. The Constitutionalists now controlled a majority in the Council of Censors. Two of the Constitutionalists who had been previously absent now appeared, and a vacancy created by the resignation of Samuel Miles was filled in a special election by George Bryan, radical supporter of the constitution. From August to the final adjournment on September 25, the Censors accomplished little. Although the Censors could not agree on defects, they were unanimous that "a capable and faithful administration" was necessary.[79]

---

[78] E. Bruce Thomas, *Political Tendencies in Pennsylvania, 1783–1794* (Philadelphia, 1938), pp. 46–82; *The Proceedings relative to Calling the Convention of 1776 and 1790 . . . together with . . . the proceedings of the Council of Censors* (Harrisburg, Pa., 1825), pp. 66–128.

[79] *Proceedings*, pp. 123, 79–80.

A month later in the elections of October 12, 1784, the radicals, or Constitutionalists, won. Sixty percent of the Assembly was newly elected. The new Assembly at once set out to rectify the "mistakes" the Republicans had made in the previous two sessions.[80] Dickinson, however, was reelected president of the Supreme Executive Council. The year that followed was strewn with difficulties. Dickinson no longer had major political backing or an Assembly likely to support any program he espoused. The Constitutionalists had programs of their own.

One major problem was paying off the state and congressional war debts. Both parties agreed that funding with interest was necessary. Claims against the state and those against the federal government had to be differentiated. After public creditors appealed to the Pennsylvania Assembly, that body empowered Dickinson to appoint two more commissioners to estimate the cost of converting the Loan Office and quartermaster and commissary certificates into specie. The president hesitated since the action involved the state's assumption of what was largely a congressional debt. He asked Congress to make the appointments, which action the Congress took, naming one commissioner rather than two. In the assumption of all debts due its citizens, the Assembly proposed paying interest from the sale of public lands, from a general tax, and from the issuing of paper money. Dickinson objected to these proposals on several grounds. He thought, for one thing, that some discrimination should be made between the original holders of certificates and the men who speculated in them. He was most concerned about the original owners, and he believed that collection of back taxes would provide sufficient funds for paying them off. Income from the sale of western lands, sold at a fixed price, could then compensate the speculators. Although paper money was the easy way out, it was the most dangerous course. Dickinson, Philadelphia merchants, the Bank of North America, and Finance Secretary Morris all opposed the measure strenuously. But the radicals were adamant, and after logrolling between eastern speculators and frontiersmen who sought titles to rich western lands, the Con-

[80] Brunhouse, p. 166.

stitutionalist won, counteracting the leadership of Dickinson and his Republican supporters.[81]

International questions were raised in the "Longchamps Affair." Charles Julian de Longchamps, a newly arrived Frenchman who had recently become an American citizen, had threatened François de Barbé-Marbois, the French consul. This caused the minister, the Chevalier de la Luzerne, to appeal to the Council for adequate punishment. The Council was concerned with the proper mode of seizing the offender and of holding him until trial. There was also the question whether now, as an American citizen, he could be turned over to the French minister who claimed him. Dickinson wrote Justice Thomas McKean of the French minister's insistence that Longchamps be arrested, stating that he believed that if the offender was not arrested and imprisoned at least until his trial, the ministers of France and the United Netherlands would leave Pennsylvania and that the king of France would insist on reparation. The Court decided the Council could not surrender Longchamps to French authority but sentenced him to a fine and two years' imprisonment. In this decision the Court failed to surrender American jurisdiction, thereby making this country an asylum for those fleeing their native land.[82]

By the constitution of 1776 the president of the Supreme Executive Council was the head of the judiciary, being ex-officio chief justice of the High Court of Errors and Appeals. As such he could sit with the judges of the Supreme Court and deliver opinions. Perhaps because of this Dickinson had a tendency to pass on to the court rather than to an attorney general queries from the Assembly on such matters as clearing titles and guaranteeing the right of

[81] See *Colonial Records*, 14:271–75, 328–42, 372; *Pennsylvania Archives*, 1st ser., 10:369–71, 405; ibid., 4th ser., 3:988–89, 991–1012. Newspapers of the period printed letters pro and con on these issues.

[82] "Longchamp Affair," Supreme Executive Council, Manuscripts, APS. See also JD to Justice McKean, May 25, 1784, McKean Papers, II, 80, HSP; G. S. Rowe with Alexander W. Knott, "Power, Justice and Foreign Affairs in the Confederation Period: The Marbois-Longchamp Affair, 1794–1796," *PMHB* 104 (1980):275–307.

habeas corpus by express provision to the people of the common-wealth.[83]

Two cases reaching the High Court of Appeals in 1784 in which Dickinson became actively involved were of particular significance. The one concerned Aaron Doan, who had been seized for robbery of collectors of public funds in Bucks County, the other an admiralty case. The first dealt with the question of life, the second with property and with court jurisdiction. After consulting the Supreme Court, Dickinson advised the Council that because of peculiarities of the particular case, the law was too unclear to legally issue a warrant for Doan's execution, and the Council determined not to do so. In *Talbot v. The Commanders and Owners of Three Brigs*, the matter was appealed from the state admiralty court. Dickinson, as chief justice, rendered the chief decision, affirming that the case could be appealed to the High Court of Errors and Appeals, rather than the confederation, or federal court.[84]

Dickinson had enemies, political and personal, but many friends. And friends were loyal, none of them more so than Benjamin Rush. John Montgomery, who as a fellow Assemblyman had sided with Dickinson nearly twenty years before in the unsuccessful fight against Franklin's effort to make the Colony royal, was now once again in the Assembly as a member from Cumberland County. Montgomery, too, was an old friend of Rush. In the summer of 1782 Rush and Montgomery sat on William Bingham's front porch with their host. Colonel Montgomery mentioned his intention to seek a state charter for the Grammar School in Carlisle, which had been in operation there for more than fifteen years. Rush immediately suggested that Montgomery seek a charter for a college rather than for a grammar school. There were many good reasons for establishing a college on the frontier. He suggested it be named "John and Mary's College" for Dickinson and his wife, both of

---

[83] Stillé, pp. 251–52.

[84] Proclamation of Outlawing against Certain Criminals, September 13, 1783, *Archives*, 4th ser., 3:924–29; *The Resolution of the High Court of Errors and Appeals for the State of Pennsylvania in the Cause of Silas Talbot, quitam, etc. against the commanders and owners of the brigs Achilles, Patty and Hibernia: January 14, 1783* (Philadelphia, 1785): I, Dallas, 180–86, 489–94.

whom he expected would be generous supporters. The president refused to allow that name to be used, but he did not demur at the college being called Dickinson. That was halfway at least toward Rush's goal. The college was chartered by the Assembly on September 9, 1783.[85] Dickinson's personal contribution to the new institution's endowment was moderate: two farms and, the best foundation of all, books from his library and from that of his father-in-law, Isaac Norris. Dickinson's assistance was also sought in obtaining financial support from the state. However, not until after he had left the presidency and the college was already in operation did the General Assembly contribute financially.

Rush had masterminded the whole concept, even the charter itself, which James Wilson and Dickinson had approved before submitting it to the legislature. On September 15, fifteen of the forty selected trustees for the new institution met at President Dickinson's house and by oath or affirmation declared their support of the college. Dickinson appropriately enough was elected president of the board. Two other meetings were held in Philadelphia, one at Rush's and the other at the State House. Meanwhile, funds for the college were solicited both in the nearby states as well as abroad. Dickinson, Rush, and the trustees who lived in central Pennsylvania then met in Carlisle on April 6, 1784.

The selection of a principal or president of the new institution now occupied Rush. He proposed the name of Charles Nisbet, a Scottish minister who had been suggested to him when Princeton, some years before, had called John Witherspoon to head its college. Dickinson, as president of the Board of Trustees, issued the formal invitation to Nisbet on September 29, 1784.

Meanwhile politics again intervened. Even the granting of the college charter, supported by Republicans but viewed with ire or suspicion by certain Constitutionalists, had run into difficulties, passing by the slim margin of four votes. The elections of October 1784 were not auspicious for continued Republican dominance. Dickinson, without Rush's knowledge, one month after his previous warm invitation to Nisbet, wrote the Scot another letter. He

[85] Sellers, *Dickinson College*, pp. 54–55; James Henry Morgan, *Dickinson College, 1783–1933* (Carlisle, Pa., 1933), p. 13; *Charter of Dickinson College*.

suggested Nisbet should not come to America until he could be assured of a more favorable prospect since matters regarding the college at the moment were "exceedingly discouraged and impeded." He feared the Constitutionalists might repeal the charter. After posting the letter, Dickinson sent a copy to Rush with his characteristically personal assurance, saying, "I have obeyed the authoritive dictates, according to my judgment, of honor and justice." Rush was furious, though he should have remembered that six weeks earlier Dickinson had suggested to Rush that "Justice certainly requires that the state of our funds should be precisely communicated" to Nisbet. But Rush overlooked that cautious note and now accused Dickinson of treacherous actions: gifts to Princeton, favoring the College of Philadelphia of which he was ex-officio member of the Board, and even corrupt election practices.[86] The good doctor, like so many others, was impotent against the president's conscience—his ever determining judgment, honor, and sense of justice. Dickinson, however, a month later wrote Nisbet that the political climate had cleared, and in 1785 Nisbet journeyed with his family across the Atlantic to the New World.

In December, Rush again became disturbed, this time over unexpected fiscal limitations of the college. John Montgomery was also gloomy. Much of the money raised for the new institution had been based on the redemption of certificates. Rush wrote his Carlisle friend: "The Assembly passed a report to pay the interest on all kinds of certificates but Mr. Dickinson has thrown a remonstrance against it from the Council which we are afraid will prevent its passing into law. His reasonings are weak but very popular. Thus he has attempted to cut off the last hopes and dependence of his college." General John Armstrong, vice-president of the Board of Trustees, wrote Rush on hearing this news that it "would draw a shade over all that has been said" and added, "There can be no doubt that the President's fears originated from that of his own estate."[87] The eventual success of Dickinson's opponents in passing

<hr />

[86] JD to Rush, October 24, 1784, Roberts Collection, Haverford College; JD to Charles Nisbet, October 24, 1784, Dickinson College Collection; JD to Rush, August 30, 1784, Winterthur.

[87] Rush to Montgomery, December 10, 13, 1784, Rush Papers, I, LCP.

the assumption bill ironically assured the continuance of the college named for him.

While never again attending a trustee meeting, Dickinson cemented a friendship with Nisbet after his arrival in Philadelphia and a few years later put $500 in a bank there for Nisbet's exclusive use. Dickinson continued his interest in a somewhat desultory way and urged the trustees to try to obtain the Public Works at the edge of Carlisle for the college's use. In 1798 he sent a hundred-dollar subscription for a new college building. This ended his involvement with the institution that bore his name.

On Monday, October 10, 1785, John Dickinson presided over his last meeting of the Pennsylvania Supreme Executive Council. He had served three years, the limit set by the state constitution. At the time of the October elections, the Republicans held some hope of organizing the Assembly. They lost. Both factions settled on the aging Franklin as the new president and more realistically focused their attention on the vice-presidency, which went to Charles Biddle, a mild Constitutionalist, who at the last Council meeting Dickinson attended was elected to fill James Irvine's seat.[88]

Success had certainly not dogged Dickinson's heels as president. Political disputes never waned. Even the college named for him had become involved in ceaseless political struggles in the three years he held office. The virulent attack by "Valerius" at the beginning of his term had been devastating. Alexander Graydon observed that Dickinson's efforts to vindicate himself "even by his political friends was thought nerveless and whining."[89] Within six months of his election the Mutiny of June and the removal of Congress had brought him still more under the shadow of criticism. Yet in that affair Dickinson had acted courageously, correctly sensing the temper of the militia and gauging the public's sympathetic attitude. His concern for the patriotic troops who had been so long unpaid; his demand that original certificate holders, as opposed to speculators, should receive first consideration in the

[88] Brunhouse, p. 180.

[89] Alexander Graydon, *Memoirs of a Life . . . in Pennsylvania* (Edinburgh, 1822), pp. 353–54.

settlement of debts owed them; and the even-handed search for fair treatment in the Wyoming disputes had placed him on the side of justice in every instance. The political tides had run against him, and those currents were strong.

There was no question where the Dickinsons would live on leaving the president's house in Market Street. Dickinson had suffered enough in Pennsylvania's political maelstrom. He and Mary Dickinson three years before had resolved to live in Wilmington. Delaware once again loomed as a refuge for them both.

☆ 10 ☆

Rewriting
Constitutions

JOHN DICKINSON'S MOVE TO WILMINGTON resulted from several factors. Mary's cousin, Deborah Norris Logan, believed the step was primarily caused by the unhappy treatment he had received from Pennsylvania political partisans. Indeed, the Dickinsons had almost decided to make it their residence in 1782, just before Dickinson's recall to political power in Pennsylvania. The town was equidistant from Philadelphia and the Dover plantation. By 1784, the year before Dickinson's retirement from the Pennsylvania Supreme Executive Council, they came to a final decision, and in October 1785, as soon as his term was up, they left for Wilmington.

A "clean, airy, neat town" with many brick houses, Wilmington had developed as a Quaker community through the efforts of William Shipley. The Delaware River was three miles distant, and the nearer Christiana Creek provided a busy thoroughfare for vessels unloading and loading cargoes at the wharves. The family goods sent down from Philadelphia arrived safely, and the weather was perfect. The Dickinsons had rented a house on the corner of Market and Ninth streets.[1] Any plan to build was deferred. Mary Dickinson reported her pleasure to her cousin Hannah Griffitts:

[1] Vaughan Journal, September 3, 1785; *Friends Historical Association Bulletin* 1 (1906):76–77.

I found a much better house than I expected, situated on the hill nearly opposite the College. Before the door is a picturesque prospect of the Delaware, Christeen and Brandywine. We have 4 rooms on a floor, 2 story and good garrets. I have a sweet nursery for my children and a door from it opens into our room [so] that I can hear them if they move—which is a Convenience wished for. Our servants are pleased which is satisfactory and I hope William's wife who we bro't with us will prove a useful hand.

A sister of Benjamin Sharpless, "staunch and solid Friends," called, and John Tatnall and his wife came by to show her the way to Meeting. Philadelphia Quakers had close relatives in the town, including the Pembertons and the Fishers, the latter interrelated with the Norrises, thus providing a changing group of visitors who brought news from Pennsylvania. Wilmington reminded Mrs. Dickinson of Philadelphia in her childhood. She had a little garden and was content, observing, "I have learnt a Lesson that Happiness is not confined to the Grandness of Life—perhaps seldom found there."[2]

The daughters were now aged fifteen and three. Sally, having left her Philadelphia teacher, in May completed her public examinations at the Wilmington school before visitors from Philadelphia and "most of the gay ladies of Wilmington." Sally recognized the elegance of certain young friends, but the serious teenager preferred the simple life. She did not mind the lack of city amusements in which she never had participated. Instead she found "an agreeable mixture of town and country here, for by walking a few yards back we are surrounded by orchards."[3] The family quickly settled down to their new life.

John Dickinson had long and earnestly devoted himself to government and its service. Removal to Wilmington did not diminish his involvement. When, in 1779, he reentered Congress as a delegate from Delaware, he carried with him that state's ratifica-

[2] Mary Dickinson to Hannah Griffitts, November 6, 1785, MDL/HSP; Mary Dickinson to Margaret Moore, December 4, Howland Collection, Haverford College.

[3] Sally Dickinson to Deborah Logan, January 3, 1786 [?], May 12, 1786, L/HSP, VII, 10–11.

tion of the Articles of Confederation. By March 1, 1781, all the states had ratified them.[4]

The Articles as first drafted under Dickinson's direction had provided for centralization, with few limits on the Congress and relatively little power guaranteed to the states. Dickinson had made sure, for example, that boundary disputes between states and western land claims would fall within the determination of the Congress. When the Articles were submitted to the states, the "national" aspects that had given strength to the first draft had disappeared. Many other changes weakened the original conservative position. Although Dickinson supported the expediency of ratification and encouraged Delaware in that action, he advised a strong declaration against certain parts of the Articles, suggesting "expectation of a revision and alteration thereof at a more convenient season to accompany it."[5]

Weaknesses showed up almost at once. The "Nationalists," of whom Dickinson was one, though he faithfully served the state interests of both Delaware and Pennsylvania as president, worked toward a revision. When he was president of the latter state, Dickinson wrote Charles Thomson for advice. Since his recommendation two years earlier that the Confederation be "strengthened and improved" had not been heeded, he thought it time to try again. He believed greater authority ought to be vested in the "Federal Council" and that powers for regulating and protecting commerce and provision for the imposition of duties on imports for revenue purposes should be uppermost among other considerations, adding, "We anxiously desire . . . that instead of being satisfied with *partial* provisions, it may lead to as *perfect* an establishment of the Union as the wisdom of *America* can desire."[6] On August 18, 1783, Dickinson sent the Pennsylvania Assembly an explicit message on the subject emphasizing his strong belief in a centralized government. He was convinced

> that to advance the dignity of the Union is the best way to advance the interest of each particular State.

[4] *American History Leaflets* (New York, 1892–1910), no. 20, March 1895.

[5] JD to Thomas Rodney, July 22, 1779, Gratz Collection, HSP.

[6] JD to Thomson, July 12, 1783, Thomson Papers, I, Library of Congress.

> When the powers of the whole shall be so combined that general and relative concerns may be firmly governed by a Federal supremacy, and a competent part of the resources of the whole can be promptly and effectually drawn forth and applied to national purposes, all the benefits of respect, tranquility, and safety, that are naturally attached to an extensive and well established Empire, may be ensured, and at a rate much cheaper and more easy than by any other method that can be devised. Indeed, without such a combination they never can be ensured.[7]

New disputes arose yearly between states; the debts of the Confederation remained unpaid and unplanned for; economic woes mounted; and not only did commerce languish but interstate trade barriers further hindered development for the new nation.[8] The lack of taxing power by the Congress was an even greater concern. Since amendments could only be added by the unanimous consent of all the states, any possible reform was blocked. Leaders within the various states found themselves divided: some certain that the states themselves could solve the problems they faced; others equally certain that national power alone would create stability.[9]

Virginia called for a convention to meet at Annapolis in September 1786 to discuss commercial reforms. Five states sent representatives; Delaware nominated five delegates, of whom only John Dickinson, Richard Bassett, and George Read attended. Dickinson was chosen chairman of the meeting and addressed the convention.[10] Among the advocates of stronger federal power present was Alexander Hamilton, who became prominent in its councils. After three days of discussion the delegates agreed that more than commercial regulation was necessary if the Confederation was to be strengthened. As a result, resolutions were prepared calling for a convention to meet in Philadelphia in May 1787. Once again

---

[7] *Pennsylvania Archives*, 3d ser., 3:894–904.

[8] John Barclay to JD, April 7, 1787, L/HSP, XLI. 99.

[9] Merrill Jensen: *The Articles of Confederation* (Madison, Wis., 1940), pp. 239–45; also, "The Progress of the Articles through Congress," pp. 249–53.

[10] John Munroe, *Federalist Delaware* (New Brunswick, N. J., 1954), pp. 104–5; Carey's *American Museum*, October 1787.

Dickinson was at the helm, playing a leading part in writing the resolves and proposing the May meeting that would officially "rewrite and amend" the Articles of Confederation. Broader instructions were required than those given the delegates to Annapolis. The Confederation Congress then forwarded notices to all the individual states.

No longer suffering anxieties as a result of political struggles, Dickinson was stronger in health and in good spirits. Much had been accomplished, and his talents were being used in advancing what he considered an important issue.

The five Delawareans asked to serve at Annapolis were again appointed delegates to the Philadelphia convention. Gunning Bedford, Jr., a prominent lawyer, and Jacob Broom of Wilmington, a young manufacturer, who had not attended the Annapolis meeting now joined their fellows in the Philadelphia convocation. George Read took particular interest in obtaining his state's support for the convention. He also saw to it that instructions to delegates were written emphasizing that each state should have but one vote in determining any alteration to the Articles.[11] Such a determination ensured Delaware's equal voice on all matters.

When the delegates assembled in Philadelphia, Dickinson was in Kent. Broom and Read both urged his immediate attendance. On May 13 Broom wrote his fellow delegate that several gentlemen at the convention had inquired about him. Both he and Read would "feel disagreeable" until their state had a quorum present. But, like other delegates, Dickinson arrived late. Indeed, the convention set to open May 14, was not organized until the twenty-fifth. Read kept Dickinson abreast of developments and engaged a room for him on Fifth Street from which Governor Edmund Randolph had moved after the arrival of his wife. Randolph, however, planned to continue to dine at the table kept by the proprietor.[12]

The convention delegations were impressive. Dr. Franklin termed it "the most august and respectable Assembly" of which he

[11] Read to JD, January 17, 1787, Read, pp. 438–39.

[12] Read to Dickinson, May 25, 1787, John Dickinson Papers, Delaware State Archives (hereafter DSA); Randolph to JD, May 13, 1787, Item 57, L-D/LCP.

had ever been a part. Benjamin Rush found the delegates united in their goal and he expected that "they will be equally united in the means of attaining them." Dickinson, writing his wife, declared, "The Convention is very busy—of excellent temper—and for abilities, exceeds I believe any assembly that ever met upon this Continent, except the first Congress."[13]

Dickinson was fifty-five and looked older than those years. His appearance deceived those who had not known him in previous conventions. The French minister described him in a report to the Foreign Office as "vieux, faible et sans influence," but the last phrase was not wholly accurate. William Pierce, delegate from Georgia, commented:

> When I saw him in the Convention I was induced to pay the greatest attention to him whenever he spoke. I had often heard that he was a great orator, but I found him an indifferent speaker. With an affected air of wisdom he labors to produce a trifle; his language is irregular and incorrect. His flourishes (for he sometimes attempts them) are like expiring flames, they just shew themselves and go out; no traces of them are left on the mind to cheer or animate it. He . . . will ever be considered one of the most important characters in the United States.[14]

That summer in Philadelphia proved particularly debilitating for Dickinson. He was frequently indisposed and unable to attend meetings. Illness, however, did not restrain his opinions, which he expressed freely.

Delaware's small size, both in geography and in population, determined the decisions of its delegates. Read and Dickinson were the nationalists of the delegation, while Bedford and Bassett more strongly favored states' rights. Dickinson understood their position and agreed that certain power should be left under state control. "National" to him did not necessarily mean centralization.

---

[13] Rush to Richard Price, June 2, 1787, "The Price Letters," *Proceedings of the Massachusetts Historical Society*, 2d ser. 17 (1903):367–68; JD to his wife, June 1787, on scrap of paper, L/HSP, VIII, 103.

[14] Max Farrand, ed., *The Records of the Federal Convention of 1787* (New Haven, 1923), 3:92.

What he sought was strong government with clarity in the division of responsibilities in the delegation of power.

Immediately on taking his seat at the convention, Dickinson assumed an active and articulate role. On May 29 Edmund Randolph presented the resolutions that became known as the Virginia Plan. After pointing out the defects in the Articles, Randolph set forth both the necessity and the means of transforming the government into a more efficient and national one. The very next day discussion of the plan was underway. Acting as a committee of the whole the convention agreed that "a national government ought to be established consisting of a supreme legislative, executive and judiciary."

Dickinson agreed with Randolph's assessment of the Confederation but thought a simpler approach to problems might be made. James McHenry of Maryland took notes on a folio sheet as Dickinson declared, "We are a nation altho' consisting of parts or States—We are also confederates, and . . . [it is to be hoped that] we shall always remain confederated." He argued that the inquiry should ask: "1. What are the legislative powers which we should vest in congress? 2. What Judiciary powers? 3. What Executive powers?" "We may resolve therefore," Dickinson continued, "in order to let us into business. That the confederation is defective; and then proceed to the definition of such powers as may be thought adequate to the objects for which it was instituted."[15]

The convention, however, avoided any such logical approach. Instead, the question of legislative representation was discussed. When the outcome of the voting indicated that representation in the national legislature "ought to be proportioned and not according to the present system" of one vote per state, Read at once moved postponement. He reminded the convention that Delaware's instructions to its delegates did not permit any change in "the rule of suffrage" and warned that should such a change be made Delaware might leave the convention. Delaware, in fact, was the only state that had limited the action of its delegates. The convention was disturbed by Delaware's position and there was no solution other than the postponement which Read sought.

[15] Ibid., 3:42. All subsequent business of the convention unless otherwise noted has been taken from Farrand.

After the convention resolved that the legislature should consist of two branches as proposed by Randolph, the method of selecting the members of each branch became cause for much debate. Such diverse voices as those of Madison, Read, Dickinson, Pierce, and James Wilson agreed that one branch should be directly elected by the people. This relationship between state and national governments Dickinson viewed as being "as politic as it was unavoidable." He then spoke eloquently of the British system and of the House of Lords as a "refining process." While Dickinson supported a strong national government, he nonetheless favored giving the states a prominent role. "The objection against making the former dependent on the latter might be obviated by giving to the Senate an authority permanent and irrevocable for three, five or seven years. Being thus independent they will speak and decide with becoming freedom."[16] George Read disagreed with Dickinson's concern for the states' positions and argued that a new government had to be established on new principles.

A motion by General Pinckney to have the state legislatures elect members to the House was defeated. The next day, on June 7, James Wilson and Gouverneur Morris proposed that the Senate should be elected by people within specially established districts. This plan Dickinson assailed in a detailed argument as impractical and unfair. The motion was lost, 10 to 1. Dickinson then submitted his own resolution. "That the members of the second branch of the national legislature ought to be chosen by the individual legislatures."[17] Wilson observed that should one branch be elected by the people and the other branch be of members chosen by the state legislatures, the two branches would rest upon different foundations. But Dickinson saw these two branches each with a different foundation as mutual checks on each other. He found a metaphor for his position, seeing such a government harmonized "and like the planetary system, the national council like the sun, would illuminate the whole—the planets revolving round it in perfect order; or like the union of several small streams, would at last form a re-

16 Ibid., 1:136.

17 Ibid., 1:149.

spectable river, gently flowing to the sea."[18] The motion won by unanimous vote.

Early on Dickinson observed that the basis of representation for each branch would have to be settled by "mutual concessions." He hoped "that each state would retain an equal voice at least in one branch of the national legislature, and [he] supposed the sums paid within each State would form a better ratio for the other branch than either the number of inhabitants or the quantum of property." The issue boiled for nearly two and a half months. Dickinson continued to argue that representation in both branches founded on numbers was "unreasonable and dangerous."[19] As for the smaller states, he feared that they would be "delivered up into the absolute power of the larger" under such proportionate measures. He even foresaw a probability that the states established in the future might come to "rule the present states as vassals."[20] He considered that the fate of the country lay in a proper and equitable solution to the prickly question.

Governor Randolph's Virginia Plan, debated in the first fortnight, was followed by that offered by William Paterson and called the New Jersey Plan. This proposal was inspired by New Jersey and Delaware, which, as small states, would find diminished power under the "national" plan of Virginia. Connecticut and New York, fearing a limitation of state power, had also looked askance at Virginia's outline and preferred supporting a weaker federation. Dickinson bluntly pointed out to Madison "the consequences of pushing things too far," as he felt the large states were doing. Although he knew some members of the smaller states were friends to a national government, he declared, "We would sooner submit to a foreign power than be deprived of an equality of suffrage, in both branches of the legislature, and thereby be thrown under the domination of the large states."[21]

[18] Ibid., 1:157 (Yates account).

[19] Notes relative to the New Jersey Plan, Item 109, L-D/LCP.

[20] Farrand, 1:112.

[21] Ibid., 1:242.

On June 19 Dickinson suggested that there were good elements in both plans. He proposed that the delegates contrast "one with the other, and consolidate such parts of them as the committee approve."[22] Two days later, tentative agreement was reached. Two houses of a congress were approved, the first branch to be elected by the people of the several states. But the question of representation in the second branch remained a subject of contention. Elbridge Gerry viewed some accommodation as an "absolutely necessary." A committee was elected to seek a solution to the problem. On July 5 the committee brought in a recommendation providing for two houses: the one house with representation apportioned according to population, with one member for every 40,000 inhabitants, and the other house providing an equal voice for each state. Slavery, taxation, and ratios remained impediments to quick approval. For ten days bitterness and misunderstandings were rampant among the delegations. Finally, on Monday, July 16, the Great Compromise of the convention ironed out the details. The states retained an equal voice in one branch of the national legislature.

Another question raised during the convention was whether the national legislature should have the power to negate state legislation. Dickinson believed that the convention "must either subject the states to the danger of being injured by the power of the national government or the latter to the danger of being injured by that of the states." To him, the greater dangers would arise from state actions. "To leave the power doubtful," he asserted, "would be opening another spring of discord." Dickinson wanted to prevent as many future conflicts as possible. But his viewpoint was not found acceptable, and even Delaware's vote was divided. The primacy of national law as opposed to state or local law was one eventually determined by the courts.

Dickinson's years in the Pennsylvania Assembly provided insight into legislative problems and organization. When the convention took up the question of the responsibilities of each branch of the legislature, he expressed his belief that money bills must originate in the lower house as the popular branch of government.

[22] Ibid., 1:327.

Any other procedure he thought autocratic and certain to be objectionable to the electorate. On the other hand, he agreed that the upper chamber might be given amendment power. Dickinson viewed the question pragmatically. Madison reported Dickinson's statement in the matter: "Experience must be our only guide. Reason may mislead us. It was not Reason that discovered the singular & admirable mechanism of the English Constitution. It was not Reason that discovered or even could have discovered the odd & in the eye of those who are governed by reason, the absurd mode of trial by jury. Accidents probably produced these discoveries, and experience has give[n] a sanction to them. This then is our guide."[23]

Just as Dickinson understood legislative organization, so he knew the needs of the executive branch. He thought it unlikely a republic could have a vigorous, strong executive. Only a monarchy could hold to this because respect and attachment made it possible. A limited monarchy, which he considered perhaps the best form of government, he recognized as out of the question. Dickinson "dreaded" a consolidation of states but sought a good national government which governed in association with the states. As president of Pennsylvania he had ruled with the advice of an Executive Council. Dickinson must have found such a multiple arrangement satisfactory. At one juncture he confessed that he feared a single executive, believing it had never been safely done. Worse, he thought a seven-year term for that office might provide a base for the president to become "a traytor to his country." He asserted "secrecy, vigor and dispatch are not the principal properties required in the Executive . . . that of responsibility is more so."[24]

Dickinson further opposed any "recital of qualification" for that office in the constitution. It was impossible to make a complete list, "and a partial one would by implication tie up the hands of the Legislature from supplying the omissions. The best defense lay in the freeholders who were to elect the Legislature." Indeed,

[23] Ibid., 2:278.

[24] Fragments of Notes, Logan Collection, HSP, pp. 107, 109; also reported by Madison on June 7, Farrand, 1:140.

Dickinson's natural aristocratic point of view was often balanced by a genuine belief in the underlying virtues of the electorate. In arguments concerning any detailing of restrictions on those eligible to serve as elected officials, Dickinson "doubted the policy of intervening into a Republican constitution a veneration for wealth. He [said that] he had always understood that a veneration for poverty and virtue, were the objects of republican encouragement. It seemed improper that any man of merit should be subjected to disabilities in a Republic where merit was understood to form the great title to public trust, honor and rewards."[25]

Correct procedure in choosing a president similarly posed a problem. Dickinson opposed an election of the executive by the national legislature or by either the legislatures or the governors of the states. He "had long leaned towards an election by the people . . . as the best and purest source." An alternative was the nomination by each state of its best citizen for the office—those most likely to be the best in each state. From this list either the national legislature or electors appointed by it could then choose.[26]

Years later in a letter to Senator George Logan, his kinsman through marriage, Dickinson recounted the final solution in the manner of electing the president.

> One morning the Committee met in the Library Room of the State House, and went upon the business. I was much indisposed during the whole time of the Convention. I did not come into the Committee till late, and found the members upon their feet.
>
> When I came in, they were pleased to read to me their minutes, containing a report to this purpose, if I remember rightly—That the President should be chosen by the legislature. The particulars I forget. I observed that the powers which we had agreed to vest in the President were so many and so great, that I did not think the people would be willing to deposit them with him, unless they themselves would be more immediately concerned in his election—That from what had passed in Convention respecting the magnitude and accumulation of those powers, we might easily judge

[25] Farrand, 2:123.

[26] Ibid., 2:114–15.

what impressions might be made on the public mind, un-
favorable to the Constitution we were framing—That if this
single Article should be rejected, the whole would be lost,
and [that] the States would have the work to go over again
under vast disadvantages—That the only true and safe principle on which these powers could be committed to an individual, was—That he should be in a strict sense of th[e]
expression, *The Man of the People*—besides, that an election by the Legislature, would form an improper dependence and connection. Having thus expressed my sentiments, Gouverneur Morris immediately said—"Come
Gentlemen, let us sit down again, and converse further on
this subject."

When they all sat down, and after some conference, James
Madison took a pen and paper, and sketched out a mode
for electing the President agreeable to the present provision.
To this we assented and reported accordingly.[27]

Removal of the chief executive from office and any vacancy that
might occur in that office posed similar problems. The disability
clause in the latter case Dickinson thought vague. "What is the extent of the term 'disability'?" he asked. "Who is to be the judge of
it?" The questions were not answered at the Convention.

At another juncture it was proposed that the executive be given
judicial power. This followed the Pennsylvania system in which
the state's president acted as a judge on the High Court of Appeals.
A similar suggestion was supported by Madison. Dickinson objected, arguing that one was the expounder and the interpreter of
the law, the other the executor of it.[28] Madison recorded that Dickinson believed that mixing the functions of the two branches was
"improper" and that responsibility could only be preserved if the
executive was left singly to discharge his assigned duties.[29]

With considerable force Dickinson pointed out that if there
were a national legislature, there ought to be a national judiciary,
and that the legislature should have the right to institute that
branch. Wilson and Madison both supported this view, observing

[27] Dickinson to Logan, November 4, 1802, folder 18, box 17–33, L-D/LCP.

[28] Farrand, 1:108, 110.

[29] Ibid., 1:140.

that there was a "distinction between establishing such tribunals absolutely, and giving a discretion to the legislature to establish or not establish them." Dickinson, however, did not believe that judges should have the power to set aside a law. He had no easy solution for this possible need; yet he was aware of at least one historical precedent for the proposal, that of the Judiciary of Aragon which by degrees went on to become the lawgiver.

Many problems concerned other aspects of the constitution. Dickinson did not slacken in either his interest or his expressions of concern. For representatives to the House he preferred triennial elections, with a rotation by annual elections of one third of the members; and he favored the same pay for both houses of the Congress.

Slavery in the new nation was brought to the fore in August. The matter arose in the proposed count of inhabitants to be made in each state for the purposes of representation and taxation. Out of the discussion came demands for cessation of the slave trade itself. South Carolina and Georgia most strongly favored its continuance. Northern states in their new constitutions had freed those slaves who were within their boundaries. Dickinson, who had manumitted his own slaves, "considered it inadmissable on every principle of honor and safety that the importation of slaves should be authorized to the states by the Constitution. The true question was whether the national happiness would be promoted or impeded by the importation, and this question ought to be left to the National Government not to the states particularly interested."[30] Although certain southern states threatened that they would not support the new constitution if the issue was not acted upon, Dickinson did not believe they would follow through on their threats. But he deemed it unlikely the "General Government" would immediately act to outlaw slavery and the slave trade. Finally, late in August, an amendment was agreed to which prevented the Congress from prohibiting the slave trade before 1808. The date had previously been suggested by Dickinson as a compromise.[31]

[30] Ibid., 2:372.

[31] Ibid., 2:416.

In this and in other arguments Dickinson noted the "best Philosophy is drawn from Experiments—the best policy from Experience."[32] He maintained his belief in the sovereign rights of small states and cautioned that the larger states, not the smaller ones, were the source of danger. Likewise, he thought that due to the proportion of slaves allowed in the total count for representatives, every importer of slaves would increase the power of his state over others, notably in the admission of the new states.[33] His surmise was all too true.

Dickinson, although plagued by physical weakness, had stuck out the convention. He and Polly wrote frequently, and Polly complained of his absence. She, too, was indisposed. He advised her to rest and, predicting an end of the sessions by mid-September, told her, "It is one of the best joys of my soul to be loved by you and I will love you with the tenderest affection."[34]

Two weeks later Dickinson was exhausted, and he abruptly decided to leave Philadelphia. He wrote George Read two notes: one, asking Read to sign his name to the constitution if it was to be signed by the convention members; the other, enclosing a bank bill to be used for the entertainment planned for "the gentlemen of the town from whom civilities had been received."[35] At almost the same time Polly and her youngest daughter were preparing to go to Pennsylvania for a week. But when Dickinson arrived home, they postponed their visit until later that month when, as was his wont, Dickinson went down to his plantation in Kent.

Dickinson supported the proposed constitution with enthusiasm. Delaware with equal zeal at once turned to its ratification. Partisanship was temporarily laid aside. Thomas Collins, the president of the state, recommended adoption and declared that it involved the prosperity, the felicity, and even perhaps the continued existence of the new nation. Accordingly, a convention was called, delegates were elected, and, on December 3, that body met and

---

[32] Fragment for a speech, 1787, Item 107, L-D/LCP.

[33] Ibid., Item 108, L-D/LCP.

[34] JD to his wife, August 30, 1787, L/HSP, VIII.

[35] JD to Read, September 15, 1787, Dickinson Papers, DSA.

ratified the new constitution—the first state to do so.[36]

Delaware had not hesitated to use John Dickinson's services. In his turn, Dickinson delayed asking for reimbursement of expenses. Not until later that year did he compute the allowances due him. These he sent Eleazer McCombe, who asked him instead to submit his bill to James Booth for presentation to the next session of the legislature. Dickinson's generous position during the earlier days of Delaware's financial difficulties is apparent in the sum owed him. This was based on

183 days attendance in Congress in 1779 @ 20s.	£183.0.0
1 year salary as president of the state	200.0.0
14 days attendance at convention in Annapolis, Sept. 1786 @ 40s.	28.0.0
74 days attendance in convention at Philadelphia in 1787 @ 40s.	148.0.0[37]

Dickinson in asking for reimbursement pointed to the difficulties of the times and "the heavy and in my judgment unreasonable taxes imposed to me. . . . [Nevertheless] I would not choose to charge the State for more than six months as a member of Congress or for more than a year as President."[38]

Although Delaware warmly supported the new Constitution, many opposed it in other states. Dickinson was alarmed by the slow pace of ratification. In an effort to stem the growing criticism he wrote nine "letters" signed "Fabius," which appeared in the *Delaware Gazette* beginning early in 1788 and subsequently were published in pamphlet form in April of that year. To ensure his anonymity, he had Dr. John Vaughan copy them and carry them to the newspaper.[39]

[36] Munroe, pp. 107–8.

[37] JD to McCombe, December 5, 1787, L/HSP, XII, 44.

[38] JD to the Auditor of Delaware, November 29, 1787, L/HSP, VIII.

[39] John Dickinson, *The Letters of Fabius . . . Observations on the Constitution* (Philadelphia, 1788); quotations are from the edition published by V. C.

The first letter noted that objections to the proposed document came both from friends of good government and from its enemies. The latter included those men who hoped to profit by a weak government or by "public convulsions" or those who had opposed the Revolution itself and now hoped that, worn down by dissensions, the people would soon return to the fold of Great Britain. Only sincere friends, Dickinson believed, deserved respect and an answer to their objections. He stated: "What concerns all, should be considered by all; and individuals may injure a whole society, by not declaring their sentiments. It is therefore not only their *right*, but their *duty*, to declare them. . . . Let everyone freely speak what he really thinks." Dickinson felt certain that "the *power of the people* pervading the proposed system, together with the strong confederation of the states" would be adequate security against every possible future danger.[40]

After taking up all the major objections regarding the frame of government as they pertained to its three branches, "Fabius" asserted that the foundations had been laid "in the most clear, strong, positive, unequivocable language" possible. Even the Magna Carta did not contain clauses "more decisive and emphatic."[41]

Not only did Dickinson analyze the governmental organization as set forth in the new constitution, but he expounded on the theory he found underlying it. He conceived of the citizens forming a society with a common stock or rights and obtaining greater benefits than one could obtain from individual efforts; thus, "in forming a confederation, each political society should *contribute* such a share of their rights, as will, from a *common stock* of these rights, produce the largest quantity of benefits for them."[42]

In his fourth letter the author suggested that "if it be considered separately, a *constitution* is the *organization* of the contributed rights in society. Government is the *exercise* of them." Nearly a

<hr />

Smyth, Wilmington, 1797. Vaughan to Deborah Logan, February 20, 1837, Miscellaneous Collection, HSP.

[40] Dickinson, *Letters*, pp. 2–3.

[41] Ibid., pp. 14–15.

[42] Ibid., p. 16.

decade later when the *Letters of Fabius* were reprinted, they were amended and added to. Dickinson again and again supplemented his original thoughts with footnotes excerpted from Thomas Paine's *Rights of Man*, published three years after the letters first appeared in newspapers.

For those who feared the "inconvenience" of a division of governmental responsibilities, Dickinson wrote that such a balance would "encrease the safety and repose of the governed" by placing restrictions against errors. He argued persuasively:

> Our government under the proposed confederation, will be guarded by a repetition of the strongest cautions against excesses. In the Senate the sovereignties of the several states will be equally represented; in the House of Representatives, the people of the whole union will be equally represented; and in the president, and the federal independent judges, so much concerned with the execution of the laws, and in the determination of their constitutionality, the sovereignties of the several states and the people of the whole union, may be considered as conjointly represented.
>
> Where was there ever and where is there now upon the face of the earth, a government so diversified and attempered?[43]

Dickinson was confident that together the states would act "prudently and honestly" but apart "foolishly and knavishly." "Fabius" warned that the seeds of liberty found in the new frame of government demanded "continual attention, unceasing diligence, and frequent conflict with difficulties: but, to object against the benefits offered to us by our Creator, by excepting to the terms annexed, is a crime to be equalled only by its folly."[44]

The influence of Dickinson's essays is impossible to gauge. The *Federalist Papers* that appeared in New York newspapers were extensive and theoretical; the *Letters of Fabius* were shorter, containing less philosophy and providing more direct answers to the main arguments raised against the Constitution. John Vaughan sent George Washington the first four letters. The general promptly acknowledged them, saying the author was a "master of his sub-

[43] Ibid., p. 31.

[44] Ibid., p. 68.

ject, he treats it with dignity, and at the same time expresses himself in such a manner as to render it intelligent to every capacity." He believed extensive publication would be valuable as a supportive force.[45]

Dickinson was constantly approached for advice and service. Shortly after his return to Wilmington in 1785, he was asked to serve as a jurist for the Confederation, adjudicating cases that came within its purview. Twice he refused. In his second letter of declination Dickinson wrote that "repose and calm" were indispensable for his health.[46] Yet in 1786 he attended the convention at Annapolis and dutifully went up to the Philadelphia convention the next year. Though often ill there, he tried not to allow his personal indisposition to interfere with his attendance. Dickinson was more inclined toward service with the state. In February 1788 Dickinson accepted appointment as a judge of the Delaware Court of Appeals. But, finding this responsibility too taxing, he did not continue long on the bench.[47]

Friends in Philadelphia wrote that summer, expressing hopes that Dickinson would become one of the first senators from Delaware. He told Tench Coxe, a Philadelphia economist, who urged him to exert efforts to have Philadelphia made the new capital, that for physical reasons he could undertake neither that requested action nor a Senate seat. In answer to a warm letter from Benjamin Rush, Dickinson similarly replied, saying, "I believe there is not a man on earth besides myself who can form any idea of the distresses, from weakness of body, that I have undergone by endeavoring to sustain a public character with some decency while laboring under such infirmities." His weak constitution tended to limit his further public service for several years.[48]

Between 1788 and 1791 Dickinson lived a life apart from active

[45] Washington to Vaughan, April 27, 1788, Fitzpatrick, *Writings of Washington*, 29:468.

[46] JD to Charles Thomson, [Dec.] 1786, draft letter, Item 7, L-D/LCP.

[47] Dickinson apparently served only a year. See Item 14, L-D/LCP and L/HSP, XXXVI, 102.

[48] JD to Coxe, July 4, 1788, Dickinson Papers, DSA; JD to Rush, August 4, 1788, Wisconsin Historical Society.

involvement either in the national government or in Delaware. In 1791, however, he responded affirmatively to another call and became a representative of New Castle County at a convention called "for the purpose of reviewing, altering and amending, the Constitution of this State [Delaware], or if they see occasion, for forming a new one." George Read, not a delegate but his political ally, twice visited him for several days in Wilmington before the convention. Dickinson that fall had also spent ten days in Kent.[49] He was clearly aware of the political climate in the lower counties as well as the issues at hand.

The convention met on Tuesday, November 29, and two days later was organized with the election of officers. John Dickinson was elected president and James Booth, secretary.[50] The convention sat until December 31, 1791, when a final draft of a new constitution was ordered printed and submitted to the General Assembly for their consideration. The convention then adjourned until May 29, when any further revisions were to be considered. Finally, on June 12, the constitution was approved. Made more harmonious with the national constitution, the new document termed the state president the governor; divided the Assembly into a senate and a house of representatives, and made the judiciary a separate branch.

Two issues of considerable importance had come before the convention. On December 22 Warner Mifflin, a fearless, indeed aggressive, Quaker from Kent County, appeared with a request that asked for the abolition of slavery in Delaware and an exemption from military duty of those people opposed to war. Although the convention had completed its major tasks, the question was considered, but no action was taken on either subject before the adjournment the following week.[51] Mifflin, a longtime acquaintance of Dickinson, aware that he seemed to assume more and more

[49] Sally N. Dickinson to Deborah Logan, December 7, 1791, Deborah Logan Correspondence, Logan Family Papers, VII, HSP.

[50] J. Thomas Scharf, *History of Delaware* (Philadelphia, 1888), 1:279; "Rough Minutes taken by Mr. Ridgely," Item 204, DSA; *Minutes of the Convention of the Delaware State* (Wilmington, 1792).

[51] Scharf, *Delaware*, 1:279.

Quaker attributes, unhappily found him to be an impartial president of the convention.

The Dickinsons had been slave owners. Dickinson as a young man writing home from London had deplored the effect of slavery upon some of his American contemporaries studying at the Temple. In the settlement of his father's estate he had been careful neither to break up families nor to sell the slaves to inconsiderate planters. In 1772 Dickinson purchased several blacks from neighbors in an apparent attempt to maintain the family ties of his slaves. In many instances his actions were motivated by charity, as in taking over by sale from a nearby estate a Negro woman and her four children from age eleven to a few months old.[52] When he had hired out any of these hands, as he frequently did, Dickinson in his agreement, as in the case of one Dinah and her two-year-old daughter, demanded of the contractor that "he and they shall treat with great kindness the said negroes and any other children she may have during the term, shall take due care of her and furnish her with proper provisions of every kind in Time of her lying in from time to time and in other sickness—shall provide her and all her children with plenty of good food and of warm and comfortable clothing and bedding during the term."[53]

Although Dickinson had manumitted his own slaves in 1781, most of them he bound to service for a period of years. In addition he accepted the voluntary indenture of others, young teenagers, for twelve to fifteen years. His actions seemed to harmonize with George Read's comments to him: "It is a mistaken plan to set those creatures to manage for themselves after a partial state of slavery." Dickinson held fast to a belief that from the time of the Declaration of Independence, slaves *"could not afterwards be imported into these states.* The Sanctions of Law, the most solemn rational acts, and the eternal Distinctions between Right and Wrong, all forbid property to spring from such a source [as slavery]."[54]

[52] R. R. Logan Papers, XXVIII, 90, 93; XXXIV, 86, 110, HSP.

[53] Ibid., XXXIV, 86, 110; see also ibid., XXVII, 27–29, XXXII, 18, XXXVI, 21, 23, XXXVII, 5.

[54] Read to JD, November 25, 1788, Loudoun Collection, HSP; JD to Tench Coxe, May 22, 1804, Tench Coxe Papers, HSP.

In 1793 Dickinson earnestly sought to have his brother free his servants from slavery. His new attitude was based on both moral and religious grounds and was indicative of his increased concern with the teachings of the Society of Friends. Philemon answered John's letter of censure with asperity, replying, "I endeavor to regulate my conduct by the principle of justice and humanity and am strongly inclined to believe you are not acquainted with my conduct towards those persons you deem so unhappy." Then, listing all his servants bound as sales or free, Philemon went into detail, asserting:

> I am far from being friendly to perpetual slavery—yet I am of opinion that people should have an Education suited to freedom—under this impression (but not viewing it in a criminal light) I would willingly subscribe to a general act for the *gradual* abolition of slavery.
>
> Not being influenced by the same motives that you are, and my situation not permitting me to make so great a sacrifice as you request, I hope I shall stand excused, even in your mind.[55]

John continued in every way to look out for the "old Black folks," as he referred to them. They lived on the Dickinson land reserved for them as well as land otherwise let by him to other tenants. In his leases Dickinson provided for their care and protection and their right to gather "wood lying on the ground for fuel—of cutting hay in the marsh for three horses and six cows and range and pasturage," as well as to keep poultry and fish on the premises.[56]

When the state constitutional convention briefly reconvened in May 1792, a Quaker delegation appeared with a memorial from a large number of Friends from New Jersey, Pennsylvania, Delaware, and Maryland who had met in Philadelphia a short while before. Over the signature of James Pemberton, clerk, the petition asked for a Delaware constitutional provision for the abolition of slavery and for freedom from military service for those holding

[55] Philemon Dickinson to JD, February 14, 1793, Item 17, L-D/LCP.

[56] Indenture with Deborah White, December 7, 1796, L/HSP, XXX, 18; see also L/HSP, XXVII, 100.

conscientious religious scruples against it.[57] Although the convention had no major business at hand and was not prepared for a long session, it agreed to consider the new requests. However, no action was taken and thus neither provision was included in the final draft of the constitution.

In general, Dickinson considered the state convention to have been one of "great harmony."[58] As chairman, his task had not been easy. His own bias had to be put aside. Yet his studied position and neutrality irked Warner Mifflin. After accusing Dickinson of having taken up the subjects of slavery and militia service on the one day he was absent at Meeting, Mifflin declared that Dickinson had sought a constitutional provision to prevent blacks from purchasing real property; that stand, supported by his conduct toward those "conscientiously scrupulous against arms," made him "an enemy to the cause of righteousness."[59] The accusations were false and unfair. Dickinson later pointed out that the constitution could not legally declare that all slaves born after the constitution was put into effect would be free, and any measure to alleviate slavery would have been constitutional sanction of that institution. Such action must be undertaken by the Assembly. He explained to James Pemberton: "Some of us thought that any pruning of this tree of bitter fruits would only strengthen it and make it last longer." Dickinson suggested to the Friends that testimony against slavery ought to continue and enclosed a bill he had drafted two or three years before and sent to the Assembly of Delaware for its action, together with his personal plea that the institution "may be gradually and totally abolished." Pemberton understood Dickinson's position and expressed a hope that the Society for Promoting the Abolition of Slavery, then inactive, might be revived at Dover and also in Wilmington and be permitted to address the Assembly on the subject. He returned the bill Dickin-

[57] Relative to the Memorial of Friends concerning exemption from Military Service and [concerning] Slavery, John Dickinson notes, Gratz collection, HSP.

[58] JD to his wife, June 5, 1792, L/HSP, VIII, 117.

[59] Mifflin to Henry Drinker, June 27, 1792, Hilda Justice, comp., *Life and Ancestry of Warner Mifflin* (Philadelphia, 1905), p. 104.

son had sent him after making some alterations to it. Dickinson, in reply, laid particular guilt for the continuation of slavery at the door of Britain as "the most guilty nation . . . that ever the sun shone on" for their engaging in the "abominable traffic" in flesh and blood.[60]

In 1804, following the purchase of Louisiana, John Dickinson as if foreseeing the future tragedy that was to be America's, wrote to Dr. George Logan then senator from Pennsylvania:

> As Congress is now to legislate for our extensive territory lately acquired, I pray to Heaven, that they may build up the system of the government, on the broad, strong, and sacred principles of freedom. Curse not the inhabitants of those regions and of the United States in general, with a permission to induce bondage.
>
> .   .   .   .   .
>
> The theme is inexhaustible. Let the pernicious project, the detestable precedent, never be sanctioned by votes of the Sons of Liberty.[61]

The second major concern presented by the Friends to the Delaware constitutional convention dealt with armed service. Pemberton wrote Dickinson that many inhabitants who by "pure conscientious motives were constrained from actively complying with military requisitions" and were penalized for their refusal could view these penalties as "species of persecution and infringement on the Rights of Conscience."[62] The convention, on receipt of the memorial of the Friends in June, expunged the second section of Article VIII in the printed draft which enjoined "the legislature to make a Militia Law without reservations."

Dickinson replied that silence on the subject seemed of some

[60] Pemberton to JD, October 22, 1792, RRL/LCP, box 3; folder 3; JD to Pemberton, November 1, 1792, Etting Collection, MOC, 1, p. 52, HSP. In 1786 Dickinson had written a bill for the gradual emancipation of slavery. See John Munroe, *Colonial Delaware* (Millwood, N. J., 1978), pp. 189–90.

[61] JD to George Logan, January 30, 1804, L/HSP, V.

[62] Pemberton to JD, June 6, 1792, L-D/LCP.

value in the writing of Pennsylvania's constitution. A clause for total exemption would have met with great difficulty. Dickinson believed considerations in this regard were more properly made through law and should not be included in the constitution. Moreover, Dickinson thought that efforts calling for total exemption would be unattainable and embarrassing to the legislature.[63]

In 1790 he had written Richard P. Hicks, whose guardian he had been, on the value of military service. Having served both as a former officer and subsequently as a private in the ranks, he could write with authority.

> Every young man should be so well instructed in military discipline as to be able to yield effectual service to his country. . . . 'Tis standing in the ranks of freedom gives dignity. . . . I wish young gentlemen of the most respected families and the largest fortunes would be emulous of serving in the militia as privates. If they see the rich and distinguished aspiring constantly to command with an implied contempt of obedience at least in its lowest form such jealousies and factions may be produced as have so often disturbed the peace of other societies. And why should they then aspire. They cannot be more honored than by the love of their countrymen. And by what can a really generous mind be more delighted?[64]

Dickinson's belief in the need for a militia was deeply rooted. In 1802 Dickinson wrote Thomas McKean on the subject, seeing lessons which made it as essential to "Liberty as to morality to 'watch always.' " In the mournful pages of history, he noted, "there has ever been an increasing struggle of the few for obtaining aggrandisement at the expense of the many." Thus, he believed, "a well-organized, well equipped and a well disciplined Militia will afford the only human means of safety for us and our posterity. The neglect of it is a prompter to internal confusion and an invitation to foreign invasion."[65]

[63] JD to Pemberton, letter draft, Gratz Collection, case 1, box 5, HSP.

[64] JD to Hicks, March 1, 1790, 41:106, L/HSP.

[65] JD to McKean, November 22, 1802, McKean Papers, III, 64, HSP.

Dickinson was satisfied with Delaware's constitution, despite a few unavoidable defects. He felt that some of these would be compensated for by the "simplicity and energy" of the judicial arrangements. Indeed, in every state the "happiness of the people will depend more upon the establishment and administration of the judicial powers, than upon the distribution and exercise of any other authority." He conceded that some regulations in the constitution should more properly have been dealt with by legislative action, but the "peculiarity of circumstances" demanded their inclusion.[66]

William Killen, the chief justice who became chancellor under the new constitution, had lived with the Dickinson family when John and his brother were children. After the first session of the convention, he wrote Dickinson that citizens in Sussex and Kent counties turned their eyes toward Dickinson as the future governor, as he was seen as the man most likely to preserve Delaware "from political insignificancy and to serve the best interests of the state." Dickinson in strong language eliminated himself, "early and directly," from this office.[67] He was then pressed to serve in the Assembly that would put the new constitution into operation. To this he did not object, suggesting, "Perhaps my infirmities may be of some service as I shall not [be] oppressed by a perpetual attention." At the same time he pointed out that he could not be useful in the Assembly if well-qualified men were not proposed elsewhere to assist in the upcoming session. Dickinson asserted the duties of the legislators would be arduous and demanding—"An extensive knowledge of the subsisting laws will be indispensibly required in order to form such as will harmonize with them under the new constitution." He also found other "several deeply interesting and embarrassing circumstances" peculiar to Delaware that required action. These exigencies Dickinson saw as demanding not only legal ability on the part of members of the legislature but also full acquaintance with public affairs. He felt that although

[66] JD to a "Friend," September 25, 1792, L/HSP, VIII, 119.

[67] JD to Killen, April 12, 1792, Loudoun Collection, HSP; "To Electors of the State of Delaware," June 21, 1792, letter draft, L/HSP, VIII, 117.

the people daily paid large sums to lawyers for their services, at the same time they were niggardly in seeking legal service for the state, that they disparaged the inclusion of lawyers in the Assembly. Dickinson went so far as to suggest the names of those he wished to have serve in that body.[68]

It annoyed Dickinson that compensation for government service was so far out of proportion to the time and study involved. He believed that public servants "should be so wisely and liberally provided for in that security [of payment] that men may be obtained to fill the offices who will not value them chiefly as *titles* to their salaries but as stations for serving their country." Without this, the best qualified men would not serve. He considered it imperative to engage "genius, knowledge and personal respectability to fill those offices thereby uniting the greatest usefulness and personal respectability, with the dignity of public station."[69]

After consenting to serve in the organizational legislature, Dickinson sought advice on matters that would assist in the implementation of the new constitution. Richard Bassett, his onetime Dover neighbor and associate, was one who answered his queries. The courts, aspects of finance, and the claims of the Penn family were particular areas on which Dickinson asked guidance. He took up his task gravely, noting, "It is a serious reflection in business that concerns thousands to know that if I err I may also cause others to err, and thus injure multitudes if not ages."[70]

The convention of 1791–92 had worn him out, and for several weeks afterwards he was confined to his house. Dickinson, however, attended the first session of the Assembly as senator from New Castle County. He had hoped to attend a second session called for May, but once again he suffered an indisposition. Dickinson felt impelled to resign. In March 1793 he drafted a message "To the Freemen of New Castle County" setting forth his continuing

[68] JD to a "Friend," September 25, 1792, Loudoun Collection, HSP; similar draft, same date, L/HSP, VIII; see next note for yet another draft.

[69] JD, letter draft, n.d., item 45, L-D/LCP.

[70] JD to Bassett, December 31, 1792, Dreer Collection (Annapolis Convention), HSP.

poor health as the reason for his resignation and forwarded it to his supporters.[71]

John Dickinson's retirement from the Assembly at the age of sixty-one marked his departure from official state and national involvement. He had served selflessly with great devotion, intelligence, and courage for thirty critical years. But withdrawal from government service did not mean any lessening of his interest or of his involvement in local, state, or national affairs as a private citizen. Dickinson was by nature a citizen always engagé, actively concerned with the best the nation could provide, critical of the country's shortcomings, and fascinated by events abroad.

[71] Draft, "To the Freemen of New Castle County," March 1793, Item 57, L-D/LCP.

☆ 11 ☆

Being a
Concerned Citizen

JOHN DICKINSON HAD INTENDED HIS MOVE to Wilmington in 1785 to free him from governmental responsibilities, although it was another eight years before his public duties came to an end. Between appointments, however, there was time for other interests. The "good works" of both John and Mary Dickinson were held as very private matters. They assisted impecunious relatives such as Hannah Griffitts, a second cousin of Mary, as well as neighbors and others whose needs were brought to their attention. At a time when all education was private, Dickinson saw to it that a poor neighboring farmer's children in Kent were sent to school, sometimes paying for six youngsters at a time. Nor did he forget the needs of his servants, some of whom he also enrolled under a schoolmaster.[1] The children of friends, such as William Hicks's orphans, received continuous support.[2]

Solicitous care for the afflicted was no casual matter for Dickin-

---

[1] For property allowed John Dickinson, Jr. (with provisions "as long as it should please John Dickinson"), see Logan Papers, XXXVII, 115-20, L/HSP. JD to Hannah Griffitts, May 5, 1754, and many other letters to her in the MDL Collection, HSP.

[2] Dickinson's Account Book, 1777-1807, Dickinson manuscript, HSP; Account with Stephen Paradee, Item 95, L-D/LCP; Account with Henry Pepper, Item 28, L-D/LCP.

son. From his early public service, in 1776, when he wrote Francis Alison that he had "made it a constant rule to apply from time to time all wages due him as a member of the Assembly towards the relief of the unhappy" and so forwarded an order "for the benefit of such widows and children of deceased clergymen as are the objects of a charitable institution in your Society," he exhibited thoughtful concern.[3] Soon after he moved to Wilmington, the relief of prisoners attracted his attention. Dickinson particularly cited those confined "on account of conscience or for debt without any distinction as to religious profession." For this purpose the Dickinsons provided ground rent income. At the same time, together they sought some "permanent provision for the proper education of poor orphan children." Both projects were put into the care of the Society of Friends. The following year John and Mary Dickinson added to their subscriptions, setting aside five acres in the Northern Liberties with a yearly rent of £7 for the Society for Relieving Miseries of Public Prisons, of which Bishop William White was chairman and James Pemberton a member of the board.[4]

The Dickinsons, late in 1786, began a more organized approach to their charitable contributions with Pemberton as adviser. As a leading Quaker, it was natural that he urged support for varied Society interests.

Dickinson's now regenerated interest in education, prison relief, and other charities raised quiet hopes that he might more definitely associate himself with the Society of Friends. Samuel Pleasants and Pemberton frequently engaged in correspondence with him in these matters. Their approach was always gentle, not directly broaching their wish for his active association, but otherwise eager in their efforts. Ann Emlen, another correspondent, was more direct. She wrote him in 1787 and expressed pleasure over Dickinson's "charitable intentions, of being a charitable contributor towards a free school." She then added:

[3] JD to Alison, January 10, 1766, Society Collection, HSP.

[4] JD to Pemberton, March 29, 1787. Etting Collection, p. 69, HSP; Indenture for "Society for Relieving Miseries," May 6, 1788, Miscellaneous Items (January Papers, etc.), L/HSP.

If thou wast became a member of [the] Society thou mightest
with just assistance of others also yoked in mind to the service become as Dr. Fothergill, a vigilant advancer of it into
execution. But that must depend on thy feelings. Perhaps
human wisdom is not yet sufficiently reduced in subjection
to the simplicity that is in Christ, to make thee as yet willing
to stoop to the foolishness of the cross sometimes appearing
in the Quaker. I do not mean an irrational or unchristian
foolishness but what appeareth foolishness to sophistry. I
suggest these things respecting thyself. I do not say they are
so. Forgive my great freedom and burn this if I do not con-
clude to save thee the trouble. If it goes let the veil of charity cover its defects. And may thou persevere this time in
that which shall induce us to address thee in the character
of—John Dickinson the Worthy—not J.D. Esq., or the Great.
Thou will say, I suppose, I am a strange girl to write as I
do.[5]

Dickinson did not become a member of the Society, but there had
been subtle change in his life and religious thought. Less than a
year after he left Pennsylvania, Dickinson began to use Quaker
address and dating in his correspondence. Soon, too, he attended
First Day Meetings with his wife and family, though he studiously
absented himself from the Monthly Meetings of the Society.

The Friends had English educational models to follow. There
the charity element in the Ackworth School under the care of the
London Monthly Meeting had been strong. A proposal had been
instituted in 1782 with the purchase of 60 acres at Nottingham in
Chester County, but only six students had been received in a small
house built there. George Dillwyn, in 1786, had urged American
Friends to locate a school similar to Ackworth in New Jersey.
Dickinson wished to assist in the establishment of such a school.
He opposed temporary measures and thought that the institution
should be for those who could not afford schooling at any great
cost and for the relief of the indigent.[6]

[5] A[nn] Emlen, Jr., to JD, December 21, 1787, Society Collection, HSP,
quoted in Isaac Sharpless, *Political leaders of Provincial Pennsylvania* (New
York, 1919), pp. 238–39.

[6] J. William Frost, *The Quaker Family in Colonial America* (New York,
1973), pp. 93–105; JD to S. Pleasants, January 22, 1788, L/HSP, XII, 45; see

Dickinson's plan for the education of the poor and orphaned was criticized as being too circumscribed. Its eventual location, he believed, ought to be within twenty miles of Philadelphia, certainly not farther away than thirty. And, in his own mind, Dickinson believed the school's curriculum should provide neither too intensive nor too broad an education. Great works had been accomplished by illiterates, he pointed out. Time for student play ought to be arranged and gardening and household management, among other subjects, taught.

Nottingham, in which Dickinson had been earlier interested, now languished for want of support and the Society had rejected the idea of a charity school. The members at the Quarterly Meeting were divided on receiving the Dickinsons' proffered trust. Owen Biddle, a Philadelphia apothecary, however, engaged the attention of the Friends with a pamphlet published in 1789 entitled *Essay on Schools*, which, at the behest of Samuel Pleasants and George Churchman, was forwarded to Dickinson. The essay met with his warm approbation. Early in January 1790 he prepared a document by which he and his wife vested part of one of their estates in the "Trustees of the Society of Friends," with the profits and income to be applied to the "Education of Poor Children." But Pleasants found the limitation Dickinson set inconsistent with decisions made at the previous yearly meeting and therefore unacceptable. There was, in short, to be no American Ackworth with a strong charitable emphasis. Three years of discussion resulted instead in the establishment of a school later known as Westtown and to which the Dickinson's subscribed.[7]

Dickinson's belief in the importance of schools, academies, and colleges was real. In 1791, following four years of reflection regarding education, he wrote his friend Dr. Rush, "I look upon the protection of education by government . . . as indispensibly neces-

---

notation on reverse of letter to J. Pleasants, March 16, 1788. Society Collection, HSP.

[7] Minutes of the Trustees, Westtown, for August 18, 1790, Westtown Library; S. Pleasants to JD, January 25, February 19, July 17, August 18, 1790; JD to S. Pleasants, letter draft, June 29, 1790, JD to Owen Biddle, July 20, 1789, August 2, 1790, February 16, 1793, Society to Heckon, HSP; Helen A. Hole, *Westtown through the Years* (Westtown, Pa., 1946), p. 3.

sary for . . . advancing the happiness of our fellow citizens as individuals and for securing the continuance of equal liberty to them in society."[8]

The Dickinsons were constant in their belief of the need for education and they were particularly concerned with those unable to receive it for financial reasons. Added to other many gifts were those to Methodists in Delaware who sought to establish a college, and that effort having failed the sum applied to the wants of superannuated ministers, widows, and orphans. Subsequently the Wilmington Monthly Meeting received funds "to facilitate the education of poor Children and the children of those not in affluent circumstances." The Brandywine Academy was established on land deeded them by Dickinson, and at a later date he supplied funds for the Wilmington Academy, of which he was a trustee.[9]

The largesse of the Dickinsons was put to good use. The State Medical Society in Delaware was given £16.17.10 for their endeavors, a gift which found James Tilton "at a loss for words" in expressing his gratitude to Dickinson. There were many other such gifts, but they were never publicized. Many sought his financial support. He and Mary sifted out what they found both possible and compatible. Aware that poverty existed in the Delaware Hundreds, Dickinson encouraged other people to go together to investigate the suffering that lay around them. Yet Dickinson's personal involvement and consideration never languished.[10]

In the twenty years from 1788 to his death in 1808, John Dickinson was increasingly involved as a man of property. Though retaining the adjoining lots in Philadelphia along Sixth Street northward to Market, he had sold his Chestnut Street house to

[8] Letter transcript, JD to Benjamin Rush, February 14, 1791, George Bancroft transcripts, 112, NYPL.

[9] L/HSP, XXXV, 110; Asbury to JD, December 10 [n.y.], L/HSP, XII, 108; Coke and Asbury to JD, November 17, 1796, JD to Coke and Asbury, January 12, 1797, HSP; L/HSP, XXXVII, 34; Brandywine Academy deed, Recorder's Office, Roll S, III, 423.

[10] Tilton to JD, June 12, 1792, L/HSP, XII, 53; Relief of the Poor, 1805, Item 14, L-D/LCP. In the different files of Dickinson papers both at the Historical Society of Pennsylvania and the Library Company of Philadelphia are many such notes and accounts.

Philemon after he moved from Philadelphia. All the Delaware lands his brother had inherited and sold, John bought back and to them he added still other farms contiguous to the original Dickinson home plantation. By 1796 Dickinson noted that "all the houses, lotts of ground, and plantations purchased in the State of Delaware, are now worth three times as much as I gave for them, and many of them four times as much."[11] He held 3,394 acres in St. Jones Hundred, 800 in Murderkill Hundred, and 1,393 in Mispillion Hundred, totaling 5,587 acres. Dickinson had acquired lands from the Pleasantons, Caesar A. Rodney and his brother Thomas, the Whethereds, the Fishers, and Nathaniel Luff, among others. All the new land he bought after his removal to Wilmington was in Delaware. The acreage of Dickinson's estate increased up to the turn of the century when problems of management tended to limit further acquisitions, although an additional 500 acres soon brought his Delaware acreage to over 6,000 in his name.[12]

In eastern Pennsylvania, by an 1805 reckoning Dickinson's holdings amounted to 1,279 acres. In addition to his few Philadelphia properties, he possessed other land in the "middle of the heart of Pennsylvania" that continually advanced in value, though the distance he lived from these properties was troublesome. Mary Norris had owed her niece a debt that predated the Dickinson marriage. Mrs. Norris, in 1788, proposed giving a tract of land in New Jersey as part payment on the account, but Dickinson refused the offer, because "by repeated experience I am convinced that land at such a distance is rather an incumbrance than a property."[13]

Dickinson's love for the land was great. The plantation at Jones Neck was a magnet in the spring and autumn and on other oc-

[11] Tax Lists, R. R. Logan Papers, HSP and LCP; see especially L/HSP, XXVI, XXVIII, and XXXVI, 116–21, and Items 14, 392, etc., L-D/LCP; For Philadelphia property, microfilm of the Philadelphia contributionship, Survey Books, and microfilm of the Independence National Historical Park Service are likewise helpful; see also JD to Tench Coxe, August 23, October 20, 1805, Tench Coxe Papers, HSP.

[12] For later acquisitions, including land extending to the bay, see L/HSP, XXV, 32, XXVI, 125–26, XXVII, 66.

[13] Mary Norris to JD, August 29, 1788, JD to Mary Norris, December 12, 1788, L/HSP, XXXVI, 96.

casions. He faithfully wrote his family when absent on these trips. In 1789 he expressed the joy he found in being at his old home:

> I always feel a melancholy kind of pleasure in being at this place where I have spent so many happy days with those that were so justly dear to me. Some of their previous remains rest in the garden. I walk, I ride, I read, I think of thee and our dear children, and humbly implore your happiness. All nature is blooming around me, and the fields are full of promises. It is surprising, how I am serenaded by heaven-taught songsters, morning and evening constantly, frequently in the day. I observed and listened yesterday for some time to a lark warbling his delight from the large Mulberry tree before the door. There is a great variety of birds and therefore of notes. A charming mocking bird every morning initiates them all. I enjoy these amusements, for I am very well.

Dickinson read continually, finding the many authors "excellent company," once noting that he was enjoying "a good deal of conversation with the justly celebrated Locke, and the truly pious Lardner."[14]

In the decade of the 1790s, Dickinson, writing his family, frequently headed his letters "Poplar Hall," as he had done decades before. Twice he referred to the plantation as Sharon, once in telling about planting "Lombardy poplars and weeping willows to give shade and pleasing objects to those who come after us."[15] The love and joy he felt for his Kent home were manifest in many ways. "Here I am, on the lands of my ancestors for several generations," he wrote on one occasion, underscoring once again the strong roots he felt in the place. One spring, having gone to Little Creek Meeting, Dickinson reported, "The country appears painted with flowers of peach trees, to whose colours cherry trees, apple trees, and even forest trees are now adding their variegated hues— This is a beautiful, favored world—but! what inhabitants! I mean not its regular innocent brutes, but its erring, sinning rationals."[16]

[14] JD to his wife, May 13, 1789, January 7, 1783, Loudoun Papers, HSP.

[15] Dickinson's letters to his family, 1793–99, Loudoun Papers, HSP.

[16] JD to his wife, April 4, 1801, and April 17, 1798, ibid.

The many acquisitions of additional land in Kent caused innumerable legal problems and disputes over the clearing of titles as well as in the unhappy task of often dispossessing tenants and other occupants. Indeed, Dickinson in 1794–95 sent letters to Nicholas Ridgely, Joseph Miller, George Read, Jr., and Nicholas Van Dyke, retaining each of them as attorneys with a fee, for all causes "in which he or his children might ever be interested."[17] A particularly disturbing suit had to do with the ejectment of Thomas and Ann Penrose in 1794. Appeals in this case extended over four years. The owner of three-tenths of five hundred disputed acres, John Mifflin, a Friend and neighbor aged seventy-six who had once lived for some time with the family of Samuel Dickinson, wrote John, with some asperity:

> The civil treatment I met with while there, has often revived in my mind and has ever since made me wish the prosperity of the family, for thee in particular I have always had a sincere regard.
>
> I was never desirous of great riches. . . . Thou has great possessions and but two children to leave them to, yet so anxious art thou, as I am told, to have more than what is really thy own, that after many years in law and a jury of honest men have given a verdict against thee, thou has still thoughts of giving the legal owners of a piece of land further trouble to come at their right.[18]

Nathaniel Luff, Jr., also wrote tellingly to Dickinson suggesting that he must find it difficult to draw the outlines of his Jones Neck property.

Much as he loved his land in Kent and looked forward to his visits there, Dickinson missed his wife and family. It was Maria, the younger daughter, whose liveliness now entertained and delighted her parents. "Let the youngest always *remember* her duties of every kind," her father wrote of the eleven-year-old, "and strive to imitate her elder sister, in giving peace to the grey hairs of her

[17] George Read, Jr., to JD, January 3, 1795, L/HSP, XXXVII, 42. See note on reverse in JD's hand.

[18] Mifflin to JD, Feb. 24, 1795, L/HSP, XII, 60; other papers, L/HSP, 21–98. Tuff to JD, "23rd 3rd Mo. 1798," L/HSP, XXVII, 97.

swiftly decaying parents." Words for her deportment were included in every letter. He urged his wife to make sure that both
children "every day of their whole lives be constant of reading at
least two chapters of the New Testament, and of offering their
prayers," suggesting that if they did not, the time would come
when the daughters would "grieve for the omission."[19] For Mary,
it was unnecessary advice.

John Dickinson, as he once wrote his wife, had the great writers
of past ages to keep him company. When in Kent overseeing repairs to the many houses and barns, he observed that "the serious
reflections of an antient come home" seemed pertinent to him. He
recounted that

> *Seneca*, when about my age, in a letter to a friend, says I
> have lately been to my villa. There, objecting to the ex-
> pense of repairs, the manager said, that with all he had
> done he could scarcely keep the house from falling on his
> head. Immediately I said to myself—when then am I who
> saw the first stone of that building laid.
>
> Walking in the orchards, I took notice to him how knotty
> and mossy the trees were grown. No wonder, replied he, for
> they are mere dotards and worn out with age. I said to my-
> self, what then am I, who helped to plant the first tree of
> that orchard.
>
> This is the substance of the story, and every part of it is
> *strictly* applicable to myself, except the complaint about
> expense.[20]

In January 1786 John Dickinson was elected a member of the
American Philosophical Society. For several decades he had been
a shareholder of the Library Company in Philadelphia and on the
"eighth day of the Ninth Month," 1788, bought a share in the
Wilmington Library Company.[21] His community activities in
Wilmington were legion. Among Dickinson's interests were tech-
nological developments. In 1787, introducing John Fitch to the

---

[19] JD to his wife, April 15, 1794, January 7, 1793, November 26, 1797, Loudoun Papers, HSP.

[20] Ibid., April 5, 1798.

[21] See L/HSP, VIII, XXXVI, for a variety of involvements.

Speaker of the Delaware legislature, he suggested that Delaware might join New York and Pennsylvania in supporting Fitch's steam engine designs "as a promotion of the public good." Dickinson helped foster the proposed canal to connect the Chesapeake and the Delaware. He later wrote Tench Coxe, who handled many of his business affairs in Philadelphia, about the promotion of manufacturing and encouraging its development in the Wilmington area, a place with "a favorable situation." As yet he was unsure whether such expansion should come about slowly or be pushed with vigor, aware, of course, that his own property would benefit.[22]

Family life in Wilmington was happy and relaxed. Mary Dickinson encouraged visits from friends, who for the most part were kinsmen and, best of all guests, Deborah Norris Logan and her family.[23] Mrs. Dickinson was a good correspondent, making up in part for any lack in her social rounds. She preferred the quiet life and was plagued by weakness and bad health from 1790 until her death. Asking Isaac Norris III, who through her had inherited Fairhill, to visit them as often as possible, she assured him that "we live in a very easy way, and if you can be satisfied with simplicity it will do—the rule here is for everybody to do as they please—eat or fast—ride or walk—read or converse—sleep or wake without the least constraint—do come and try."

Mary larded her letters with piety. A dozen years before her death she announced to Isaac that she was preparing "for her end" and told him: "Let me entreat thee, dear Isaac, to consider deeply before it is too late for what purpose thee was placed here."[24] Her days were not "numbered" as she had written him, but it did not keep her in other letters from asking him to "repent" from unexplained wrongdoing and reminding him of the stories of the Prodigal Son and of the Lost Sheep. Yet there were, apparently, long periods of ill health for Mary, although at times she looked so well that her visiting relatives could scarcely believe she was so often

[22] JD to Coxe, April 15, 1793, September 17, 1804, April 25, 1905, Tench Coxe Papers, HSP.

[23] Norris Family Papers, I and II, HSP.

[24] Mary Dickinson to Isaac Norris III, October 10, 1791, and December 5, 1791, ibid., I, 80.

ill.[25] This quiet and gentle wife was increasingly dear to Dickinson. Her devotion was matched only by his love and tenderness for her, which he expressed in a brief note sent up from Dover. "My Love, I have but one moment to thank thee for thy letter, to express my happiness in hearing of thy being better and of our children being well, to assure thee that I am very hearty, and that thou art dearer if possible to thy own."[26]

Sally Dickinson in 1789 was a young woman of eighteen, and Dr. William Thornton, the inventor and architect, paid suit to her that year. Susanna Dillwyn relayed that news to her father in England, commenting "whether he will be successful in his pursuit is very doubtful. . . . He told me he was intimate with Doctor Lettsom and is, I suppose, not more of a friend [Quaker] than he. That I suppose would be a principal objection with J.D. who is much more of a Friend than formerly."[27] But the marriage was not to be. The following year Dr. Thornton married Anne Bordeau of Philadelphia and sailed home with his bride to Tortola in the Virgin Islands.

Every First Day, Dickinson accompanied his family to Meeting, but his religious reservations concerning the Society remained. The Quaker James Bringhurst, writing in 1799, believed Dickinson "to be an improving Christian" and thought it was Sally who had brought about the change. Once, in a "free and open" conversation in Wilmington, Bringhurst said Dickinson told him that while president of Pennsylvania he had proposed that Sally learn dancing and had offered to provide a teacher for the purpose. When Sally hesitated, Dickinson asked his daughter to think it over. Later, she had replied, "If Father pleases I had much rather be a Friend." "That," Bringhurst suggested, "with some other parts of her conduct [had] put him upon closer thinking of the cause" and had effected "a change in him who was in great exaltation as to worldly eminence."[28]

[25] Mary Norris to Hannah Griffitts, November 28, 1794, ibid., II, 80.

[26] JD to his wife, May 15, 1793, Loudoun Papers, HSP.

[27] Susanna Dillwyn to her father, September 20, 1789, Dillwyn Papers, LCP.

[28] Sharpless, quoting James Bringhurst, letter dated 8th of 10th mo., 1799, pp. 239–41.

Both Wilmington and Kent County Friends, with whom Dickinson was now almost exclusively connected, never lost hope that he would declare himself one of them. Yet he strictly held the view he had expressed in September 1788 to Richard Penn Hicks, who had declared himself a Deist: "I have always acted consistent with my own ideas of religion which were that there was no necessity to become a member of any particular sect as the intent of each sect is the same and I suppose that in less than a century there will be no such distinctions but that, people thinking on a larger scale, all religions will unite under one head."[29]

Dickinson, whose whole adult life had dealt with colonial, state, and national governments, became deeply interested in international developments during the 1790s. His enthusiasm for France knew no bounds. That country's attitude toward America following the peace, however, had cooled. Any "Gallomania" that once may have existed in America had also ended. The very year of Washington's inauguration, the French Revolution had begun, leading to the execution of Louis XVI in 1792. In the meanwhile, the United States had accused Britain of avoiding living up to provisions in the Treaty of 1783. John Jay was commissioned to secure a new treaty with Britain that would compensate for vessels seized, open its West Indian ports to trade, arrange the British evacuation of the Old Northwest, and, if possible, negotiate a commercial treaty.

When the details of the treaty Jay negotiated reached the states in 1795, many reacted furiously against it. The only significant concession by Britain was seen as a renewed promise to abandon the western posts. The commercial aspects were considered humiliating, restrictive, and exceedingly limited; other matters were ignored. In their angry response to the treaty, the opponents overlooked the provisions for settling other disputes by arbitration. Since the Constitution provided that a treaty must have a two-thirds approval by the Senate, protest meetings were held throughout the country to influence that body.

On August 4, 1795, Wilmington citizens gathered at four in the

[29] JD to Hicks, September 13, 1788, L/HSP, XLI, 100.

afternoon in the upper Market House to discuss the treaty. Dr. James Tilton was chairman, and Robert Coram was appointed secretary. So great was the attendance that the meeting was adjourned to the larger Presbyterian Meeting House near the Academy. It was estimated that five hundred people were present.[30]

Caesar A. Rodney opened the meeting with a resolution: "Resolved, that it is the constitutional right of freemen to assemble together and express their opinions of public measures." The resolution was unanimously adopted. A discussion followed as to whether the treaty should be read. Some argued that everyone knew its contents, but a majority favored a reading, which Coram then gave.

Now turning to Dickinson, Rodney said that "he wished to hear the sentiments of a venerable Patriot . . . whose head had grown grey in the faithful discharge of his duties in the legislative, judicial, and executive departments of government." Dickinson rose and acknowledged that it was a citizen's duty to make observations on the treaty, but, with the "hand of age and infirmity" upon him, he called on some younger man present "to take the labouring oar into his hand and break the way." Then he, the elder, might more easily follow and express his own sentiments.

Rodney himself answered Dickinson's call. He termed the president's appointment of Chief Justice Jay as the envoy, a violation of both the spirit and the letter of the Constitution and its clause mandating the "advice and consent" of the Senate. The speaker declared the treaty "fraught with more evils than Pandora's box." As Rodney saw it, the lives, liberties and fortunes of all citizens were involved. His concluded to a "unanimous burst of applause."

The proper stage having been set, Dickinson then rose and began an oration "in a strain of dignified eloquence." A newspaper reporter declared that he despaired giving his readers "even the faintest imitation of the speech." Dickinson maintained that the treaty involved not only the dearest interests of America but its independence as well. The United States had given up essential rights of sovereignty by it. Those who believed that treaty oppo-

[30] Two manuscript accounts, Brown Collection, HSD.

nents were advocates of war were mistaken; rather, agreement to the provisions under consideration would put America in league against France.

Dickinson listed all his objections to the treaty. As to "the inequality of our leaving the settlement of the [boundary] lines and British debts to Commissioners and especially by their taking away the trials by jury" in cases dealing with British creditors, he pointed out that the latter was also a contradiction of Britain's own policy.

Dickinson spoke for two hours. Coram, who had been taking notes, could not keep up with him: "He enlarged on all these [above] heads but when he had finished the last part mentioned I got w[e]ary and left the meeting—what remarks he made afterwards I did not hear." The audience, however, greeted his discourse with appreciative applause, and the newspaper account asserted: "Such was the efficacy of Mr. Dickison's convincing detail of facts and irresistable eloquence that many who had been wavering on the subject of the treaty were [now] found against it and even those few who supported it felt their opinions entirely changed."

Six months later, Alexander H. Rowan, a British visitor, came to Wilmington, where he remained for some time. Bearing a letter of introduction from Deborah Logan, he called on Dickinson. Greatly pleased and impressed, Rowan recorded his impressions of that statesman, noting, "He is greatly opposed to the late British treaty but says he wishes it may be carried into effect now it has been ratified."[31]

Although the execution of Louis XVI and the sad tales of refugees somewhat stemmed America's enthusiasm for the new French government, Dickinson continued to sympathize with the French. He was distressed by Britain's failure to support the principle that "free ships made free goods." The British seizure of American men and vessels on the open sea alarmed him, while he saw the restrictions on American neutral shipping imposed by the French Directory merely as the result of its war with Britain. France had

[31] Observation, April 16, 1796, William H. Drummond, ed., A. H. Rowan, *Autobiography of Alexander H. Rowan* (Dublin, 1840), p. 292.

once been this country's loyal ally and now was struggling to become a republic.

Just as he had once put his thoughts into poetic form in a "Freedom Song" before the American Revolution, in January 1797 he wrote an ode to the citizens of the French Republic which was warmly sympathetic to the French cause.[32] First appearing in the *New World*, a Philadelphia newspaper, the verses were amended and republished on several occasions, including an appearance in the *Mirror of the Times and General Advertiser* of Wilmington at the time of Jefferson's inauguration. Two stanzas embody the theme he sounded:

> Oppression's guilty chiefs alarm'd
> Their Hordes in impious Union arm'd
> The Sons of Liberty to bind,
> And Blast THE HOPES OF HUMAN KIND.
>
> Go on—go on—heroic bands!
> And publish to the listening lands
> The Worth of Equal Rights and Laws—
> The cause of FRANCE IS FREEDOM'S cause.

Dickinson found morality and religion combined in his support of the French cause. He was deeply disturbed by what he saw as the Federalists' neglect of justice and humanity in foreign relations.

Within three months of the first publication of the ode, Dickinson began a new series of letters signed "Fabius." These also were published in Philadelphia's *New World*.[33] The spark that aroused Dickinson's ire was the "extraordinary call of Congress" on March 25, 1797, to act on the Franco-American dispute that became known as the XYZ affair.

These new letters of "Fabius" added up to fifteen in number.[34]

---

[32] William G. Soler, "John Dickinson's Attitude toward the French, 1791–1801," *Delaware History* 6 (1955):294–98 and "John Dickinson's 'Ode to the French Revolution,'" *American Literature* 25 (1953):287–92; manuscripts, L/HSP, XI, and Loudoun Papers, HSP.

[33] Philadelphia *New World* beginning with the issue of April 10, 1797.

[34] *The Letters of Fabius in 1788 on the Federal Constitution; and in 1797 on the Present Situation of Public Affairs* (Wilmington, 1797).

Dickinson derided the "ambition and duplicity" with which the combined powers of Europe had moved against France. Asserting that "the French are contending for the rights granted them by the charter of their creation (no language can be too strong, when we speak of the right of man to liberty)," he wrote:

> Our path is very plain. Let us not be inveigled from it, by a mean desire to cover our own faults by the fanciful notions of a *political refinement*, or by an unjustifiable rage for *speculations* upon the welfare of us and our posterity. Let us assert and maintain OUR TRUE CHARACTER—*Sincerity* of thought, and rectitude of action; and convince the world, that no man, or body of men, whatever advantages may for a while be taken of our unsuspecting confidence, shall ever be able to draw this nation out of the direct road of an open, candid, and generous conduct.[35]

Dickinson praised France not only for its establishment of a republic but also for its victory over despotism. As Rome had triumphed over Carthage, France as a continental power, he believed, was bound to triumph over Great Britain. All advantages seemed to lie with France. It deserved America's support; it was in our national interest to side with France, and assisting it was the honorable position to take. The letters were at once collected and published in book form together with the previous letters he had written in defense of the Constitution.

The letters, Dr. Rush assured Dickinson, were the "most practical and useful things published on the [French] controversy." Dickinson hoped that the *Letters of Fabius* might be published in France and sought assistance from both Rush and McKean. To the latter he confided that if they were published abroad, his name then could be given as the author.[36]

Dickinson continued to worry about America's foreign policy. He wrote McKean that he feared his efforts in writing the *Letters of Fabius* were in vain and not strong enough to encounter the "ignorance, passion, selfishness and the phrenzy of political speculation." Dickinson viewed the situation darkly; to Rush he prayed,

[35] Ibid., pp. 183–85.

[36] Rush to JD, October 11, 1797, L/HSP, IX, 10.

"May the Morning of Peace soon open upon this agitated globe; and may its mild beams soon bless our Country." McKean agreed with his correspondent and wrote that he believed the administration was actuated more by passion than by true policy.[37]

On May 3, 1798, Dickinson again wrote McKean, declaring that "never was the happiness of a people more wantonly exposed to hazard" than in the impending break of relations with France. He felt certain that the people did not realize the dangers facing them, making it all too easy for the administration to whip up anger over the insults dealt to the American ministers to France. Thinking that his Fabius letters were perhaps "too feeble," he again sat down at his desk. The result was a small pamphlet entitled *A Caution; or Reflections on the Present Contest between France and Great Britain*, advertised in the Philadelphia *Aurora* as a publication "containing a view of the practicability of a descent on England from France: and the fatal consequences of our being involved in war with France." In the twelve-page essay, to which Dickinson appended a revision of his ode on the French Revolution, he laid bare the situation in his first paragraphs:

> These States are at present exposed to very threatening dangers. Whether *France* has been justly provoked by the conduct of the late President and his successors, or by the temper that placed the last in his situation, will not now be enquired. The *fact* is, that *France* is provoked. What the resentment may be, demands our most serious consideration.
>
> She still believes, that a great body of *American* citizens regards her and the cause in which she is engaged, with the warmest affection. She believes rightly: but it is possible, and probable too—that a single manoeuver of our *constituted authorities* may convince her, that the nation is hostile to her and her cause; and this conviction may instantly snap the thread by which a naked sword is suspended over our head.
>
> SOME MANOEUVER OF THIS KIND IS MEDITATED.

Dickinson warned that Americans deceived themselves if they thought a French invasion of Great Britain was impossible, and

[37] JD to McKean, McKean Papers, III, 14, HSP; JD to Rush, May 30, 1798, Winterthur; McKean to JD, July 30, 1798, L/HSP, XII, 79.

he discussed at some length the military and naval means which could be employed.[38]

Dickinson's pamphlets made little impression. The Federalist–Democratic-Republican political struggle was itself worsening. Dickinson increasingly missed conversations with his Philadelphia friends. Lacking such discussions and frustrated by the national and international scene, Dickinson by 1799 could only see "a germination of wars, oppressions, and calamities . . . ahead."[39]

The political tide turned with Thomas Jefferson's election as president. Dickinson now hoped for renewed friendly relations with France. He was convinced that the vast majority of American citizens held that country in esteem, which in no way was lessened "by any novelties introduced into their form of government, for whatever that form may be *the People* of France are the objects of our regards, and they have a right to establish such a form as they please." Developments in Europe, however, with Napoleon's conquests of Spain, parts of Italy, Germany and Bavaria, as well as France's acquisition of Louisiana, soon changed Dickinson's viewpoint. Suddenly he became alarmed. Not waiting for others to take the initiative, Dickinson wrote out his new thoughts on the subject. The result was *An Address on the Past, Present and Eventual Relations of the United States to France*, signed "Anticipation." It affected to be an "Address of the President and Congress to the People of the United States."[40]

The *Address* was carefully wrought. Dickinson reviewed the warm attachment Americans felt toward France. He then suggested tolerantly that "France, however ardent her love of liberty, may not, perhaps, be yet prepared for a government of the best form." But he was not blind to facts and observed:

[38] *A Caution: or Reflections on the Present Contest between France and Great Britain* (Philadelphia, 1798); William G. Soler, "A Reattribution: John Dickinson's Authorship of the Pamphlet 'A Caution,' 1798," *PMHB* 77 (1953): 24–31 and Soler, "A Note on John Dickinson's Pamphlet 'A Caution,' " *PMHB* 79 (1955):100–101; Philadelphia *Aurora*, February 19, 1798.

[39] JD to McKean, August 9, 1799, McKean Papers, III, 29, HSP.

[40] *An Address on the Past, Present and Eventual Relations of the United States to France* (New York, 1803).

The conquest of one country leads to the conquest of another. The rage for obtaining wealth by pillage is never sated. It grows, by being constantly fed, to a height altogether monstrous. Every conquest adds not only a new strength, but a new appetite to the devouring power. . . .

There is no trust to be placed in those whose thirst of empire disdains all limits. . . .

The area is arrived when no nation can be safe that stands by itself. There must be an union, cemented by noble sentiments and generous resolutions. . . .

With common consent a system must be devised and adopted, that will faithfully aim at the wellfare of ALL. Such an union will arrest the career of *France* on the *European* continent.[41]

Dickinson foresaw only war and devastation if reason did not survive. He predicted war between France and Great Britain if the former should occupy the Netherlands. The acquisition of Louisiana seemed to portend a desire "to acquire dominion over all America." Should negotiations fail and "things come to extremities," he then proposed:

Let Britain open to us the unshackled commerce of all her dominions in every quarter of the globe; and the spring we shall give to her manufacture . . . will produce an increase of wealth and stability which it is impossible for her in any other manner to obtain: but, in the first place, let her forever abolish the *African* slave-trade, that enormous sin which . . . menaces to sink her into perdition. (Let her also establish a construction of the Laws of nations relative to the Rights of neutral powers that shall be satisfactory to them.)

All impediments being removed, and a confederacy framed, of which the objects shall be uniformly justifiable, a conjunction of the naval powers of *Britain* and *these States* may, in a short time, seize every island held by France and her associates. It may do more.[42]

---

[41] Ibid., pp. 15–17.

[42] Ibid., p. 10. The parenthetical sentence in the quotation is an addition in Dickinson's handwriting in his own copy of the publication in HSP.

Happily, the United States avoided such involvement. And, even as Dickinson was writing, this country was negotiating for the purchase of Louisiana, an action about which he was patently unaware. Nevertheless, the Napoleonic wars advanced, and repercussions were felt on this side of the Atlantic.

So, as had many others, John Dickinson's political interest in the 1790s turned from the purely domestic political arena to the country's international relations. His published opinions obscured the private individual whom posterity would not know. Dickinson had become a "sage" in Delaware. Visitors sought him out. Guests ranged from such old friends as Thomas McKean and George Read to Thaddeus Kosciusko, Aaron Burr, Noah Webster, and John Fitch.[43]

Philemon in Philadelphia was conscious of his brother's isolation and always looked for opportunities that might interest him. When the United States Mint was about to be established, he suggested that the position of director could undoubtedly be John's were he to wish it. Robert Edge Pine was busy painting portraits and events of the Revolution. John repeatedly declined to sit for him, pleading "indisposition" and also refusing because he considered it an impropriety to be part of the "Independence" tableau since he had opposed the "Declaration at the time when it was made." He did, however, ask Philemon to subscribe his name to a set of the prints proposed for publication.[44]

When the Dickinsons moved to Wilmington they had rented a house on the northwest corner of Ninth and Market streets. But he soon purchased a lot and house on the corner of Market and Kent (Eighth Street) which ran back to Shipley. Once again he immersed himself in architectural reverie, studying plates in Abraham Swann's *Book of Architecture*, reflecting on and planning for a new home. As he had done with the house he built in Philadelphia, Dickinson added a residential front to the smaller standing

[43] McKean to JD, September 14, 1801, McKean Papers; Kosciusko to JD, November 24, [n.y.], Gratz Collection, HSP.

[44] Philemon Dickinson to JD, February 12, 1792, JD to Philemon Dickinson, April 12, 1792, Loudoun Papers, HSP.

building. He drew up certain details relative to its construction and then wrote David Evans of Philadelphia, who had worked on the house in Chestnut Street, for advice.[45] Dickinson's studies of style and construction were manifold, enabling him to give exact instructions to the builders from the removal and reconstruction of an old staircase to precise measurements for Ionic columns. When he had completed his design, Dickinson wrote out four descriptive pages to be followed in the construction, beginning: "A house 45 feet square from out to out—2 stories high, one of them about 12 or 13 feet, and the other about 10 or 11 feet—the first floor to be about 3 feet and a half from the ground, the house to consist of 2 rooms back, each of them about 21 feet wide and 23 feet long and of 2 Rooms and a passage in front."[46]

Dickinson wrote a detailed memorandum for two Wilmington carpenters, Warrenton and Askew, contractors for the job, who planned a trip to Philadelphia for supplies and observations. He directed them "to examine carefully the doors, windows, chimnies, mantels, staircases, etc., etc.," of the houses of William Bingham, Henry Hills, George Clymer, Thomas Fitzsimmons, and others, as well as "Dr. Franklin's bath in Market Street, and the Public Baths in Sassafras on Arch Street." At the same time he requested the men "to get two Doric and Ionic pillars made by—a famous turner who lives on the northside of Union Street between 2nd and 3rd Streets. . . . The bases and capitals in the best manner [and] of mahogany to guard effectively against the heat of the sun." Dickinson asked them "to get a plan for a dumb waiter" and suggested they see the one made for Thomas Jefferson in one of Lieper's houses and go to Henry Hill's house to examine the kitchen there.[47] The front door was to be topped by a fanlight for which an engraving in Swann was selected. The door itself was designed according to a draft sent by Dr. William Thornton, the old family

[45] JD to Evans, August 4, 1798, L/HSP, XXXI; and in XLVI, HSP, detailed instructions; Elizabeth Montgomery, *Reminiscenses of Wilmington* (Wilmington, 1872), p. 298.

[46] L/HSP, XXXI, 38.

[47] Letters, Memoranda, etc., L/HSP, XXXII, 4–11.

friend, now a notable amateur architect whose work included designs for the Capitol in Washington. The finished house was a handsome and imposing residence.

Its completion, however, resulted in a regrettable dispute. The estimate agreed upon by Dickinson and the contractors was for £3,074.3.3; the final cost tallied £4,413.17.3. David Evans and William Garrigues were appointed to "referee" the matter, with all their expenses paid by Dickinson for what he described as "peace making business." Dickinson's dominance over the issue and the probable inability of Warrenton and Askew to estimate the costs of items with which they were very possibly unfamiliar put the contractors at a disadvantage. The matter was settled in due course, but it was an unpleasant end to what should have been a happy conclusion. They moved in before the turn of the century.

In April 1799 Dickinson wrote Charles Willson Peale that the canvases of the family portraits Peale had painted needed repair. He also sought some prints after Francis Wheatly, particularly "Rural Benevolence" and "Rural Simplicity," and one of "Howard's Visit to the Distressed in Prison." Dickinson expressed a preference for representation of scriptural subjects, which he deemed "very useful to young persons," and asked Peale for prints of Raphael's "Transfiguration" and "Ascension."[48] The subjects of this order, perhaps more than anything else, revealed John Dickinson as a man who had changed in many ways. The prints were not merely a matter of artistic preference, as the handsome furniture and decorative items he sought thirty years before had been. The subjects were indicative of the new life he now lived.

[48] JD to Charles Willson Peale, April 24, 1799, APS.

☆ 12 ☆

An End
Must Come

IN 1782 THE REVEREND JOHN MILLER, a Presbyterian minister and old family friend who lived near Dover, had written Dickinson voicing strong approval of his gubernatorial proclamation against vice and immorality. In answer Dickinson replied that he was convinced "that the happiness of men in this life as well as in the next depends on the prevalence of piety and virtue among them."[1]

In the decade of the seventeen-nineties, religion, quite as much as national affairs, claimed Dickinson's attention, even more perhaps because the subject was one he had so long avoided save in an abstract way. In 1796 he published some of his thoughts in a pamphlet entitled *A Fragment*. He wrote out a few brief statements in defense of the Christian religion and sought the assistance of Benjamin Rush in having them published as a tract. Dickinson explained that "my ardent desire, my fervent prayer is that my fellow creatures may be happy and I am certain they cannot be so without religion." If only one youth were put on guard against ideas contrary to virtue and piety, he felt his effort would be justified. In print the pamphlet contained an introduction of three

---

[1] JD to Miller, January 19, 1782, John Miller Collection, Princeton University (hereafter cited as PUL).

pages, a "short, simple, strong" statement of eleven pages, and, in typical Dickinson fashion, thirty-two pages of footnotes to buttress the text. As with his other writings, the author sought anonymity.[2]

In the introduction Dickinson suggested that the pamphlet was "deleted from a Treatise designed for instruction of youth, which a weak state of health may most probably prevent being completed." Dickinson viewed religion as a stalk from which various observations might branch. Here the main branch represented the "blossoming of a reverence, fed by the meditation of a mature mind illuminated by continued research." Indeed, Dickinson's study of art, science, literature, and the Bible seemed to culminate in this work.

Dickinson saw man as "a beautiful prodigy—composed of dust and spirit—the wonderful connection of two worlds." He believed it was man's "PRIVILEGE, *to be good*—It is his DUTY, *to be happy*." Dickinson's views of the universe and his general philosophy were echoes of his time, of scientific curiosity, and the growth of his religious convictions. He noted that the Creator could destroy even as he could create, but it was the goodness of the Creator he stressed. He believed man should habitually practice self-examination, citing Saint Paul's letter to the Philippians. Dickinson urged his readers to demonstrate that "we are *truly wise*, by improving in ourselves and others the *lively* and *habitual* influence of this principle: that, WE ARE OF DIVINE EXTRACTION."

Dickinson soon got to work on a proposed "Essay towards Religious Instruction of Youth."[3] He covered many pages of manuscript, but he did not find a satisfactory publishable form for this study. Dickinson jotted down many thoughts for the projected essay: "There is a relation between the principles of religion and the principles of Civil Society. . . . Education of children [is] the most important office that can be performed by human creatures. . . . As every duty is allied to a blessing, so every right is allied to a

---

[2] *A Fragment* (Philadelphia, 1796); JD to Rush, February 24, 1796, letter draft L/HSP, II, 62; Dobson to JD, March 31, 1796, L/HSP, XII, 64; JD to Rush, March 4, 1796, L/HSP, XII, 64.

[3] There are many manuscripts and separate notations with this title in the R. R. Logan Collection, HSP. There is no evidence that any were published.

duty." At times he considered a question-and-answer format, as in a catechism.

In a letter to Joseph Bringhurst, Dickinson asserted that there was "gross ignorance among youth concerning the progress of human affairs." He believed that the caution the Friends exercised in the books they allowed their children to read was excessive. Other Christian societies, he noted, had good authors who produced worthwhile writings.[4] Dickinson himself was studying the Old and New Testaments with scholarly interest. He wrote and put aside "Notes on the Bible," "The New Covenant commonly called the New Testament," "Alterations of the Old Testament," "The Gospel according to Matthew," jottings regarding translations, and other observations.[5] Even as he was so engaged, Charles Thomson, his old friend and kinsman, now removed from the political fray, was translating the New Testament from the Greek.

After the turn of the century Dickinson began a lively correspondence with Tench Coxe of Philadelphia and the Reverend Samuel Miller, Presbyterian minister of New York, son of the Reverend John Miller of Dover. These letters, coupled with earlier ones to Rush and to Bringhurst, reveal the extent of Dickinson's religious thought, his belief in revelation and Christian evidence.

Dickinson missed the political and intellectual life that his health forbade him. In 1801 Hezekiah Niles and Vincent Bonsal, printers in Wilmington, published two volumes of his political writings. No other American had had his political writings so collected and issued. Dr. John Vaughan, the Wilmington physician, initiated the idea, which the printers immediately encouraged. Dickinson hesitated at first, but having finally agreed to the printing, he cooperated wholeheartedly. The publication he saw in a sense redeeming his faded reputation. The preface purported to be written by the editors but bore every evidence of John Dickinson's mind and literary style. It declared that the selected political papers were to provide the opportunity "to trace our momentous controversy with *Great Britain*, from its commencement in her injustice, to its termination in our independence," for which the

[4] JD to Bringhurst, July 1, 1799, Haverford College Library.

[5] See the R. R. Logan Collection, HSP, for these and other notes.

editor believed "every friend to mankind must rejoice, in contemplating the actual and probable consequences of our revolution to other nations."[6]

The project, of course, presented a happy opportunity for Dickinson to set before the American people the many contributions he had made in the great struggle for American liberty. And they did add up to an impressive total. The writings themselves at times were introduced, or followed, by the insertions of "testimonies" which showed the high opinion of the public toward the essays and documents at the time they were first published. The warm and sincere admiration of those who knew Dickinson intimately was also evident in the Wilmington publication. The venture, however, proved financially disastrous for the partners; their association ended as a result of the failure of the enterprise. Thirteen years later, another printing was made;[7] its origin and financial fate are unknown.

Niles, who later moved to Baltimore, where he published his successful *Weekly Register*, regarded Dickinson highly. Many years later he recalled that, passing Dickinson's house one noon in 1801, when repeal of the Judiciary Act was being argued in Congress, he saw him standing in the doorway. After a greeting, Dickinson invited Niles inside. Years later he recorded the visit in the *Register*.

> He had been a little unwell, he said. He would have a glass of old wine with me, the first he had drank for six weeks. After taking a couple of glasses of wine in instant succession, he suddenly sat down, and abruptly asked me what I thought of the discussion then going on in Congress on the great question about the Judiciary. Having very briefly given my opinion, he said in a sprightly manner, "I'll tell thee mine,"—on which he began an argument, soon became animated, and was uneasy in his seat. As he proceeded he elevated his voice, and finally, rising slowly and uncon-

[6] *Political Writings*, 1:xv; Leon de Valinger, Jr., and Virginia Shaw, ed. and comp., *A Calendar of Ridgely Family Letters* (Dover, Del., 1948), 1:197.

[7] Other editions of the two-volume *Political Writings* were by Dunott (Wilmington), 1814, and by Bonsal (Wilmington), 1861.

sciously from his chair, he put forth his hand, and addressed me as if I had been the chairman of a legislative body, with all its members present. I have never heard a discourse that was comparable to his speech, for its fire and spirit poured forth in a torrent, and clothed in the most beautiful and persuasive language. The graceful gestures of the orator, his fine and venerable figure, interesting countenance, and locks "white as wool," formed a tout ensemble that riveted me to my chair with admiration. His delirium, if it may be called so, lasted for nearly half an hour, when it was interrupted by one of the family entering the room. He stopped instantly, with a word half finished on his lips, and sat down in great confusion, apologized for his strange behavior, and entirely dropped the subject. . . . It was his soul, rather than his person, that acted on the occasion, and a master spirit it was.[8]

Age and ill health had taken their toll on Dickinson. His wife, too, was ill, as she had been for the past dozen years. In 1798 Mary Dickinson told her Aunt that her "pilgrimage" seemed at an end. She was consoled, she wrote, by "a great blessing in a most affectionate husband and no person has a better child than Sallie. She takes care of me and relieves me from domestic care." Mary's health caused Dickinson to change the executorship of his will two years later with Sally first named and, if she were not living, then Maria. Finally, in April 1803 Mary Dickinson became seriously ill, and on July 23 she died. "A most unaffectedly good and amiable woman," her cousin Debbie Logan wrote. "Most affectionate, humble, generous and pious. My love to her was great and sincere."[9]

---

[8] *Niles' Weekly Register*, 13 (January 8, 1818): 300–301. If, as Niles suggested, Dickinson was abetted in his oration by the glasses of wine, it is interesting to note that in an earlier if unknown year, in a letter addressed to his wife, he declared, "I verily believe that my habitual temperance has been blessed to protect me. Oh holy and innocent sobriety! Pleasing to the Deity—a friend of nature—the daughter of Reason—the sister of all the virtues (etc. . .)" (Loudoun Papers, HSP).

[9] Mary Dickinson to Mary Norris, 1798, L/HSP; will of John Dickinson, 1803, Item 393 (incl. codicils), LCP; Deborah Logan Diary, L/HSP, VII, 87; see also L/HSP, XIV, 66.

Dickinson and Sally, deeply stricken, were outwardly composed; Maria, always emotional, was half fainting and overcome with grief. John was seventy-one, Sally, thirty-two, and Maria, twenty. A year later Dickinson found himself sinking into fits of depression. "My mind is continually engaged in contemplating it and seems to delight in sorrow," he wrote Coxe, "[although] I am perfectly convinced that I ought not to grieve as those 'who have no hope.' "[10] But it was difficult not to do so.

That spring of 1804 Dickinson had other reasons to be depressed. In March, James Kimmy, a tenant at Jones Neck, wrote that the Dickinson mansion there had burned to the ground on Saturday the third. A spark from the chimney, fanned by a northwest wind, had caused the destruction. Part of the household furniture had been carried to safety, the "new room" and kitchen saved, but the main house was entirely destroyed, and the walls appeared too cracked to be used again.[11]

Dickinson immediately notified the Insurance Company of North America of his loss. The insurance adjuster estimated the cost of rebuilding at $3,000. The company, however, offered to pay only $2,400 of the total cost. Dickinson finally agreed to have the house rebuilt "in a very plain manner" without charging for marbles, glass, painting, wainscoting, or any inside carpenter's work whatever, with the company then repaying any costs beyond the original offer.

The house was rebuilt largely as originally laid out. Dickinson wrote out explicit instructions for the restoration. He wrote his painter that there were to be three coats of paint everywhere, "of a handsome stone color" similar to that in the halls of his Wilmington house. The exceptions were the doors and handrail of the stairs, which were to be an exact imitation of mahogany, while the cappings of the surbase and washboards were to be a dark

[10] Ann Ridgely to her mother, July 24, 1803, Ridgely Collection, DSA; JD to Coxe, May 22, 1804, Tench Coxe Papers, HSP.

[11] Nathan Burrow to JD, March 5, 1804, Kimmey to JD, March 13, 1804, Thomas Canaday to JD, March 19, 1804, L/HSP. The "new room" was probably only new in the sense that it had been constructed later than the mansion as originally built.

brown color.[12] Costs far exceeded the sum set by the insurance company. The most noticeable change was the omission of the front triangular pediment at the roofline. For this Dickinson did not charge the company "nor for the porch at the front door that was burnt." Two rooms in the third story were retained, now probably smaller than the "two handsome chambers" with three windows each that had existed there before the fire. This charge and that for all the bricks and plastering were also omitted from Dickinson's final account.[13] Though he saw that the work was done thoroughly, Dickinson lacked the enthusiasm for this task that he had shown in his other building projects.

There were two marriageable daughters now at home. Sally was past the years for ardent suitors. Maria, however, was being courted. Williamina Ridgely, who lived near Dover, in May 1802 declared Maria, then aged eighteen, the "prettiest girl in town," but on a subsequent trip in December, she reversed that judgment. "Sally," she wrote her mother, "looks to be at least one hundred and is the primmest thing in the world, she talks tho' but is disagreeable. Maria is in my opinion very far from pretty. She is extremely awkward, very tall and was dressed in a course calico short gown with a striped purple worsted petticoat tho' near one o'clock." In the spring of 1803, Williamina wrote again at length on Maria's suitors. One was Tom Cadwalader, a Dickinson cousin, who had often visited the family the previous summer. Williamina now considered Maria as a "very sensible agreeable girl"; she regretted that Tom Cadwalader had stopped his calls on Maria because he had a pleasing personality and sterling character; "What is [of] still greater consequence to the old man, he has a pretty Fortune, is in business now, and is very attentive to it." Williamina also had heard that Maria was "engaged to Dr. [George] Logan's son, a disagreeable schoolboy."[14] That rumor was not confirmed until five years later.

[12] JD to David Train, patiner, August 2, 1804, L/HSP, XXX, 121. For many other building details, see L/HSP, XXX, 58–63, 73–76.

[13] JD to Charles Petit, Insurance Company of North America [1806], letter draft, L/HSP, XII, 102.

[14] Williamina Ridgely to Mrs. Charles Ridgely, May 2, December 20, 1802, April 27, July 8, 1803, *Ridgely Calendar*, 1:215, 230–31, 238.

All the Dickinson friends commented on the obvious differences in the personalities of the two young women. Sally was quiet and composed, Maria always bubbling with vivacity. Susanna Dillwyn Emlen wrote a long letter to her father about the two of them. She enjoyed watching "the different effect of their valuable father's manners on their differently constructed minds," and wrote that "Cousin Dickinson though a most affectionate parent governed with absolute authority to which Sally, I believe, never in her whole life offer'd much [resistance] unless she was authorized in a few instances to do so by the most serious consideration. If there was any partiality in his love of his children it appeared in favour of the youngest (Maria)."[15]

There was an extraordinary closeness in the family. Dickinson, recognizably singular in many ways, was for very many engaging and delightful, possessing both intelligence and charm. Whether it was recounting his dreams which so fascinated his daughters that they recorded them,[16] impressing Hezekiah Niles by his magnetic personality, or simply spending the evening playing "How do you like it" and other games with guests, John Dickinson was a memorable individual. Even Williamina Ridgely came to wonder why it was so "clever," or pleasant, at the Dickinsons.[17]

New avenues of study and reflections on religion in no way dimmed Dickinson's continuous curiosity about and opinions of the world about him. In his later years he engaged in steady correspondence with Tench Coxe and with Dr. George Logan. Coxe's political turnabouts had finally placed that gentleman in the Democratic-Republican column. His opinions and analysis of current affairs Dickinson found of great interest. Dr. Logan, the husband of Deborah Norris, was chosen a Jeffersonian senator for Pennsylvania in 1801 and was close to every action in Washington. The change of administrations from Adams to Jefferson delighted Dickinson and excited him to write Caesar A. Rodney: "I look

[15] Emlen to William Dillwyn, March 23, 1809, Dillwyn Papers, HSP.

[16] The recorded dreams all had a strange religious overtone, even those that occurred in 1775 (R. R. Logan Papers, HSP).

[17] Williamina Ridgely to her mother, April 6, 1803, Miss A. Catherine Wethered to Ann Ridgely, February 19, 1805, *Ridgely Calendar*, 1:229, 334.

upon Republicanism to be the Gospel of policy. It embraces its several objects with mildness and benevolence. In primitive times the *heathen* used to say—'Behold! how these Christians love one another.' Let the *heathens*—I mean the enemies of truth—in our days be forced to exclaim—'Behold! how the Republicans love one another.'" Dickinson wrote a warm letter of congratulations to Jefferson on his election to the presidency. Undoubtedly, the president was bemused to read Dickinson's declaration that, "As far as I am enabled to form a judgment, I believe, that our minds have been in perfect unison." That certainly was true only after the formation of the Union.[18]

Coxe sent him a manuscript essay on the militia he had written. Dickinson read it with approval and told Coxe that until the states established militia so that half a million citizens could be called into the field "in perfect preparation" within ten days, all the "executive and legislative provisions are inscriptions on the leaves of the Sybils—the sport of every wind." Unless the negligent states were persuaded to adopt a contrary policy, "our liberties would be very short lived." Indeed, Dickinson added, he had written President Jefferson several times concerning public defense, believing that "a general militia, well provided, seem to be essential not only to the welfare but to the independence of the states." "What can be done to arouse our fellow citizens from their deep slumbers on the very brink of Destruction?" he asked. Dickinson's ideas about the militia were reflected in what was called his favorite maxim, "that an armed people and an armed magistracy was the best security for freedom."[19]

As a lawyer Dickinson frequently commented on the law and the judicial system. The national government had not been in operation six months when he queried George Read, "Is it possible, or agreeable to the Constitution to establish an appeal from the Decisions of the Supreme Court in cases where that Court has original, exclusive jurisdiction? Or is it right & best that the single

[18] JD to Rodney, November 9, 1803, Gratz Collection, Case 1, box 21, HSP. JD to Jefferson, February 21, 1801, copy, NYHS.

[19] JD to Coxe, January 24, 1807, Tench Coxe Papers, HSP; *Niles' Weekly Register*, 12 (May 17, 1811):178.

Determination of that Court in such cases should be irreversible?"
Witnessing the operation of the courts and the relationship of the
judiciary to the other branches of government, Dickinson was
aroused to write Dr. Logan in 1801 suggesting that the judicial
system

> must be regulated in such a manner, that there cannot pos-
> sibly be a conflict between the Judicial and Legislative au-
> thorities, the one solemnly making laws, and the other as
> solemnly repealing them, or, in other words declaring them
> unconstitutional and void.
>
> ... Would it be a sufficient precaution, if provision should
> be made that unless the Supreme Court of the United States
> should within a fixed period, by a written address to the
> Executive, declare a law to be unconstitutional, no objec-
> tion should afterwards be made to its Constitutionality?
> And if such an address should be made to the Executive,
> should there not be some mode established for deciding
> forthwith between the two clashing authorities?[20]

Dickinson did not shy from expressing his opinions of actions
already taken or in offering Dr. Logan proposals for others. Both
opinions and proposals were frequent. In December 1806 he did
not know whether there was reason "to rejoice or to mourn" over
the situation in foreign affairs. He had approved the Nonimportation Act when it was passed; with a change in the British ministry,
Dickinson now thought it improper. Disturbed about the revolt
in San Domingo, he believed the United States should observe the
strictest neutrality in that situation, and he was disgusted by the
rapacity of commercial interests which sold goods to the rebellious
citizens there. Devoted as he was to the chief executive, he wrote
Logan that he thought a "momentous error" had been committed
in the government's negotiations with Spain in what he considered
careless disregard for the settling of the east and west boundary
lines of Louisiana. Dickinson feared that passions were so aroused
over the situation that war was possible, an action he considered a

[20] JD to Read, June 24, 1789, Read Papers, HSD; JD to Logan, January 8,
1801, Loudoun Papers, HSP.

mad attempt to control what was in large part a wilderness.[21]

The Pennsylvania senator interceded on occasion on behalf of his cousin by marriage. When John Marshall wrote his *Life of George Washington,* he implied that Dickinson had not been the author of the Address to the King sent by the First Continental Congress. In high dudgeon over that misrepresentation, Dickinson asked Logan to inform Marshall of the error, enclosing evidence to support his claim as author. At other times he addressed long letters to the senator, intending that his ideas be forwarded to Jefferson. Occasionally the president became exasperated. When Dickinson indirectly offered his opinions on how to get France to come to terms on spoilations and a settlement of Louisiana's borders, Jefferson assured Dr. Logan that "nobody's judgment is entitled to more respect than Mr. Dickinson's when truly informed of facts, nor does anybody respect it more than Thomas Jefferson. But he seems to have been uninformed of the only fact which obliges us to take serious ground."[22] Dickinson's letters to Jefferson were almost ingratiatingly humble in tone but frequent, particularly in the beginning of the administration. Dickinson wrote letters of introduction to the president for his friends, offered to give advice in recommending Delaware Democratic-Republicans to appointive office, and sent congratulations and approbation of various actions taken. As the correspondence developed, Dickinson invariably concluded his letters to Jefferson, "I am truly Thy affectionate Friend." The correspondence continued until Dickinson's death near the end of Jefferson's second term. Jefferson answered each letter with considerable kindness.

In discussing the newly acquired western territory, Dickinson considered the means of settling the area and exploring it. He stressed the necessity of an organized militia to Jefferson. He was also concerned about the threat of civil dissension; the "ominous" and continuous hatred held by the Federalists "afflicted" him unhappily. "If such a temper can be cherished and supported in the

---

[21] JD to Logan, 1805 and February 7, 1805 (?), L/HSP, V, 62 and 70; ibid., February 11, December 19, 1805, December 17, 1806, MDL/HSP.

[22] Jefferson to Dr. George Logan, April 7, 1806, MaHS.

youth of our commonwealth and under such an administration, and in so much prosperity, as we have for several years enjoyed," he asked, "what peace can we look for, when future circumstances shall hold out to unprincipled ambition stronger temptations to fraud and violence,"[23] The partisan enmity of the Federalists puzzled Dickinson. He saw them "incessantly agitated by a spirit of hostility" against all who differed with them, the more strange because of the benefits Jefferson's administration had produced. Looking around him, Dickinson found "peace and liberty" and wondered why more of the oppressed of Europe did not come to America. He believed, however, "It is probable that they will increase. May they contribute to the happiness of wanderers and our own."[24]

On July 2, after the British frigate *Leopard* had fired upon the American *Chesapeake* near Hampton Roads and seized four men from her crew, President Jefferson issued a proclamation protesting the "wanton disregard" of law, interdicting American harbors and waters to British ships of war, and forbidding all commerce with them until apologies and recompense were made. Dickinson praised the proclamation as admirable for "sentiment, temper and language." A town meeting in Wilmington was held to discuss the affair and support the government's stand. Dickinson reported that the inhabitants quite properly saw the event as a "horrible outrage committed against humanity and our Country." He at first pointed to his "age and infirmities" as reason not to attend, but, being pressed, he went to the meeting. Dickinson, however, took no hand in drafting the resolutions. Had he been consulted, he later said, he would have suggested they be styled as a proclamation and correspond more with the president's "firm, calm and dignified manner" than they did.[25]

Dickinson confessedly was fascinated by Europe. Angered by the actions of Britain, he went so far as to predict that the country would soon fall into ruin. He suggested that "if an angel from Heaven should preach to Great Britain the terms of political sal-

[23] JD to Jefferson, January 22, 1806, copy NYHS.

[24] JD to Coxe, February 9, February 25, 1807, Tench Coxe Papers, HSP.

[25] Ibid., July 6, 1807; JD to George Logan, July 7, 1807, L/HSP, IX, 31.

vation, he would descend in vain."²⁶ Dickinson especially feared the effect of the raging British and European disputes on America and its future peace and liberty. Preparedness was one answer, and Dickinson proposed that fifteen or twenty gunboats should immediately be stationed to guard the Delaware. France at the moment seemed to aim at "Universal Empire," but it was Great Britain that gave him most pain. The world's hostility toward that country inevitably would lead to its fall and bring ruin to others. "What in this crisis of difficulties can we wish for? Her destruction?" he asked Rush. "Then the domination of France will be established for ages to come. Her triumph? Then her insolence will be madly outrageous."²⁷ Dickinson arrived at the unhappy conclusion that this country should "take a solemn, honest, forbidding distance from both sides." He regretted an embargo but thought the consequences better than "the calamities of war," asking, "If we shrink from the privations and suffering of such a state, what is our national character?"²⁸

The admiration and affection Delaware tendered John Dickinson continued until the end of his life. In 1801 friends sought to nominate Dickinson for governor, going so far as to ask Aaron Burr to intercede for them when he stopped on one of his trips through Wilmington.²⁹ But Dickinson refused. On another occasion he was proposed for Congress. An anonymous writer from Kent County to the *Mirror*, however, pointed out that the three congressmen from Delaware all came from New Castle County. Since Dickinson's name was being mentioned as a candidate, the writer suggested that because of his "great information and experience" he should rather be given a seat in the Senate.³⁰ Again he turned down the proposal. Finally, in 1807, when Dickinson was seventy-five, members of the Democratic-Republican party of Delaware convened and unanimously resolved that John Dickin-

²⁶ JD to Tench Coxe, September 22, 1807, Tench Coxe Papers, HSP.

²⁷ JD to Rush, November 16, 1807, Rush Papers, LCP.

²⁸ JD to Tench Coxe, January 22, 1808, Tench Coxe Papers, HSP.

²⁹ T. Mendenhall to John Mason, March 21, 1801, HSP.

³⁰ Manuscript letter, "To the Mirror," Brown Collection, HSD.

son be the Democratic-Republic candidate at the ensuing election "to represent the State in the Congress of the United States."[31] Dickinson was touched by the compliment, but the confidence reposed in him also disturbed him. He pointed out that he had repeatedly said he could not serve in any such capacity due to "the infirmities of a weakly constitution." Further, Dickinson noted that, if chosen, "a sense of duty" would compel him to resign at once, and consequently "the State would be put to the trouble and expense of a new election."[32]

John Dickinson and his two daughters lived happily if simply but, as their cousin Debbie Logan wrote, "in great comfort and hospitality." Sally on rare occasions visited her relatives in Philadelphia. She attended the Yearly Meeting there in 1805 and two years later spent ten days with the Logans at Stenton. For the most part she remained at home, ran the household smoothly, and acted as her father's amanuensis. It was with her that John now discussed charities and the good works which the Dickinson fortune supported.

By the spring of 1807, Maria and her second cousin Albanus Logan had decided to marry. Susanna Emlen summed up the groom's qualities to her brother William Dillwyn:

> Albanus has been carefully educated: not much in the way of Friends to be sure. If he had he would not have suited Maria nor her father but he appears to have an honest frankness that is engaging and has been much preserved from the vices of the age. He has something "entre nous" of the turbulent temper of his father's family but tis hoped advancing reason and an amiable companion will correct that very important failing. This match also more closely connects two families always very intimate and, lastly, what to dear Sally is very material, it will secure Maria from falling into the fashionable dissipations as they are to live in the country.[33]

[31] Broadside, LCP 47–2a, no. Am-1807 Dem/Rep.

[32] Draft for letter, 1807, Item 47, L-D/LCP.

[33] Emlen to Dillwyn, May 30, 1808, LCP.

The marriage was planned according to the Society of Friends, a decision reported as "an unspeakable comfort" as well as "the most earnest wish" of Maria's sister Sally. Their father concurred in the arrangement. The couple announced their intentions before the Friends' Monthly Meeting on February 4, 1808.

From his youth John Dickinson had suffered one illness or indisposition after another, about which he all too frequently complained. At times it was merely a general weakness; at other times it was pronounced to be gout or some other identifiable distress. For the last two decades of his life, Dickinson wrote incessantly about the infirmities of age and his approaching demise. Yet when he was seventy-three, after saying he had pains in the small of his back which were sometimes severe, he boasted that he could "see and hear and walk and ride as well as I did in my youth."[34]

Dickinson's white hair and his elegant manner remained with him, but in his last year or two he became "more fleshy" and had "the look of age." Although he looked older, his guests noted his "faculties [were] bright and perfect and he [was] agreeable and cheerful." Dickinson was increasingly conscious that the end of his life was approaching. He spoke of it frequently. Sally recollected that he was "for several months in so heavenly a state of mind that she thought no feeling mind could doubt his being like a shock of corn fully ripe, and ready to be gathered into the garner of eternal rest."[35]

On February 8, 1808, Dickinson felt abnormally weary and early in the evening he went upstairs, assisted by his black servant. Sensing that he was deathly ill, he mentioned his presentiment to the servant but asked him not to tell his daughters and then added some advice for this man who had so long been devoted to him. That night Dickinson grew weak with coughing and hiccuping. The next day he had a high fever. Each succeeding day for a week his strength ebbed. Dr. Logan, his wife, Debbie, and their son Albanus were sent for. Dickinson became delirious and often lost

[34] JD to Mercy Warren, December 22, 1806, MaHS.

[35] Susanna Emlen to William Dillwyn, February 17, March 21, May 30, 1808, LCP.

understanding. On the morning of the fourteenth, John Dickinson died.[36] Burial was in the grounds of the Friends Meeting House in Wilmington. His charity, benignity, and all his living actions warranted his resting in death beside the grave of his wife.

Dickinson's every outward move had seemed to place him once again as an active member of the Society of Friends. His regular attendance at First Day Meetings, the many charitable concerns he put under their protection, his intimate association with Quaker kin and neighbors, and, not least, his newly adopted intimate form of address and numerical dating (thus avoiding days and months with pagan names) had encouraged such a supposition. But, in his heart and mind, he resisted any formal commitment to that Society. In a fugitive jotting, Dickinson stated his belief that

> Christianity is an active, affectionate and social religion, chiefly consisting in a discharge of duties to our fellow creatures. It therefore requires no separation from them. Tho enjoining that we "be not conformed to the world," in following this direction, the utmost attention is necessary lest distinctions from others by plainness of manners and customs assume the place of virtues, and thus become snares. Such distinctions are not in the least value in themselves because they are no part of the Divine Laws; but they may be exceedingly beneficial by promoting "moderation" in ourselves and others and especially in young persons. For with respect to these, they may be preservatives against an indulgence in vain fashions and customs, that have a tendency to estrange the mind from a steady exercise of its faculties and a just regard for serious things.[37]

In the century that followed Dickinson's death, Friends, because of his burial in the Friends' burying ground in Wilmington, wondered if he had been a member of their Society. Both his parents had been born into that religious persuasion. His father, though never disowned, had forsaken it; his sons had followed his exam-

---

[36] Ibid., February 17, March 21, 1808. Sarah Rhodes to "Cousin Logan," February 19, 1808, R. R. Logan Papers, HSP, describes in detail Dickinson's final illness.

[37] From uncatalogued notes in the R. R. Logan Papers, HSP.

ple. Residence in Wilmington and close family relationships had tempered John's early criticisms. But he never assumed full association. In January 1807 Dickinson wrote Tench Coxe: "I am on all proper occasions an advocate for the lawfulness of defensive war. This principle has prevented me from union with Friends." That conviction was only one factor that had restrained him. In August of the same year he wrote the Reverend Samuel Miller that he believed any group of Christians had the right to form themselves into a church and that ministers approved by them as pious men were properly ministers of the Gospel. Then Dickinson asserted, "I am not, and probably never shall be united to any religious Society, because each of them as a Society, holds principles I cannot adopt."[38] Half a year later Dickinson died. His burial in the Quaker Graveyard, therefore, was in recognition of his Friendly spirit, his birth, and his family's devotion, rather than any formal acknowledgment on his part of all that Society's views.

Encomiums came from many quarters: from Thomas Jefferson in the White House to friends and neighbors. When word reached the new Federal City on the banks of the Potomac, the reaction of Congress was immediate. Both the House and the Senate unanimously agreed to wear black crepe armbands in his memory. Those such as George Read, Jr., who knew him intimately treasured their heartwarming recollections:

> I have a vivid impression of the man, tall and spare, his hair white as snow, his face uniting with the severe simplicity of his sect a neatness and elegance peculiarly in keeping with it; his manners a beautiful emanation of the great Christian principle of love, with that gentleness and affectionateness which, whatever may be the cause, the Friends, or at least individuals among them, exhibit more than others, combining the politeness of a man of the world familiar with society in its most polished forms with conventional canons of behavior. Truly he lives in my memory as the realization of my beau-ideal of a gentleman.[39]

[38] JD to Coxe, January 24, 1807, Tench Coxe Papers, HSP; JD to Miller, August 10, 1807, Samuel Miller Papers, PUL.

[39] Read, ed., *Read*, p. 570.

There was, however, yet another, more formal legacy that Dickinson left to all Americans whether or not they had enjoyed the compelling charm of his person. His integrity, courage, and intelligence had combined to awaken America to the meaning and the necessity of liberty. The virtue he championed he himself had heeded. Fearless of public opinion, he ever boldly asserted the truth as he saw it, conscious of the future rather than the moment. John Dickinson never bowed to public opinion. He sought to lead it, taking a stand regardless of the consequences. As Jefferson noted, "Among the first of the advocates of the rights of his country when assailed by Great Britain, he continued to the last the orthodox advocate of the true principles of our new government."[40]

Dickinson's contributions to the new nation had been striking. Small wonder that Tench Coxe soon wrote Charles Thomson seeking materials for a history of Dickinson's life. Such a biography, Coxe believed, would "reflect credit upon the middle states and honor upon our country at large, nor will it have an indifferent effect upon the character of mankind."[41]

Dickinson acquaintances, whether members of the Society of Friends or associates in other endeavors, expressed curiosity about his will. Sally was the sole executor, and the large estate was divided between the two daughters. The only other bequest was a farm left to William Dickinson, his distant cousin and son of "Shuffling John," who had fared badly in worldly affairs. Susanna Emlen in her correspondence with her brother reported that many persons were disappointed that no legacies had been left to others, either individuals or charities, but, as she pointed out, John Dickinson was liberal while living and perhaps believed he had done his part.[42] Other family intimates suggested that it was because Sally knew what charities her father favored. She had also received a larger share of the estate. Her father knew of Maria's impending

---

[40] Jefferson to Joseph Bringhurst, February 24, 1808, Andrew A. Lipscomb, ed., *The Writings of Thomas Jefferson*, Library ed. (Washington, D. C., 1904), 11:435–36.

[41] Coxe to Thomson, September 26, 1808, deCoppet Collection, PUL.

[42] Emlen to Dillwyn, March 21, 1808, LCP. See also John Fisher to Thomas Rodney, May 15, 1808, Fisher Papers, HSP.

marriage and, friends reasoned, was confident that the Logans could take good care of her. The marriage of Maria and Albanus took place in early April. The young Logans lived with Sally for a year.

The impress of John Dickinson on the minds and actions of Americans in the years of this nation's birth and infancy cannot be measured. Often the violent partisanship of the years in which he was active in the councils of government sullied his stunning contributions to the Revolutionary era. America with good reason can honor John Dickinson not only as the best-known politician and writer in the decade leading to the Revolution but also, subsequently, as an intellectual force in the nation's development. Ever cautious, he sought union and foreign support before any break with England. Author of the first draft of the Articles of Confederation, he saw many of his ideas manifested in the present Constitution. Favoring a strong central government, as president of Pennsylvania in 1783 he wisely protected that state's authority when it was intimidated by the Congress. He clearly saw the necessary division of power between the states and the central government. After the new beginning of the nation in 1787, there was no diminution of Dickinson's concern for the country in whose very establishment he was so prominent. He never slacked in his fight for liberty—both domestic and foreign, in his assertion of the responsibilities of citizenship, in his efforts to protect the individual from arbitrary government and in hope for peace at home and among nations. For his country he was ever on call in the maintenance of truth and in the perpetuation of its honor by pen and voice.

Selected Bibliography

Any study of John Dickinson must first depend on the manuscript collections of his letters, notes, and preliminary drafts of his published documents and opinions, and then on Dickinson's published writings.

Manuscript collections in the Library Company of Philadelphia and the Historical Society of Pennsylvania are particularly rich lodes of information, notably in the Logan Collections of Dickinson's papers. These collections must shape any biography of John Dickinson. Both libraries also reward in letters found in related collections, particularly in those of Gratz, McKean, Dreer, and Loudoun. Other libraries with important letters are the Historical Society of Delaware (the R. S. Rodney Collection), the Delaware State Archives, and the Massachusetts Historical Society. Manuscript holdings in the Library of Congress, the American Philosophical Society, New-York Historical Society, Harvard, Yale, and Princeton universities, Dickinson College, and Winterthur are also useful.

These letters are supplemented by published letters and other writings of Dickinson's contemporaries: William T. Read, ed., *The Life and Correspondence of George Read* (Philadelphia, 1870); William B. Reed, ed., *Life and Correspondence of Joseph Reed*, 2 vols. (Philadelphia, 1847); George W. Ryden, ed., *Letters to and from Caesar Rodney, 1756–1784* (Philadelphia, 1933); John C. Fitzpatrick, ed., *The Writings of George Washington*, 39 vols. (Washington, D.C., 1931–44); Julian P. Boyd et al., eds., *The Papers of Thomas Jefferson*, 20 vols. (Princeton, 1950–74); Andrew A. Lipscomb et al., eds., *The Writings of Thomas Jefferson*, 20 vols. (Washington, D.C., 1903–4); Charles

Francis Adams, ed., *The Works of John Adams* (Boston, 1850–56); Charles Francis Adams, ed., *Familiar Letters of John Adams to His Wife Abigail during the Revolution* (Boston, 1875); Lyman H. Butterfield, ed., *Diary and Autobiography of John Adams*, 4 vols. (Cambridge, Mass., 1961); *Warren-Adams Letters, 1743–1814* (Boston, 1850–56); Leon de Valinger, Jr., and Virginia E. Swan, eds., *A Calendar of Ridgely Family Letters, 1742–1899*, 3 vols. (Dover, Del., 1948–61); Worthington C. Ford, ed., *Letters of William Lee* (Brooklyn, 1891); Richard Henry Lee, *Life of Arthur Lee*, 2 vols. (Boston, 1829); Richard H. Lee, *Memoir of the Life of Richard Henry Lee*, 2 vols. (Philadelphia, 1825); Carl Van Doren, ed., *Life and Papers of Benjamin Franklin and Richard Jackson, 1753–1785* (Philadelphia, 1947); Leonard W. Labaree, ed., *Papers of Benjamin Franklin*, 21 vols. (New Haven, 1959–78).

In addition these primary sources: Christopher Marshall, Diaries, 1773–93, fragments of the journal kept by Samuel Foulke, the Memorandum Book and Register of William Bradford, Jr., the Diary of Jacob Hiltzheimer, and Deborah Logan's Diary are illuminating. Joseph Reed's narrative of early revolutionary events, in the collections of the New-York Historical Society, is valuable as is Charles Thomson's own observations in the same collection. In addition, miscellaneous Delaware papers in that state's archives, *Minutes of the Council of Delaware State from 1776–1792* (Dover, 1886), are important sources.

The known publications of pamphlets or broadsides written by Dickinson, excluding official documents published by Congress or the states of Delaware and Pennsylvania, are:

A Speech, Delivered in the House of Assembly of the Province of Pennsylvania, May 24th, 1764. By John Dickinson, Esq. One of the Members for the County of Philadelphia. On occasion of a petition, drawn up by Order, and then under Consideration of the House; praying his Majesty for a Change of the Government of this Province. . . . Printed and sold by William Bradford. Philadelphia. MDCCLXIV.

Second edition three weeks later.

London edition, J. Whiston and B. White, in *Fleet Street*. MDCCLXIV. All title pages include the following:

"As for me, I will assuredly contend for that glorious plan of *Liberty*/ handed down to us from our ancestors; but whether my Labours/ shall prove successful, or in vain, depends wholly on you, my dear/ Countrymen!"

Eine Rede, gehalten in dem Hause der Assembly der Provinz Pennsylvanien, am 24ten May, 1764 . . . Bey Gelegenheit einer bittschrift, die auf Befehl des Hauses aufgesetzt. . . . Henrich Miller, Printer, Philadelphia [1764].

To the King's Most Excellent Majesty in Council, the Representation and Petition of Your Majesty's dutiful and loyal Subjects, Freeholders and Inhabitants of the Province of Pennsylvania. [Philadelphia, 1764. Broadside.]
Also a German edition.

A Reply To a Piece called The Speech of Joseph Galloway, Esquire, by John Dickinson . . . Philadelphia: Printed and sold by William Bradford, MDCCLXIV.
London reprint. J. Whiston and B. White, *Fleet Street,* MDCCLXIV.

To the Public. Last Tuesday Morning Mr. Galloway carried a writing containing some reflections on me to a printer in this city . . . [William Bradford, printer. Untitled 4-page pamphlet.] Philadelphia, 1764.

A Receipt to Make a Speech By J . . . . . G . . . . , Esquire. [William Bradford. Philadelphia, 1764.]

Protestation gegen die Bestellung Herrn Benjamin Franklin's zu Ugenten fur diese Provinz . . . Germantown. Christoph Saur. 1764.

Friends and Countrymen. The Critical time is now come, when you are reduced to the necessity of forming a Resolution. [Philadelphia, 1765(?) Broadside.]

The Late Regulations respecting the British Colonies on the continent of America considered, In a Letter from a Gentleman in Philadelphia to his Friend in London. Philadelphia. Printed and sold by William Bradford. MDCCLXV.
Two London editions with slight variations. Reprinted for J. Almon. MDCCLXV [actually 1766].

An Address to the Committee of Correspondence in Barbados. Occasioned by a late letter from them to Their Agent in London. By a North-American . . . Philadelphia, Printed and sold by William Bradford, 1766.

Letters from a Farmer In Pennsylvania, To the Inhabitants of the British Colonies. Philadelphia. Printed by David Hall, and William Sellers, MDCCLXVIII.
Second edition.
Third edition printed by William and Thomas Bradford, MDCCLXIX.
Boston. Edes and Gill, MDCCLXVIII.
Boston. Printed by Mein & Fleming, MDCCLXVIII.

New York. Reprinted by John Holt, 1768.

London. [Preface by Benjamin Franklin.] Printed for J. Almon. MDCCLXVIII.

Letters From a Farmer in Pennsylvania to the Inhabitants of the British Colonies; Regarding the Right of Taxation, and several other Important Points. To which are Added, as an Appendix, the Speeches of Lord Chatham, and Lord Camden, the one upon the Stamp Act, the other on the Declaratory Bill, with a Preface by the Dublin editor. [Also reprints earlier Preface by Benjamin Franklin.] Dublin. Printed for J. Sheppard, MDCCLXVIII.

Lettres d'un Fermier de Pennsylvanie, aux Habitans de l'Amerique Septentrionale, Traduites de l'Anglois. Amsterdam, Aux depens de la Compagnie. MDCCLXIX. [Translated and edited by Jean Barbeu Dubourg, it was actually printed in Paris. Franklin's preface and two other pieces were included in this edition.]

The Farmer's and Monitor's Letters to the Inhabitants of the British Colonies. William Rind, Williamsburg, MDCCLXIX. [This included a preface by Richard Henry Lee.]

The following/address/was read at a Meeting of the Merchants, at the Lodge, in Philadelphia, on Monday/ the 25th of April, 1768. [Broadside, 1768.]

A New Song to the tune of Hearts of Oak. . . . Philadelphia. Hall & Sellers, 1768. [Broadside.]

A copy of a letter from a Gentleman of Virginia to a Merchant in Philadelphia. [Broadside, 1768.]

To the Public . . . [Relative to the renewal of the nonimportation agreement.] Philadelphia, William Goddard, 1768.

A Letter from the Country, to a Gentlemon in Philadelphia. (Signed) Rusticus. [Philadelphia, 1773. Broadside.]

Reprinted with prefatory note by the "Association of the Sons of Liberty." New York, 1773.

An Essay on the Constitutional Power of Great Britain over the Colonies in America; with the Resolves of the Committee for the Province of Pennsylvania, and their Instructions to their Representatives in Assembly. Philadelphia. 1774.

London edition entitled *A new essay (by the Pennsylvania farmer) on the Constitutional Power of Great Britain.* 1774.

The Writings of John Dickinson, 1764–1774, edited by Paul Leicester

Ford (Philadelphia, 1895), mention the following more fugitive writings of the period preceding:

A Protest against a Resolution of the Assembly of Pennsylvania for petitioning the King to change the Colony of Pennsylvania . . . to a Royal Government. Pennsylvania Gazette, July 26, 1764.

A protest against the appointment of Benjamin Franklin as agent for the Colony of Pennsylvania. Pennsylvania Journal, Nov. 1, 1764. Printed in German as a pamphlet.

Observations on Mr. Franklin's Remarks on a Late Protest. Nov. 1764. [Manuscript HSP.]

Resolutions adopted by the Assembly of Pennsylvania relative to the Stamp Act. Sept. 21, 1765. Draft by John Dickinson, HSP.

The Declaration of Rights adopted by the Stamp Act Congress. Oct. 19, 1765. Drafted by John Dickinson.

A Petition to the King from the Stamp Act Congress. Oct. 19, 1765. Drafted by John Dickinson.

A Petition from the Assembly of Pennsylvania to the King. March 9, 1771.

Letters to the Inhabitants of the British Colonies. Pennsylvania Journal, May 25, June 1, June 8, June 15, 1774.

Other writings are:

A Circular letter addressed to the State Societies of the Cincinnati, by the general meeting, convened at Philadelphia, May 3, 1784. Together with the constitution, as altered and amended. Philadelphia: Printed by E. Oswald and D. Humphreys, 1784.

A Caution; or Reflections on the Present Contest Between France and Great Britain. Philadelphia. Printed by Benjamin Franklin Bache, MDCCXCVIII.

The Letters of Fabius, in 1788, on the Federal Constitution; and in 1797 on the Present Situation of Public Affairs . . . From the office of the Delaware Gazette, Wilmington, by W. C. Smyth, 1797.

A Fragment. Philadelphia. Printed by Thomas Dolson. 1796.

The Political Writings of John Dickinson, Esquire, Late President of the State of Delaware, and of the Commonwealth of Pennsylvania . . . Wilmington, Del. Printed and sold by Bonsal and Niles, 1801.

An Address on the Past, Present, and Eventual Relations of the United States to France. New York: Printed by T. and J. Swords, 1803.

Richard J. Hooker ("John Dickinson on Church and State") ascribes three essays of a series of twenty-one under the heading "The Centinel" to John Dickinson. These opposed the Anglican move for an American episcopate. Dickinson's authorship is attached to nos. six, seven, and eight (*Pennsylvania Journal; and Weekly Advertiser,* April 28, May 5, and May 12, 1768).

The Political Writings of John Dickinson, vol. 2 (Wilmington, 1801) includes the following official papers, not listed above:

The Address of Congress to the Inhabitants of Quebec. October 26, 1774.

The [first] Petition of Congress to the King, 1774.

Second Petition of Congress to the King, 1775.

A Declaration by the Representatives of the United Colonies of North America, now met in General Congress at Philadelphia, setting forth the Causes and Necessity of their Taking up Arms. Philadelphia, Printed by William and Thomas Bradford. 1779.

Address of Congress to the several states on the present situation of affairs. May 26, 1779.

An Appendix—added notes to the *Letters of Fabius* published in 1797.

There has only been one biography of John Dickinson, that by Charles J. Stillé, *The Life and Times of John Dickinson* (Philadelphia, 1891). One valuable aspect of this work is the republication of Dickinson's so-called *Vindication.* David L. Jacobson, *John Dickinson and the Revolution in Pennsylvania, 1764–1776* (Berkeley, Calif., 1965), covers his early life and activities utilizing manuscripts unavailable to the earlier writer and succeeds admirably in his work. An excellent appraisal is Bernard Bailyn, ed., *Pamphlets of the American Revolution* (Cambridge, Mass., 1965).

The following pamphlets cover various aspects dealing with Dickinson: Leon de Valinger, Jr., *The John Dickinson Mansion* (Dover, Del., n.d.); George H. Moore, *John Dickinson, the Author of the Declaration of Taking Up Arms in 1775* (New York, 1890); J. H. Powell, *The House on Jones Neck: The Dickinson Mansion* (Wilmington [?], 1954); Robert A. Richards, *The Life and Character of John Dickinson* (The Historical Society of Delaware, Wilmington, 1901); Edwin Wolf, 2nd, *John Dickinson: Forgotten Patriot* (Wilmington, 1968).

Many significant articles dealing directly with Dickinson's life, letters, and thought include Julian Boyd, "The Disputed Authorship of the Declaration of Causes of Taking Up Arms," *Pennsylvania Maga-*

zine of History and Biography (hereafter *PMHB*) 74 (1950):51–73; H. Trevor Colbourn, "A Pennsylvania Farmer at the Court of King George: John Dickinson's London Letters, 1754–1756," *PMHB* 86 (1962):241–86, 417–53; idem, "The Historical Perspective of John Dickinson," *Bulwark of Liberty* 3 (1961):3–37; Leon de Valinger, Jr., "Handwriting of John Dickinson," *Autograph Collectors' Journal* 3, no. 4 (1951); Wharton Dickinson, "John Dickinson, L.L.D.," *Magazine of American History* 10 (1883):223–34; Richard M. Gummere, "John Dickinson, the Classical Penman of the Revolution," *Classical Journal* 52, no. 2 (1960):81–88; Jean Holder, "The Historical Misrepresentation of John Dickinson," *Journal of Historical Studies* 1 (1976):1–20; Richard J. Hooker, "John Dickinson on Church and State," *American Literature* 16 (1944–45):82–98; David L. Jacobson, "John Dickinson's Fight against Royal Government, 1764," *William and Mary Quarterly*, 3d ser., 19 (1962):64–85; Stanley K. Johannesen, "John Dickinson and the American Revolution," *Historical Reflections/Reflections Historique* 2 (1975):29–49; Carl F. Kaestle, "The Public Reaction to John Dickinson's Farmer's Letters," *Proceedings of the American Antiquarian Society* 78, pt. 2 (1969):323–53; Bernhard Knollenberg, "John Dickinson vs. John Adams, 1774–1776," *Proceedings of the American Philosophical Society* 197, no. 2 (1962):135–44; John H. Powell has many studies to his credit: "John Dickinson and the Constitution," *PMHB* 60 (1936):1–14; idem, "Speech of John Dickinson Opposing the Declaration of Independence," *PMHB* 65 (1941):458–81; idem, "John Dickinson: Character of a Revolutionist," in E. P. Bartlett, *Friends in Wilmington* (Wilmington, Del., 1938) pp. 87–95; idem, "John Dickinson, President of the Delaware State, 1781–1782," pts. 1 and 2, *Delaware History* 1 (1946):1–54, 111–34; idem, "The Debate on American Independence, July 1, 1776," *Delaware Notes*, 23d ser. (1950):37–62; idem, "John Dickinson as President of Pennsylvania," *Pennsylvania History* 28 (1961):254–67; idem, "A Certain Great Fortune and Piddling Genius," *Bulwark of Liberty* 197, no. 3 (1961):41–72; idem, "A Certain Great Fortune and Piddling Genius, July 5–25, 1775," in *General Washington and the Jackass* (South Brunswick, N.J. 1969), pp. 86–118, also note, pp. 314–18; and idem, "The Day of American Independence, July 1, 1776," pp. 119–75; also note, pp. 318–23; Martha Calvert Slotten, "John Dickinson on Independence, July 25, 1776," *Manuscripts* 28, no. 3 (1976):188–94; William G. Soler, "John Dickinson's Attitude toward the French, 1797–1801," *Delaware History* 6 (1955):294–98; idem, "A Reattribution: John Dickinson's Authorship of the Pamphlet 'A Caution,' 1798," *PMHB* 77 (1953):24–31; idem,

"John Dickinson's 'Ode, On the French Revolution,'" *American Literature* 25 (1953):287–92; idem, "A Note on John Dickinson's Pamphlet 'A Caution,'" *PMHB* 79 (1955):100–101; Frederick B. Tolles, "John Dickinson and the Quakers," *Bulwark of Liberty* 2 (1956):67–88; James M. Tunnell, Jr., "John Dickinson and the Federal Constitution," *Delaware History* 6 (1955):288–93; see also *Bulwark of Liberty* 2 (1956):60–66; Edwin Wolf, 2nd, "The Authorship of The 1774 Address to the King Restudied," *William and Mary Quarterly*, 2d ser., 22 (1965):189–224.

There are also these dissertations: David L. Jacobson, "John Dickinson and Joseph Galloway, 1764–1766: A Study in Contrasts," Princeton Univ., 1959; John H. Powell, "John Dickinson: Penman of the Revolution," Univ. of Iowa, 1938; Stanley K. Johannsen, "Constitution and Empire in the Life and Thought of John Dickinson," Univ. of Missouri, Columbia, 1973; William G. Soler, "Some Important Influences upon John Dickinson: Chiefly Bacon, Locke, and Pope," Temple Univ. 1953.

The files of the *Pennsylvania Magazine of History and Biography*, with its *Index*, are invaluable for background articles. *Pennsylvania History* is less important. *Delaware History*, as noted, is here significant in the two articles on Dickinson's Presidency of that state. The *William and Mary Quarterly* also yields articles valuable in colonial background studies. The *Proceedings of the Massachusetts Historical Society* have been helpful. Specific articles here used are found in the footnotes.

The Commonwealth of Pennsylvania in its *Colonial Archives*, as the volumes including the Minutes of the Provincial Council of Pennsylvania and Minutes of the Council of Safety are commonly referred to, and the *Pennsylvania Archives*, ser. 8, particularly vol. 8, contains minutes of the Pennsylvania Assembly to July, 1776. Edmund C. Burnett, ed., *Letters of Members of the Continental Congress*, 8 vols. (Washington, D.C., 1921–38 is helpful. Burnett has been superseded by the Paul H. Smith, ed., *Letters of Delegates to Congress, 1774–1789*, 7 vols. (Washington, D.C. 1976–); Max Farrand, ed., *The Records of the Federal Convention of 1787*, 4 vols., rev. ed. (New Haven, 1937); Worthington Chauncey Ford, ed., *Journals of the Continental Congress, 1774–1789*, 32 vols. (Washington, D.C., 1904–36) are rich mines of documentary importance. Frank Moore, *Diary of the American Revolution* (New York, 1859) has unexpected, useful information. More important is Peter Force, *American Archives*, 4th and 5th ser. (Washington, D.C., 1837–53); Hezekiah Niles, *Weekly Register* (Baltimore), vol. 13 (Jan. 8, 1818). To all the above must be added the news-paper files of the *Pennsylvania Gazette*, *Pennsylvania Packet*, and *Pennsylvania Evening Post*.

Background studies are basic to any interpretation of events in each period, whether one agrees with the writer's conclusions or not. Among these are Moses Coit Tyler, *The Literary History of the American People*, 2 vols. (Putnam, N.Y., 1891); Vernon L. Parrington, *Main Currents in American Thought* (New York, 1930), are old but still interesting studies. Classic, according to the historical periods concerned, are Caroline Robbins, *The Eighteenth Century Commonwealthman* (Cambridge, Mass., 1959); Carl and Jessica Bridenbaugh, *Rebels and Gentlemen: Philadelphia in the Age of Franklin* (New York, 1962); Michael Kammen, *Empire and Interest: The American Colonies and the Politics of Mercantilism* (Philadelphia, 1970); Bernard Bailyn, *Ideological Origins of the American Revolution* (Chapel Hill, N.C., 1965); Pauline Maier, *From Resistance to Revolution: Colonial Radicals and the Development of American Opposition to Britain, 1765–1776* (New York, 1972); Edmund S. Morgan and Helen M. Morgan, *The Stamp Act Congress* (Chapel Hill, N.C., 1953). Of equal significance and importance are Jack N. Rakove, *The Beginnings of National Politics* (New York, 1979); Gordon S. Wood, *The Creation of the American Republic, 1776–1787* (Chapel Hill, N.C., 1969); John Munroe, *Federalist Delaware, 1775–1815* (New Brunswick, N.J., 1954); Merrill Jensen, *The Articles of Confederation: An Interpretation of the Social-Constitutional History of the American Revolution, 1774–1781* (Madison, 1940); Andrew C. McLaughlin, *The Confederation and the Constitution, 1783–1789* (New York, 1905).

Quaker life, in general, is covered in Richard Bauman, *For the Reputation of Truth* (Baltimore, 1971) and gives a good understanding of early Quaker life. J. William Frost, *The Quaker Family in Colonial America* (New York, 1973) and Frederick B. Tolles, *Meeting House and Counting House: The Quaker Merchants in Colonial Philadelphia, 1682–1761* (Chapel Hill, N.C., 1948) provide background as indeed does the more pertinent older study by Isaac Sharpless, *The Quakers in the Revolution* (Philadelphia, 1899).

The first major political events in Dickinson's life are touched in the pioneer work of Charles H. Lincoln, *The Revolutionary Movement in Pennsylvania, 1760–1776* (Philadelphia, 1901) and less happily in Theodore G. Thayer's *Pennsylvania Politics and the Growth of Democracy* (Harrisburg, Pa., 1953). The movement for royal government is elucidated further in Oliver C. Kuntzleman, *Joseph Galloway, Loy-*

alist (Philadelphia, 1941); Benjamin H. Newcomb, *Franklin and Galloway: A Political Partnership* (New Haven, 1972), and James H. Hutson, *Pennsylvania Politics, 1746–1770* (Princeton, 1972).

Richard Alan Ryerson, *The Revolution Is Now Begun: The Radical Committees of Philadelphia, 1765–1776* (Philadelphia, 1978), has forged new ground in analyzing committee structures, while Charles S. Olten, *Artisans for Independence; Philadelphia Mechanics and the Revolution* (Syracuse, N.Y., 1975) also plumbs new areas. David Hawke, *In the Midst of Revolution* (Philadelphia, 1961) more than measures up to its objective and deals with Pennsylvania's Constitution of 1776.

Both Helen A. Hole, *Westtown through the Years* (Westtown, Pa., 1942) and Charles Coleman Sellers, *Dickinson College* (Middletown, Conn., 1973) touch on Dickinson's educational interests. Dickinson's taste is indicated in Joseph Downs, *Philadelphia Furniture: The Queen Anne and Chippendale Periods* (New York, 1972); William McPherson Horner, *Blue Book of Philadelphia Furniture* (Philadelphia, 1935); Elizabeth Montgomery, *Reminiscenses of Wilmington* (Wilmington, Del., 1872), and Nicholas B. Wainwright, *Colonial Grandeur in Philadelphia* (Philadelphia, 1964).

Biographies of Dickinson's associates in the colonial, Revolutionary and post-Revolutionary years are not here mentioned. George Read, Joseph Reed, and the Lees are seen in letters only. Those of McKean, Wilson, and others are limited. The various biographies of John Adams and Alexander Hamilton (James Thomas Flexner, *The Young Hamilton: A Biography* [Boston, 1978]) yield little pertinent to Dickinson's career although the latter includes Hamilton's opinion of Dickinson during the Mutiny of 1782.

SUBSCRIBERS

The Reverend and Mrs. Richard S. Bailey

Mr. and Mrs. James A. Bayard

Mr. Walter J. Beadle

Mr. Sewell C. Biggs

Mrs. Alfred E. Bissell

Mr. and Mrs. George P. Bissell, Jr.

The Honorable J. Caleb Boggs

Bredin Foundation

Mrs. Thomas E. Brittingham

Mrs. Donald F. Carpenter

Mr. and Mrs. Edward W. Cooch, Jr.

Mr. and Mrs. Lammot du Pont Copeland

Mrs. David Craven

Mr. Vernon B. Derrickson

Mr. and Mrs. Earl R. Downs

Mrs. E. Paul du Pont
in memory of
E. Paul du Pont
Charles F. Gillette
Edward S. Paxon

Mrs. H. B. du Pont

Mrs. Margaret Lewis du Pont

Mr. George P. Edmonds

Mrs. Elwyn Evans

Mrs. Geoffrey S. Garstin

Mr. and Mrs. Robert H. George

Mr. and Mrs. James S. Grant, Jr.
in memory of
Theodore Marvin

Mr. and Mrs. T. Jefferson Gray, Jr.

Miss Dorothy W. Greer

Mr. Harold Hancock

Mr. and Mrs. Willis F. Harrington, Jr.

Mr. and Mrs. Anthony Higgins

Mr. Albert W. Holmes, Jr.

Mr. and Mrs. William S. Ingram, Jr.

Mr. Joseph Y. Jeanes, Jr.

Capt. and Mrs. Andrew F. Knopp, Jr.

Mr. and Mrs. Rodney M. Layton

Mrs. Herbert C. McDaniel

Mrs. Theodore Marvin

Mr. and Mrs. John A. Munroe

Mrs. G. Burton Pearson, Jr.

Mr. and Mrs. Donald Cargill Pease

Mrs. Eugene K. Quigg

Mr. Charles Lee Reese, Jr.

Mrs. Charles F. Richards

Mr. William F. Richardson

Mr. and Mrs. Harlan Scott

Mr. William C. Scott

Miss M. Carol Short

Mr. Mark A. Showell

Mr. and Mrs. William V. Sipple, Jr.

The Honorable Edwin D. Steel, Jr.

Mr. John A. H. Sweeney

Mr. and Mrs. Sigurd S. Swensson

The Honorable and Mrs. James M. Tunnell, Jr.

Mr. John Warner

Mr. and Mrs. William A. Worth

Index

France (*cont.*)
  birth of dauphin celebrated, 207
  peace talks and obligations of confederacy, 204, 206–7, 217
  support for colonies sought, 158, 163
  treaties and peace negotiations, 191–92
  XYZ affair, 277
Franklin, Benjamin, 85
  agent to London, 46–47
  objections of Dickinson, 50
  Articles of Confederation, 159
  bathhouse, 283
  charging whigs as seditious and rebellious, 121
  Committee of Safety, 134
  Confederation Congress, 239
  Continental Congress, 117
  Cool Thoughts on the Present Situation of Our Public Affairs, 35, 77
  Farmer's Letters, 69
  and John Dickinson, 34–35
  militia and defense appropriations, 32–34, 40
  morals questioned, 44
  nonimportation agreement, 72, 74
  North Atlantic fishing rights, 190, 193
  Pennsylvania Assembly, 31, 44–45, 147
  perpetual union for colonies proposed, 135–36
  petition to king, 131
  Popular party opposing, 76–77
  president of Pennsylvania, 233
  proprietary estates, taxation of, 30–37
  royal government proposed, 35–37
  Second Continental Congress, 124, 144, 154
  Speaker of Pennsylvania Assembly, 39–40, 43
  Stamp Act controversy, 50
  support of foreign states sought, 158
  trade, open for colonies, 136
  treaties with foreign powers, 159

  trees for Fairhill estate, 85
Franklin, Sarah, 45
Franklin, Thomas, 171
Franklin, William, 70, 141
Freeman's Journal, attacks on Dickinson, 211
Free press, Dickinson supporting, 176
Frontier Pennsylvania and taxation for military defense, 30–35, 39

Gage, Thomas, 137
Galloway, Grace, 214
Galloway, Joseph, 23, 31, 94, 214
  blows exchanged with Dickinson, 42
  A Candid Examination of the Mutual Claims of Great Britain, 121
  challenged to duel, 41
  confederation of colonies, 160
  Continental Congress
    colonial unity, 106, 108, 120
    delegate selection, 111–12, 124
    deposed as Speaker of Assembly, 118
  Farmer's Letters, 63–64, 70
  First Continental Congress, 111, 113
  John Dickinson dispute, 37–45
  nonimportation agreement, 71, 73, 75
  Pennsylvania Chronicle sponsor, 63
  Popular party opposing, 76–77
  preventing destruction of Fairhill, 187
  Second Continental Congress, 121
  Stamp Act controversy, 51, 54, 59
  Thomson dispute, 73
  To the Public, 43–44
  Townshend Acts, 62–63
  whigs charged with sedition and rebellion, 121
Garrick, David, 14
Garrigues, Jacob, 170
Garrigues, William, 284
Gaspee (revenue cutter), 96
George III, king of England, 35
  declaring colonists in rebellion, 140–41
Gerard (minister to France), 192

Index